BEATING
GOLIATH

BEATING GOLIATH

Why Insurgencies Win

JEFFREY RECORD

Potomac Books, Inc.
Washington, D.C.

The views expressed in this book are the author's alone and do not necessarily represent those of the Air War College, the Air Force, the Department of Defense, or any other federal agency.

Library of Congress Cataloging-in-Publication Data
Record, Jeffrey.
  Beating Goliath : why insurgencies win / Jeffrey Record. — 1st ed.
    p. cm.
  Includes bibliographical references and index.
  ISBN 978-1-59797-090-7 (alk. paper)
  1. Insurgency—History—20th century. 2. Insurgency—History—21st century. 3. Iraq War, 2003–
4. Vietnam War, 1961–1975. 5. United States—History, Military—20th century. 6. United States—
History, Military—21st century. I. Title.
  D431.R43 2007
  355.02'18—dc22

                                                                                    2007001847

Printed in the United States of America on acid-free paper that meets the American National Standards Institute Z39-48 Standard.

Potomac Books, Inc.
22841 Quicksilver Drive
Dulles, Virginia 20166

First Edition

10 9 8 7 6 5 4 3 2

Contents

Introduction

The continuing insurgency in Iraq underscores the capacity of the weak to impose considerable military and political pain on the strong. Whether that pain will compel the United States to abandon its agenda in Iraq remains to be seen.

What is not in dispute is that all major failed U.S. uses of force since 1945—in Vietnam, Lebanon, and Somalia (the jury is still out on Iraq)—have been against materially weaker enemies. In wars both hot and cold, the United States has fared consistently well against such powerful enemies as Nazi Germany, Imperial Japan, and the Soviet Union, but the record against lesser foes is decidedly mixed. Though it easily polished off Slobodan Miloševic's Serbia and Saddam Hussein's Iraq, the United States failed to defeat Vietnamese infantry in Indochina, terrorists in Lebanon, and warlords in Somalia. In each case the American Goliath was militarily checked or politically defeated by the local David. Most recently, the United States was surprised by the tenacious insurgency that exploded in post-Baathist Iraq, an insurgency now in its fifth year with no end in sight. An estimated 20,000 insurgents have battled 140,000 U.S. troops and an increasing number of Iraqi government soldiers and police to a military stalemate. What was expected to be a cakewalk became a quagmire.

The phenomenon of the weak defeating the strong, though exceptional, is as old as war itself. Sparta finally beat Athens; Frederick the Great always punched well above his weight; American rebels overturned British rule in the Thirteen Colonies; the Spanish guerrilla bled Napoleon white; Jewish terrorists forced the

British out of Palestine; Vietnamese Communists drove France and then the United States out of Indochina; and mujahideen handed the Soviet Union its own Vietnam in Afghanistan. Relative military power is a very imperfect predictor of war outcomes. Carl von Clausewitz believed that "superiority of numbers is the most common element of victory" and declared that the "best strategy is always *to be very strong*." But the great Prussian philosopher of war also recognized that "superiority of numbers in a given engagement is only one of the factors that determines victory. Superior numbers, far from contributing everything, or even a substantial part, to victory, may actually be contributing very little, depending on the circumstances."[1]

Why do the strong lose? Indeed, what is meant by "strong"? As used here, the term means the side with greater material resources at its disposal—i.e., the side with numerical superiority in population, territory, industrial resources, financial power, and conventional military forces, especially firepower. Often, though not always, attending these material advantages is technological superiority. The stronger side (the heavyweight) usually beats the weaker side (the lightweight), all things else being equal. The problem is that all things else are often not equal. The United States enjoys unprecedented global conventional military primacy, yet its military difficulties in Iraq testify to the limits of that primacy against an irregular adversary whose fighting power stems primarily from nonmaterial factors.

One of the most obvious cases of a decisive military victory arguably predetermined by crushing material superiority was Japan's defeat in the Pacific War of 1941–45. In attacking Pearl Harbor, the Japanese entered a war with an enemy that dwarfed Japan in financial, industrial, and latent conventional military power; it was also an enemy with an enormous superiority in war-related sciences and engineering capacity that doomed Japan to technological defeat. (Both the atomic bomb and the B-29 that carried it lay beyond Japan's technological reach.) Whatever nonmaterial advantages the Japanese may have initially enjoyed—combat experience, the element of surprise—could not begin to offset Japan's relative material poverty. Under these circumstances the Japanese were driven to a desperate theory of victory based on the hope that their racial and spiritual superiority would provide a defense of their Pacific island empire tenacious and bloody enough to compel the Americans to accept a termination of hostilities that would leave Japan the dominant power in East Asia if not the

Pacific. The Japanese pitted what they believed to be a superior willingness to die against a superior American capacity to kill.

Twenty years after Japan's unconditional surrender, a much stronger United States entered another war in Asia against an enemy much weaker than the Japanese were during World War II. Yet the United States proved unable to defeat that enemy and, after eight years of heavy fighting, withdrew from the conflict.

Why did the United States beat the Japanese yet lose to the Vietnamese Communists? Why do Goliaths lose to Davids? The biblical David nailed the biblical Goliath with a single slingshot to the head, just as a safari hunter brings down a charging rhinoceros with a single rifle shot. Such instant and cheap victories based on technological superiority, however, are not available to the weak in wars against the strong.

In attempting to answer the question of why the strong lose to the weak, I focus on states fighting non-state actors—specifically, states facing insurgencies within their own territory or overseas. The former include any organized movement aimed at overthrowing a constituted government via subversion and armed conflict, including terrorism, guerrilla warfare, and traditional military operations; the latter include all armed rebellions against foreign government rule or military occupation. The key military characteristic of insurgent wars is the clash between regular government forces and irregular insurgent forces. Such wars are "small wars" as classically defined by C. E. Callwell in 1896: "Small war . . . may be said to include all campaigns other than those where both sides consist of regular troops"—i.e., "operations of regular armies against irregular, or comparatively speaking irregular forces."[2] This definition is echoed in the U.S. Marine Corps' 1940 *Small Wars Manual*, which was reissued without alteration in 1990: "The ordinary expedition of the Marine Corps which does not involve a major effort in regular warfare against a first-rate power may be termed a small war."[3] Counterinsurgency is by definition small war because it involves operations by regular government forces against irregular insurgent forces. Small wars are thus qualitatively different from wars in which both sides employ regular forces against each other.

In terms of regularity, conventional wars are thus symmetric, whereas small wars are asymmetric. Asymmetry is not a constant in all small wars, however. Maoist revolutionary war theory and practice embraces the evolution of insurgency from asymmetrical to symmetrical conflict; third-phase military operations based on insurgent transition from the weaker to the stronger side entail predominately conventional mobile and positional military operations supported by guerrilla warfare. The outcomes of both the Chinese civil war and the Vietnam War were decided by massive conventional military operations.

I am not interested in the objectives or "cause" of particular insurgencies, nor their methods of violence, except in so far as either influences the course and outcome of hostilities. Insurgencies, because they are militarily weak, almost invariably employ some combination of guerrilla warfare and terrorism, methods of violence that are no guarantee of success. Indeed, guerrilla warfare may fail against a politically skilled and militarily careful adversary, and excessive reliance on terrorism, often testimony to lack of popular support, can be self-defeating. The Iraqi insurgency's videotaped beheadings of hostages and large-scale employment of suicide bombings in crowded streets stand in considerable contrast to the Vietnamese Communists' selective use of terror against government officials and "class" enemies. No less a terrorist mastermind than al Qaeda's Ayman al-Zawahiri was prompted in October 2005 to chastise Abu Musab al-Zarqawi for the Jordanian-born terrorist's unnecessary alienation of Iraqi Shia and international Muslim opinion via al-Zarqawi's exceptionally bloodthirsty and indiscriminate acts of terror.[4]

Finally, in seeking to understand why states lose to insurgencies, I distinguish between general factors that seem common to many cases of state defeat by insurgencies and factors that, if not peculiar to the United States, are manifestly distinctive. Most states that lose to insurgencies appear to suffer from some combination of inferior political will, inferior war strategy, and an inability to isolate insurgent forces from external support. In the theater of operations they either lack popular support to begin with (e.g., the Israelis in the West Bank) or they lose it through military excess and political mistakes (e.g., the Americans in Vietnam). But other factors worked against the United States there. America has both a distinctive approach to strategy and a distinctive way of war rooted in its history, culture, political values, and geopolitical circumstances. All of these influences have combined to produce, among other things, not only an apolitical view of war, which encourages the pursuit of military victory for its own sake, but also a profound professional military aversion to counterinsurgency, which hands insurgent enemies a major strategic advantage.

The following chapter reviews the recent literature about why the strong lose. That literature has postulated strong-actor inferiority of political will, bad strategy, and type of government as explanations for defeat. Each of these explanations sheds much light on the phenomenon of beaten Goliaths, but neither individually nor even in combination do they provide a completely satisfactory explanation. Great powers often display a lesser strength of political will in fights against weaker enemies, but they nonetheless go on to win more often than not—testimony to the advantage of being a great power. Overwhelming material superiority can also compensate for bad strategy—indeed, render strategy irrelevant. Native Americans, for example, had no effective strategic choices to block the Europeans' westward advance across North America in the nineteenth century. And while modern democracies have displayed greater difficulty than dictatorships in sustaining protracted wars against irregular adversaries, there are enough instances of democratic success against insurgent foes (and insurgent victories over dictatorships) to deprive regime type as a reliable predictor of strong-side defeat in guerrilla wars.

A critical factor in insurgent success is foreign help, which is the subject of chapter 2. External assistance is certainly no guarantee of victory in insurgent wars, but there are few examples of unassisted insurgent success against governments or occupations not already on the verge of collapse. Chapter 2 examines six examples of assisted insurgencies: the American War of Independence (1775–83), the Spanish guerrilla against the French (1808–14), the Chinese Communist defeat of the Nationalist Government (1945–49), the French-Indochina War (1946–54), the Vietnam War (1965–75), and the Soviet-Afghan War (1979–89). To illustrate the military impact of absent or denied external help, the chapter also looks at the American Civil War (1861–65), the Boer War (1899–1902), the Malayan Emergency (1948–60), and the Algerian War (1954–62).

Chapter 3 applies explanations of strong-actor defeat to the ongoing war in Iraq. Though the outcome of that conflict remains undetermined, there has been sufficient war experience there to make tentative judgments on the strength of U.S. interests in Iraq and the quality of U.S. strategy relative to those of the insurgent enemy, on the capacity of early twenty-first-century American democracy to sustain the war, and on the actual and potential role of foreign assistance in determining the war's outcome. To sharpen the analysis of prospects for strong-actor success/failure in Iraq, I employ previously published research comparing the Vietnam and Iraq wars.[5] Comparison to Vietnam does not—and is not intended to—suggest the inevitability or even likelihood of U.S. defeat in Iraq; the differences between the two wars, including the size and fighting power of the enemy, greatly outnumber the similarities. Comparison nonetheless provides important insights on the Iraq War, especially on the challenges of overseas state-building and sustaining domestic political support for a protracted war against a seemingly undefeatable enemy.

Chapters 4 and 5 examine America's strategic culture and methods of war as impediments to success in counterinsurgent conflicts. An abiding American embrace of war as a substitute for politics has bred a general aversion to limited wars and a particular dislike of intervention in foreign internal wars. Once the shooting starts, Americans tend to view military victory as an end independent of the reasons for war in the first place. This approach can and has produced politically sterile military successes. Reinforcing national aversion to limited war is the professional military's acute distaste for counterinsurgency, which is in large part a function of preference for the conventional warfare it wages so well. This dread of counterinsurgency is troubling because irregular warfare is increasingly supplanting conventional combat as a means of resolving violent disputes within and among states.

The final chapter presents the study's major findings. There is no convincing single-factor explanation for strong-actor defeats. Goliaths usually win, but their exceptional defeats are almost always the result of a combination of inferior political will, ineffective strategic interaction with the enemy, and failure to isolate the weaker side from foreign help. Indeed, external assistance appears to be the most common enabler of insurgent success. And it does not help if the Goliath in question is a modern democracy. Democratic Goliaths do indeed suffer inherent disadvantages in conducting long wars against irregular enemies, though, at least in the United States, the impact of casualties on domestic political opinion is a function primarily of military action's perceived costs, benefits, and chances of success. That said, America's peculiar political system and scientific approach to war greatly impede its ability to conduct counterinsurgent warfare—to the point where a strong case can be made for adopting a policy of refusing U.S. involvement in foreign internal wars altogether.

1

Explaining Goliath Defeats:
Will, Strategy, and Type of Government

During the cold war, serious intellectual examination of the phenomenon of the strong succumbing to the weak was provoked by a series of events: the success of the Chinese Communists in 1949, the rapid and largely unexpected disintegration of European colonial empires in Asia and Africa, France's violent defeat in Indochina and Algeria, and above all the defeat and humiliation of the United States in Vietnam. Western conventional military superiority over non-Western adversaries, which had been a source of European imperial success since the days of the Conquistadores, was exposed after World War II as vulnerable to irregular and politically revolutionary warfare. Maybe the West was not as strong as it appeared. Perhaps it was irreparably weakened by the European civil wars of 1914–18 and 1939–45. The United States had emerged from World War II stronger than any Western power before it, yet had gone on to be defeated by the same enemy that had vanquished the French. What accounted for the remarkable success of the Vietnamese Communists against two far more powerful Western states?

In seeking the common cause that explains the stronger side's loss to the weaker, Andrew Mack, in his pioneering 1975 assessment, "Why Big Nations Lose Small Wars: The Politics of Asymmetric Conflict," argued that the answer lay in differentials in political will to fight and prevail that were rooted in different perceptions of the stakes at hand. By focusing on will to fight, Mack embraced Carl von Clausewitz's conception of war as, at bottom, a contest of wills. Calling

1

war "nothing but a duel on a larger scale," the great Prussian philosopher of war defined it as "an act of force to compel our enemy to do our will." Force was but "the *means* of war; to impose our will upon the enemy is its object."[1]

Mack began his assessment by observing that the combination of the West's record of military success in the third world during the nineteenth and early twentieth centuries and the Allied experience in World Wars I and II "served to reinforce and rigidify the pervasive notion that superiority in military capability (conventionally defined) will mean victory in war."[2] Yet the notion that military and technological superiority was a reliable guide to the outcome of wars offered no explanation for post-1945 European losses in wars in the third world or the outcome of the Vietnam War. Power obviously meant more, perhaps much more, than simple capability.

In his examination of the wars of decolonization, Mack observed that "although the metropolitan powers did not *win* militarily, neither were they *defeated* militarily." Indeed,

> The military defeat of the metropolis [great-power homeland] itself was impossible since the insurgents lacked an invasion capability. In every case, success for the insurgents arose not from a military victory on the ground—though military success may have been a contributory cause— but rather from the progressive attrition of their opponents' *political* capability to wage war. In such asymmetric conflicts, insurgents may gain political victory from a situation of military stalemate or *even defeat*.[3]

Mack went on to observe that in both the French-Indochina War and the American war in Vietnam the outcome was decided by not by a conclusive military victory on the Communist side but rather by a collapse of political will on the anti-Communist side. "If the external power's 'will' to continue the struggle is destroyed, then its military capability—no matter how powerful—is totally irrelevant." Indeed, "in certain types of conflict, conventional military superiority is not merely useless, but actually may be counter-productive."[4] Mack noted that even in cases where "military victory over the insurgents is unambiguous—as in General Massu's destruction of the FLN infrastructure in the notorious Battle of Algiers—this is still no sure guide to the outcome of the conflict. Despite the fact that the FLN never regained the initiative, the French abandoned their struggle within four years."[5]

In Mack's view, post-1945 successful rebellions against European colonial rule as well as the Vietnamese struggle against the United States all had one thing in common: the materially weaker insurgent was more politically determined to win because it had much more riding on the outcome of war than did the stronger external power, for whom the stakes were lower. In such cases

> the *relationship* between the belligerents is *asymmetric.* The insurgents can pose no direct threat to the survival of the external power because . . . they lack an invasion capability. On the other hand, the metropolitan power poses not simply the threat of invasion, but the reality of occupation. This fact is so obvious that its implications have been ignored. It means, crudely speaking, that for the insurgents the war is "total," while for the external power it is necessarily "limited." Full mobilization of the total military resources of the external power is simply *not* politically possible. . . . Not only is full mobilization impossible politically, it is not thought to be in the least *necessary.* The asymmetry in conventional military capability is so great and the confidence that military might will prevail is so pervasive that expectation of victory is one of the hallmarks of the initial endeavor.[6]

Superior strength of commitment thus compensates for military inferiority. Because the outcome of the war can never be as important to the outside power as it is to the indigenous insurgents who have staked their very existence on victory, the weaker side fights harder, displaying a willingness to incur blood losses that would be unacceptable to the stronger side. The stronger side employs but a fraction of its power, whereas the weaker side uses all of its available power, thus reducing the actual disparity of power in the theater of operations. Because the struggle is a limited war for the stronger side and a total war for the weaker side, the stronger side has lower political tolerance of blood and treasure losses.

The signers of the Declaration of Independence risked their lives, fortunes, and sacred honor in what became a contest with an imperial giant for which North America was (after 1778) a secondary theater of operations in a much larger war between European powers. For the American rebel leadership, defeat meant the hangman's noose. For British commanders in North America, it meant reassignment to another command or a return to the comforts and pleasures of London society. In his definitive assessment of the American War of Independence from the British perspective, Piers Mackesy observes the contrast between the timidity of British generalship and that of the Americans:

> At the very top of the [British command] there was petrification. While the American commanders were products of a revolutionary situation in which timid men did not rise, learning the trade of war as they practiced it, with everything to lose by defeat and everything to gain by victory, [British generals] Howe and Clinton were members of a stable political community who had arrived and could not be shaken from their perch. They had only to play the game safely to draw their emoluments and retain their position. Their fertility of invention was spent in devising reasons for inaction.[7]

The tables were reversed in Vietnam. There, the United States attempted to suppress a revolution against foreign domination mounted by an enemy waging a total war against a stronger power, a power for which the outcome of that war could never be remotely as important as it was to the insurgents. The United States could and did wreak enormous destruction in Vietnam, but nothing that happened in Vietnam could or did threaten core overseas U.S. security interests, much less the survival of the United States.[8] It did not help that the United States had little material interest in Indochina or that the official rationales proffered for intervention and subsequently staying the course were abstractions—containing Communism, maintaining the credibility of U.S. commitments worldwide, achieving peace with honor. Thus, whereas the Vietnamese Communists invested all their energy and available resources in waging war, U.S. annual defense spending during the war averaged only 7.5 percent of its gross national product and included other large military commitments in Europe and Northeast Asia.[9] Far more important to President Lyndon Johnson than securing South Vietnam was securing the enactment of his expensive Great Society program of social reform. Indeed, after he left the White House he bemoaned the resource competition between "that bitch of the war on the other side of the world" and "the woman I really loved—the Great Society."[10]

Key Vietnam War players in the Johnson administration grasped neither the disparity in interests and will that separated the United States and the Vietnamese Communists nor its consequences. They could find no reason for the enemy's tenacity and staying power. In 1965, U.S. ambassador to South Vietnam (and former Chairman of the Joint Chiefs of Staff) Maxwell Taylor marveled, "The ability of the Vietcong continuously to rebuild their units and make good their losses is one of the mysteries of this guerrilla war. We still find no plausible explanation for the continued strength of the Vietcong. . . . [They] have the recuperative power of the phoenix [and] an amazing ability to maintain morale."[11] A year later, Secretary of Defense Robert McNamara remarked to an acquaintance, "I never thought [the war] would go like this. I didn't think these people had the capacity to fight this way. If I had thought they could take this punishment and fight this well, could enjoy fighting like this, I would have thought differently at the start."[12] Secretary of State Dean Rusk later confessed, "Hanoi's persistence was incredible. I don't understand it, even to this day."[13] Even Gen. William C. Westmoreland, commander of U.S. forces in Vietnam (1964–68), conceded that the U.S. leadership "underestimated the toughness of the Vietnamese."[14]

Nothing testifies more to the disparity in willingness to sacrifice in the Vietnam War than the difference in casualty tolerance. The United States withdrew from Vietnam after suffering 58,000 dead—a miniscule fraction of its total population of about 194 million (in 1965) and only 2 percent of the total of 2.85 million U.S. military personnel who served in Southeast Asia during the Vietnam War. In contrast were the "total war" losses of the Vietnamese Communists. In April 1995 the government in Hanoi announced that Communist forces during the "American period" of the Vietnam War had sustained a loss of 1.1 million dead, a figure that presumably included the Communists' 300,000 missing in action. (Hanoi also estimated 2 million civilian dead.)[15] The military dead represented 5.5 percent of the Communist population base during the Vietnam War of 20 million (16 million in North Vietnam and 4 million in those areas of South Vietnam effectively controlled by the Communists). No other major belligerent in a twentieth-century war sustained such a high *military* death toll proportional to its population.[16] (French military dead in World War I amounted to 3.4 percent of France's total population.[17]) Another way of putting the 5.5 percent loss in perspective: it would equal about 16.5 million dead from the current U.S. population of almost 300 million. (The 600,000 dead in the American Civil War, by far the deadliest of all of America's wars, represented but 1.9 percent of the nation's 1860 population of 31 million.)[18] Richard K. Betts has commented on the effects of the "fundamental asymmetry of national interests" at stake in Vietnam:

The Vietnamese Communists were fighting for their country as well as their principles, while the Americans had only principles at stake—and as the antiwar case became steadily more persuasive, even those principles were discredited. The only possibility for decisive victory for the United States lay in the complete obliteration of North Vietnam, an alternative unthinkably barbaric, unimaginably dangerous and pointless. Hanoi bent but never broke because it preferred endless war to defeat; Washington bent and finally did break because the public preferred defeat to endless war.[19]

Reinforcing U.S. blindness to the fact and implications of the Vietnam Communists' commitment to total war were an ignorance of Vietnamese history and culture and an arrogant confidence in American ability to determine the future of South Vietnam. Surely, a Pentagon that had defeated Germany and Japan and that had saved South Korea from the Chinese Communist menace would prevail over an Asian peasant insurgency. And surely, there was nothing to learn from France's defeat in Indochina: when was the last time the French had won a war?

The United States also had an inferior strategy. Indeed, superior political will—a greater commitment to the fight—would not, alone, seem sufficient to defeat a stronger enemy. Having a significant edge in resolve cannot overcome a strategy that pits insurgent military weakness against the bigger enemy's military strengths. The Tet Offensive was a military disaster from which the Vietcong never recovered because Communist forces came out in the open and tried to take and hold fixed positions, thereby exposing themselves to crushing U.S. firepower. (The Taliban made the same mistake in Afghanistan thirty-three years later.) Tough is one thing. Tough and stupid is quite another.

But Tet was exceptional. What was not exceptional was the American military command's persistent pursuit of an attritional, firepower-based "search-and-destroy" strategy that simultaneously generated a steady flow of recruits for the Communist side and fanned hostility to the South Vietnamese regime the Americans were fighting to save. Gen. William C. Westmoreland never comprehended the political consequences of his strategy because he saw the Vietnam War as a military contest, not a political struggle. Even militarily, attrition was doomed to failure against an enemy who could and did withdraw from combat when it suited him to do so. A strategy of attrition guaranteed a military stalemate, which in turn guaranteed attrition of American political will.

In explaining the phenomenon of Goliaths losing to Davids, Andrew Mack did not assign much importance to strategy, at least the stronger side's strategy. He believed that

> the process of political attrition of the metropolitan power's capability to wage war is *not* the consequence of errors of generalship, though these may well occur. Rather, it is a function of the *structure* of the conflict, of the nature of the conflictual relationship between the belligerents. Where the war is perceived [by the metropolitan power] as "limited"—because the opponent is "weak" and can pose no direct threat—the prosecution of the war does not take automatic primacy over other goals pursued by factions within the government, or bureaucracies or other groups pursuing interests which compete for state resources. In a situation of total war, the prosecution of the war *does* take automatic primacy over all other goals. Controversies over "guns or butter" are not only conceivable in a Vietnam-type conflict, but inevitable. In a total war situation they would be inconceivable; guns would get *automatic* priority.[20]

On the other hand, Mack regarded the weaker side's strategy choice as crucial to prospects for insurgent success. The metropolitan power could not be vanquished militarily, but it could be defeated politically. Wearing down the stronger side's weaker political will dictated a Maoist strategy of protracted irregular warfare that combined political mobilization of the indigenous population and the insurgents' imposition of a "steady accumulation of 'costs' on their opponents."[21] Just such a strategy had delivered insurgent victories in China in 1949, Indochina in 1954, and Vietnam in 1975—the year that Mack published his analysis. Mack concluded his assessment with a warning:

> Governments which become committed to such wars for whatever reason should realize that, over time, the costs of the war will inevitably generate widespread opposition at home. The causes of dissent lie beyond the control of the political elite; they lie in the structure of the conflict itself—in the type of war being pursued and in the asymmetries which form its distinctive character. Anti-war movements, on the other hand, have tended to underestimate their political effectiveness. They

have failed to realize that where the external power has been forced to withdraw, it has been as a consequence of internal dissent.[22]

Mack's postulation of a built-in asymmetry of interest and attendant willingness to sacrifice in wars between governments and insurgents is a major insight into the phenomenon of defeated Goliaths. Differentials in stakes, motivation, and pain tolerance can and have more than offset material weakness. His analysis, however, has an air of structural determination about it because it suggests that governments are doomed to defeat in wars with foreign insurgent enemies because of inherent imbalances in political will between the stronger and weaker sides. In fact, in irregular as in regular conflicts, the materially stronger side prevails more often than not. Wealth, numbers, and firepower count—as the Germans discovered in two world wars and as most insurgencies have discovered throughout history from Roman times. Steven Peter Rosen, in his survey of 39 wars from 1848 through 1945, found that the materially stronger side won 80 percent of the time. Rosen, who published his findings in 1972, examined two theories of war power, "one emphasizing the importance of [material] strength in producing victory, the other emphasizing willingness to suffer. Reliance on force," he observed, "is characteristic of conventional forces, such as those of the United States, whereas reliance on superior cost-tolerance," best measured as "losses of life . . . relative to population size . . . is typical of guerrilla forces such as the Viet Cong."[23] It is the insurgents' greater strength of interest in the fight and attendant willingness to sacrifice that defeats the stronger side.

> The very essence of the doctrine of guerrilla struggle is that it is a form of struggle designed to combat a materially stronger opponent; the basic idea is that the regime has the guns, but the guerrillas have the hearts of the people. The guerrilla's superiority is not his ability to harm, but in his greater willingness to be harmed. Ho Chi Minh formulated this in a classic way with his familiar prediction that "In the end, the Americans will have killed ten of us for every American soldier who died, but it is they who will tire first."[24]

The problem is, argues Rosen, based on his survey data, "that while superior cost-tolerance may occasionally give the advantage to the weaker party, having less strength but more cost-tolerance more often results in defeat."[25]

Rosen's argument seems intuitive. Strength matters. It is always better to be stronger than it is to be weaker. All armed entities, be they states, insurgencies, gangs, or otherwise, seek strength because strength protects, confers security choices, and works—not always, but most of the time. Guerrilla warfare is hardly the preferred choice of the weaker side; on the contrary, it is dictated by weakness. Observes British strategist Colin Gray, "In irregular warfare a relatively materially resource-rich regular force is pitted against a resource-challenged foe. Of necessity, the latter must operate by stealth, and has to avoid open combat except under conditions of its own choice."[26] Mao himself rejected guerrilla warfare as the means to decisive victory; it was but a preparatory stage to gaining the ability to conduct operations from superior strength—final-phase, conventional military operations.

It is perhaps no coincidence that Mack's analysis makes no reference to examples of metropolitan-government military and political defeats of foreign insurgencies such as Great Britain's defeat of the Indian Mutiny (1857), the Boers in South Africa (1899–1902), and the Malayan Races Liberation Army in Malaya (1948–60); Spain's defeat of the Rif rebellion in Spanish Morocco (1921–26); and the U.S. defeat of the Aguinaldo rebellion in the Philippines (1899–1901) and the Sandino insurrection in Nicaragua (1926–33). These and other cases suggest that factors other than political will are at work. Even the strongest will, if hitched to a bad strategy or denied minimum material resources, can be defeated. Perhaps no twentieth-century leader possessed a stronger political will than Adolf Hitler, but he could not will closure of the fatal gap between his unlimited territorial ambitions in Europe and the means at his disposal to fulfill them. Nor could he will immunity from such gross strategic errors of judgment as taking on Russia before finishing off Britain and gratuitously declaring war on the United States in 1941. Post-Bismarckian German statecraft and war planning displayed a persistent willingness to sacrifice strategy on the altar of operational considerations. The result was strategic defeat in both world wars. Will is indispensable to success in war but so too is sound strategy.

Mack's analysis warrants two further comments. First, the disparity in material strength between the stronger and weaker sides is almost always misleading in great-power wars against foreign insurgencies because, as Mack observes, great powers never commit but a fraction of their military power to such fights. As great powers they must always prepare first and foremost for war against other extant or emerging great powers, and they may have other overseas military commitments to boot. What counts is not the gross power relationship—with a few nuclear weapons the United States could have wiped out North Vietnam in a matter of minutes—but rather the balance of power within the theater of combat operations. Going further, within the theater of operations, what counts first and foremost is the balance between those directly engaged in the fighting—combat as opposed to support forces. Distance dilutes combat power. Great powers use expeditionary forces to wage overseas wars, and expeditionary forces, especially those technology-addicted and creature-comforted forces of the United States, are notorious consumers of combat support and combat-service support.

Second, while hindsight argues strongly that losing great powers had no vital interests at stake in wars against vitally interested winning insurgencies, calibration of interest is hardly an objective undertaking. The farther one ventures from homeland physical security, the more subjective the term "vital interest" becomes. Neither Imperial Japan nor Nazi Germany were in a position to attack the continental United States, which accounts in no small measure for President Franklin D. Roosevelt's inability to mobilize domestic political opinion for war absent the reckless Japanese attack on Pearl Harbor and Hitler's subsequent and even more idiotic declaration of war on the United States. Who defines vital interests and by what criteria? And are not political leaders, at least in democratic states, compelled to sell virtually all major resorts to force as wars of necessity (as opposed to wars of choice), which in turn require the invocation of threatened "vital" interests? In the case of the United States, even obvious wars of choice—the Korean, Vietnam, Gulf, and Iraq wars—are embraced as crusades against the forces of evil, with the attendant demonization of enemy leaders and ideologies. No great power abjures wars of choice, which indeed are a distinguishing feature of great powers; vital interests are not the only interests warranting threatened and actual use of force. That said, the postulation of interest ignores not only the definitional subjectivity of interest but also the fact that the stakes may appear to be far more important on the eve of war than afterward, especially if it is a costly lost war. If the United States had decisively won the Vietnam War in 1965 or 1966, the Johnson administration's prewar claim that America had critical interests in preserving an independent non-Communist South Vietnam would likely have escaped convincing challenge. Military victory tends to render moot leadership claims of high stakes as well as leadership exertion to sustain public opinion.[27]

Ivan Arreguin-Toft, in his seminal 2001 assessment, "How the Weak Win Wars: A Theory of Asymmetric Conflict" (and a subsequent book of the same title[28]), has taken up where Mack left off. Contending that Mack was the "one scholar [who] has advanced a strong general explanation of asymmetric conflict outcomes"—namely, that "the actor with the most resolve wins, regardless of material power resources," Arreguin-Toft focuses instead on "how a weak actor's strategy can make a strong actor's power irrelevant." His starting point is that "strategy . . . can multiply or divide power."[29] He contends that "the best predictor of asymmetric conflict is strategic interaction" and that "strong actors will lose asymmetric conflicts when they use the wrong strategy vis-à-vis their opponents' strategy."[30]

In his view, the strong actor has two strategies available. The first is "direct attack," or "the use of the military to capture or eliminate an adversary's armed forces, thereby gaining control of that opponent's values" (e.g., "a capital city, an industrial or communications center, or a bridge"). Direct attack's "main goal is to win the war by destroying the adversary's capacity to resist with armed forces. Both attrition and blitzkrieg are direct-attack strategies."[31] The second strategy available to the strong actor is "barbarism," or "the systematic violation of the laws of war in pursuit of a military or political objective." Unlike direct attack, barbarism is aimed at destroying the weak actor's political will to fight via such depredations against civilian populations as crop destruction, forcible population relocation, collective punishment, hostage-taking, reprisals, rape, murder, torture, and indiscriminate bombing.[32] Reliance on barbarism to suppress rebellion has been common to imperial states from the Roman Empire through the Third Reich, and even democratic states have employed at least some elements of the strategy (e.g., Britain in South Africa, France in Algeria, the United States in Vietnam, Israel in the West Bank and Gaza Strip).

Two strategies are also available to the weaker side: "direct defense," which entails "the use of armed forces to thwart the stronger side's attempt to capture or destroy values such as territory, population, and strategic resources," and "guerrilla warfare" (and its related strategy of terrorism), which involves "the organization of a portion of society for the purpose of imposing costs on an adversary using armed forces trained to avoid direct confrontation."[33] A guerrilla warfare strategy requires a supportive population and a physical or political sanctuary. In Arreguin-Toft's view, "the universe of potential strategies can be reduced to two ideal-type strategic approaches: direct and indirect. Direct approaches target an adversary's armed forces in order to destroy that adversary's capacity to fight. Indirect approaches seek to destroy an adversary's will to fight."[34] A guerrilla warfare strategy targets enemy soldiers, but it does so for the purpose of wearing down the enemy's political will over time. Indeed, time is the indispensable ingredient of any successful guerrilla warfare strategy; denied the physical capacity to gain a quick and decisive victory over the stronger enemy, the weaker side must employ protraction of hostilities as its main weapon against the weaker-willed. And it certainly helps if, characteristically, the stronger side is overconfident.

> In asymmetric conflicts when strategic interaction causes an unexpected delay between the commitment of armed forces and the attainment of military or political objectives, strong actors tend to lose for two reasons. First, although all combatants tend to have inflated expectations of victory, strong actors in asymmetric conflicts are particularly susceptible to this problem. If power implies victory, then an overwhelming power advantage implies an overwhelming—and rapid—victory. As war against a Lilliputian opponent drags on, however, dramatic overestimates of success force political and military elites in the strong state to escalate the use of force to meet expectations (thus increasing the costs of a conflict) or risk looking increasingly incompetent. . . . Strong actors also lose asymmetric wars when, in attempting to avoid increasing costs—such as declaring war, mobilizing reserves, raising taxes, or sustaining casualties—they yield to the temptation to employ barbarism. Barbarism conserves friendly forces, but even when militarily effective it is risky. Barbarism carries the possibility of domestic political discovery (and opposition) as well as external intervention.[35]

Arreguin-Toft contends that the stronger side is most likely to lose when it attacks with a direct strategy and the weak side defends using an indirect strategy, all other things being equal. Why?

> Unlike direct strategies, which involve the use of forces trained and equipped to fight as organized units against other similarly trained and equipped forces, indirect defense strategies typically rely on irregular

armed forces (i.e., forces difficult to distinguish from noncombatants when not in actual combat). As a result, an attacker's forces tend to kill or injure noncombatants during operations, which tends to stimulate weak-actor resistance. Most important, because indirect defense strategies sacrifice values [territory, population, resources, etc.] for time, they necessarily take longer to resolve so long as weak actors continue to have access to sanctuary and social support. In asymmetric conflict, delay favors the weak.[36]

This was pretty much what happened in Vietnam. The United States opted for a direct "search-and-destroy" strategy against enemy field forces practicing (with the exception of Tet) an indirect strategy of guerrilla warfare. The result, for the stronger side, was a politically intolerable protraction of bloody and indecisive hostilities. Both Westmoreland and Vo Nguyen Giap pursued a strategy of military attrition aimed at breaking the other side's political will, and the Communists prevailed because they always had the stronger will as well as a strategy based on that fact. The British in North America also pursued a direct strategy against American forces, which were waging what amounted to a protracted guerrilla war. The colonial militia fought as irregulars, and after 1776 Gen. George Washington was careful not to risk the survival of the regular Continental Army. He was always prepared to run away from superior British force. Both the Vietnamese Communist and American rebel leaderships understood a critical reality that their stronger opponents failed to grasp: the insurgent can win simply by not losing, whereas the counterinsurgent power can lose by not winning.

Indirect defense via irregular warfare is in most cases the only sensible strategy for the weaker side because a direct defense is an invitation to swift defeat. The principal elements of irregular warfare are protraction, attrition, and deception. Protraction and attrition are dictated by the conventional enemy's military superiority. Because the weaker side has no hope of quick and decisive victory, it employs time and the steady infliction of casualties and other war costs to subvert the enemy's political will to continue fighting. Protraction also requires a willingness to trade space and resources for time because attempted territorial defense plays to the conventional enemy's superiority in firepower. Anonymity, or the capacity to dissolve into the local population and terrain (natural and man-made), shields irregular forces from the potentially catastrophic consequences of the enemy's firepower superiority and can provoke the enemy to inflict politically self-defeating collateral damage on the civilian population.

In the twentieth century, Mao Tse-tung crafted a theory and practice of irregular warfare known as "protracted war" or "revolutionary war" that delivered Communist victories in China and Indochina and inspired other insurgents elsewhere in the third world. When the United States encountered this particular brand of irregular warfare in Vietnam, it grasped neither the essentially political nature of the conflict nor the limits of its own conventional military power in the Indochinese political and operational setting. It waged the only war it knew how to fight but was stalemated by an enemy with a ferociously superior will to win and a strategy of warfare that denied decisive application of U.S. military strengths. The United States picked the wrong strategy.

But if the stronger side can pick the wrong strategy, so too can the weaker side. Positional warfare is the stronger side's best game, and for the weaker side to attempt to play that game, or at least play it prematurely, is to invite impalement on the stronger side's firepower. The battles of Rorke's Drift (1879) and Omdurman (1898) are but two of many colonial warfare examples of inevitably defeated weaker-side frontal assaults against prepared stronger-side defenses. The Boers in the Orange Free State and Transvaal initially attempted positional warfare against advancing stronger British forces, were defeated, and then switched to irregular warfare.[37] Insurgencies that attempt to transition from guerrilla to conventional warfare before the balance of strength at least approaches parity with the regular enemy risk operational and even strategic defeat. The Communist-led insurgency in post–World War II Greece made this mistake, as did the Vietcong in mounting the Tet Offensive in 1968. Tet was a military calamity for the Vietcong because it sought to take and hold ground against vastly firepower-superior U.S. and South Vietnamese forces. The weaker side must never lose respect for the stronger side's conventional superiority.

Arreguin-Toft's analysis rests on a review of all asymmetric (i.e., strong actor versus weak actor) wars fought from 1800 to 2005[38] and on case studies of the Murid War (Russia's conquest of the Caucasus, 1830–59), the Boer War (1899–1902), the Italo-Ethiopian War (1935–40), the Vietnam War (1965–75), and the Soviet-Afghan War (1979–89). He forcefully argues that strategic interaction is a better predictor of asymmetric war outcomes than any other factor, including interest, political will, strong-actor regime type, and foreign assistance to the weak actor. With respect to foreign help, he dismisses it as a significant contributor in all his case studies except the Soviet-Afghan War, in which U.S.-supplied handheld surface-to-air missiles enabled Afghan resistance forces to impose unacceptable losses on Soviet heliborne infantry operations.[39] His analysis rejects the view that "weak actors could . . . be winning asymmetric conflicts because they are supplied from the outside, rather than because they use a favorable counterstrategy." In fact, he claims his data show that "even when they receive no external support, weak actors are more likely to win opposite-approach interactions than they are same-approach interactions. Essentially, the effects of strategic interaction overwhelm the effects of external support for weak actors."[40]

And what of the influence of the strong-actor regime type? The stronger side's vulnerability to defeat in protracted conflicts against irregular foes is arguably heightened if it is a democracy. Indeed, the nature of the stronger side's government is a key variable in the predicting prospects for insurgent success. Chances for victory are virtually nonexistent against powerful and ruthless dictatorships, which are not answerable to public or parliamentary opinion and are accustomed to violence and the threat of violence in getting what they want. Resistance movements in Nazi-occupied Europe were never in a position to liberate their countries on their own; German forces were too powerful and the Nazi state was exceptionally barbarous. Similarly, captive peoples in Eastern Europe had no prospect of overthrowing Soviet rule as long as Moscow retained the will and capacity to use force; Eastern Europe freed itself from Communist tyranny only when Soviet leader Mikhail Gorbachev renounced Soviet use of force to preserve its European empire. Insurgent prospects improve against weak dictatorships and strong democracies, however. The former may in fact be weaker than the supposedly "weak" insurgent side, or at least not in possession of a strategically significant measure of physical superiority. And though modern democracies may be exceptionally powerful, they face internal constraints on the use of force that most dictatorships do not.

Gil Merom, in his persuasive study, *How Democracies Lose Small Wars*, examines France in Algeria, Israel in Lebanon, and the United States in Vietnam. "How," he asks, "do democracies lose [small] wars in spite of their military superiority?" Put succinctly,

> democracies fail in small wars because they find it extremely difficult to escalate the level of violence and brutality to that which can secure victory.

They are restricted by their domestic structure, and in particular by the
creed of some of their most articulate citizens and the opportunities their
institutional makeup presents such citizens. Other states are not prone to
lose such wars. . . . Furthermore, while democracies are inclined to fail in
protracted small wars, they are not disposed to fail in others types of wars.
In a nutshell, then, the profound answer to the puzzle involves the nature
of the domestic structure of democracies and the ways by which it inter-
acts with ground military conflict in insurgency situations.[41]

Merom accepts the importance of motivation and strategy in determining the
outcome of state-versus-insurgency wars, but he believes that "the nature of the
strong contender—that is, its domestic structure—remains the most important
determinant of the outcomes of small wars."[42] Specifically, for democracies, "what
dooms the prospects of political victory in protracted small wars involves an
almost impossible trade-off between expedient and moral dicta that arise from an
intricate interplay between forces in the battlefield and at home."[43]

For Merom, the expedient strategy against an insurgency would be that of
Arreguin-Toft's "barbarism" against the weaker side's noncombatant political
and social support base, a strategy commonly practiced by dictatorships confronted with rebellion.

The ensuing brutality, however, invigorates moral opposition to the war.
Depicted as immoral, the war objectives and casualties seem even less
sensible. In the final analysis, then, events in the battlefield of small wars
and the political requirements they entail create a front against the war
that operates in the marketplace of ideas at home. This front alone can
convince democracies to relinquish the initiative and become defensive
in the battlefield, if only in order to minimize the pressure at home. In
such a case, the war initiative shifts to the insurgents, and retreat becomes only a matter of time.[44]

Merom believes that "what fails democracies in small wars is the interaction of
sensitivity to casualties, repugnance to brutal military behavior, and commitment
to democratic life." Democracies fail in small wars because they are unable to
resolve three related dilemmas: "how to reconcile the humanitarian values of a portion of the educated class with the brutal requirements of

counterinsurgency warfare, . . . how to find a domestically acceptable trade-off between brutality and sacrifice, [and] how to preserve support for the war without undermining the democratic order."[45]

There is no question that domestic, elite political opinion, much of it morally repulsed by brutality in the use of force, played a major role in the withdrawals of France from Algeria, the United States from Vietnam, and Israel from Lebanon. But was an articulate minority's moral revulsion over military methods a more powerful factor in determining the outcome of hostilities than the course of hostilities itself? Perhaps it was in the case of France in Algeria, where war-induced metropolitan political exhaustion occurred against a backdrop accelerating insurgent defeat. In the case of Vietnam, however, growing public disaffection over the war stemmed primarily from the fact of a costly and seemingly endless military stalemate; presidential candidate George McGovern, who made the morality of the war his central campaign issue, went down in one of the worst political defeats in American history. Richard C. Eichenberg, in his exhaustive study of U.S. public opinion and the use of force from 1981 to 2005, concludes that most Americans approach the use of force on the basis of perceived costs and benefits, and it is not casualties per se or moral considerations, but rather "the principal policy objective and the success or failure of military operations [that] are [the] crucial factors determining the level of civilian support and its aftermath."[46] Christopher Gelpi, Peter D. Feaver, and Jason Reifler reach a similar conclusion:

> [T]he U.S. public's tolerance for the human costs of war is primarily shaped by the intersection of two crucial attitudes: beliefs about the rightness or wrongness of the war, and beliefs about a war's likely success. The impact of each attitude depends upon the other. Ultimately, however, we find that beliefs about the likelihood of success matter most in determining the public's willingness to tolerate U.S. military deaths in combat. . . . U.S. casualties stand as a cost of war, but they are a cost that the public is willing to pay if it thinks the initial decision to launch the war was correct, and if it thinks the United States will prevail.[47]

And is barbarism the only effective counterinsurgent strategy? It proved militarily potent if politically self-defeating in Algeria, but is the counterinsurgent

choice, as implied by Merom and Arreguin-Toft, restricted simply to going barbaric or going down to defeat? Such a strategy was not employed by the British
in Malaya or by the Philippine government against the Huks, two cases of successful counterinsurgency by democracies employing a combination of political
and social reform and highly discreet use of force. Indeed, in Vietnam, but for the
North's conventional military intervention, the Communists almost certainly would
have lost the war in South Vietnam; by 1970–71 the Vietcong insurgency had
been broken by a combination of horrendous military losses, land reform, and
economic progress. Barbarism as a counterinsurgency strategy may be morally
and politically foreclosed to modern democracies (although many believe Israeli
behavior on the West Bank is barbaric), but a strategy of military restraint and
accommodation of genuine political grievances (which for Israel would mean
withdrawal from the West Bank) is certainly not. All three of Merom's cases
involved, in varying degree, a hated foreign military presence that left the stronger side no real choice other than barbarism or withdrawal. No political middle
ground could have accommodated both the aspirations of the occupied and the
perceived strategic interests of the occupiers. This is Israel's situation today in
the West Bank. No political concession short of evacuation will satisfy the Palestinian nation, yet refusal to leave mandates a policy of harsh repression and con-
demns Israelis and Palestinians to an endless cycle of violence. The strategic
logic that dictated Israel's withdrawal from Lebanon and the Gaza Strip applies
to the West Bank as well, although in the West Bank strategic logic has taken a
backseat to lingering imperial ambitions.

Furthermore, all three of Merom's cases involved stronger-side reliance on
conscripted armies and the incursion of substantial casualties. How salient is his
argument for a democracy that relies on a volunteer professional army and has
perfected means of warfare that minimize casualties? Merom admits that professional armies give leaders of democratic states greater domestic political latitude
in using force abroad,[48] though he does not address the issue of technologies and
tactics that lower blood costs. The United States abandoned conscription in the
wake of the Vietnam War and over the next three decades developed new military technologies and tactics that dramatically reduced traditional casualty rates
in the wars it fought during the 1990s and early twenty-first century in the Persian Gulf, the Balkans, and Iraq. Even in the nasty Iraqi insurgency U.S. losses
proportional to the size of the force committed have been substantially lower

than those incurred in Vietnam notwithstanding U.S. inability to neutralize road-side bombs, the insurgents' simple but deadliest weapons.

Does relative immunity from traditional blood costs of combat increase the political staying power of democracies in small wars? For the United States, which has led the technical and tactical casualty minimization revolution, the evidence is inconclusive. Public and congressional support for intervention in Bosnia and Kosovo was at best modest, notwithstanding the lack of U.S. combat casualties. Losses in Afghanistan and especially Iraq have been politically significant, with public support for the war in Iraq sharply declining. But the reasons for this decline may stem less from casualties alone than from the fact that they are being incurred against the backdrop of failure to discover weapons of mass destruction in Iraq or evidence of a collaborative relationship between the Baathist regime and al Qaeda, which were the primary rationales for the war. Making matters worse was the Bush administration's manifest unpreparedness to deal with the state-building challenges it encountered in post-Baathist Iraq, most notably a surprise insurgency that has seemingly stalemated U.S. military power there.

Regime type can affect the outcome of military operations in another way as well: as Merom asserts, insurgents recognize that democracies, in contrast to dictatorships, have inherent and significant political difficulties in sustaining protracted small wars. Insurgents seem to grasp democracies' lower tolerance for such wars. "The internal struggle in democracies does not escape insurgents," he observes. "Rather, it emboldens them, influences their feasibility calculations, and provides them with strategic targets outside the battlefield."[49] Merom's contention that insurgents grasp democracies' low tolerance for protracted small wars has been validated by subsequent analysis. Robert Pape, in *Dying to Win*, a landmark study of suicide terrorism from 1980 through 2003, discovered that almost all suicide attacks during that period, including those in Iraq, were motivated primarily by nationalism and conducted against the territory or forces of democracies and quasi-democracies—specifically, the United States, France, India, Israel, Russia, Sri Lanka, and Turkey—perceived to be occupying, or supporting the occupation of, territory the terrorists considered to be their homeland. (Post-2003 actual and thwarted suicide attacks in Spain, Great Britain, and Australia, which participated in the U.S.-led occupation in Iraq, are consistent with Pape's findings.)

Pape believes that suicide terrorism, which, like guerrilla warfare, is "a strategy of coercion, a means to compel a target government to change policy,"[50] targets democracies for three reasons. First, democracies "are thought to be especially vulnerable to coercive punishment. Domestic critics and international rivals, as well as terrorists, often view democracies as 'soft,' usually on the grounds that their publics have low thresholds of cost tolerance and high ability to affect state policy." Second,

> suicide terrorism is a tool of the weak, which means that, regardless of how much punishment the terrorists inflict, the target state almost always has the capacity to retaliate with far more extreme punishment or even by exterminating the terrorists' community. Accordingly, suicide terrorists must not only have high interests at stake, they must also be confident that their opponent will be at least somewhat restrained. Democracies are widely perceived as less likely to harm civilians, and no democratic regime has committed genocide in the twentieth century.

Third, "suicide attacks may also be harder to organize or publicize in authoritarian police states, although these possibilities are weakened by the fact that weak authoritarian states are also not targets."[51] Pape notes, for example, that not a single suicide attack was conducted in Iraq during the twenty-five years of Baathist rule, even though al Qaeda and other radical Islamist groups regarded Saddam Hussein's secular state as an apostate regime. Saddam Hussein had effectively monopolized terrorism in Iraq.

Democracies may not have a military center of gravity within insurgent reach, but they have a political center of gravity that is vulnerable to indirect pressure: finite public tolerance for protracted war against an irregular enemy. According to Bui Tin, a former North Vietnamese official and military commander, "[The U.S. antiwar movement] was essential to our strategy. . . . The American rear was vulnerable. Every day our leadership would listen to the world news over the radio to follow the growth of the American antiwar movement. . . . It gave us confidence that we should hold on in the face of battlefield reverses." The "conscience of America," he declared, "was part of its war-making capability, and we were turning that power in our favor. America lost the war because of its democracy."[52]

A key element in Saddam Hussein's 1990 decision to invade Kuwait and his subsequent refusal to evacuate that country, even as a huge U.S.-orchestrated coalition force massed to evict him, was his conviction that the United States had little stomach for war, that its tolerance for incurring casualties in third world conflicts was low to the point of barring risky military intervention. (He apparently failed to grasp the great disparity in U.S. strategic interest in the Persian Gulf and Indochina.) The chilling effect of the Vietnam War, manifest in the Pentagon's self-proclaimed restrictive use-of-force doctrine and reinforced by disastrous U.S. military intervention in Lebanon, persuaded Saddam that the United States was not prepared to risk a desert Vietnam, which he mistakenly thought he could impose on the United States.[53]

Al Qaeda leaders also believe they can break America's political will—in this case, the will to maintain U.S. military power and political influence in the Middle East and Persian Gulf. They too have been quite impressed by the U.S. behavior in Vietnam and Lebanon, and even more so by that in Somalia—evidence, in their view, of American cowardice. In his 1996 declaration of war against the United States, Osama bin Laden noted the "false courage" of the United States in permitting a single suicide bomber to compel the withdrawal of U.S. forces from Lebanon in 1983–84. He continued,

> But your most disgraceful case was Somalia, where after vigorous propaganda about the power of the USA and its post–Cold War leadership of the new world order you moved tens of thousands of international forces, including twenty-eight thousand American soldiers to Somalia. However, when tens of your soldiers were killed in minor battles and one American pilot was dragged in the streets of Mogadishu you left the area carrying disappointment, humiliation, defeat and your dead with you.[54]

A month after the 9/11 attacks, Ayman al-Zawahiri, bin Laden's right-hand man, again referred to American fecklessness. "People of America, your government is leading you into a losing battle," he declared in a statement released by al Jazeera satellite television. "Remember that your government was defeated in Vietnam, fled in panic from Lebanon, rushed out of Somalia and was slapped across the face in Aden [the bombing of the USS *Cole*]."[55]

Democracies have a very impressive record of waging conventional wars, even long and bloody ones, against autocratic and totalitarian states.[56] They defeated Imperial Germany in World War I and Imperial Japan and Nazi Germany in World War II. They then waged a long, twilight struggle against the Soviet Union and its Communist empire in Europe, which culminated in the dissolution of both. Fully aroused, democratic great powers have impressive staying power in trials of strength against undemocratic enemies. But democracies, at least since World War II, have displayed limited tolerance for overseas wars against determined insurgents waging protracted irregular combat. Such conflicts have rarely engaged the democracies' vital interests, and with few exceptions the democracies have been bested or at least stalemated by superior will and strategy. Insurgent material weakness, not enemy regime type, dictates insurgent selection of irregular warfare as a strategy. That strategy's prospects for success, however, are greater against democracies than dictatorships.

Mack, Arreguin-Toft, and Merom offer path-breaking insights on the phenomenon of the strong losing to the weak. Disparities in strength of interest and willingness to sacrifice, the dynamics of strategic interaction, and the relative vulnerability of democratic states to coercion via properly conducted irregular warfare go a long way in explaining the outcome of many "unequal" wars, especially insurgencies conducted against foreign occupiers.

2

The Role of External Assistance

The explanatory power of Mack's, Arreguin-Toft's, and Merom's theses regarding stronger-side losses, while formidably insightful, are nonetheless inadequate because they fail to explain why most insurgencies fail or why almost all successful insurgencies have in common something other than superior motivation and strategy: external assistance. Indeed, the presence or absence of external assistance may be the single most important determinant of insurgent war outcomes. There are few if any examples of colonial or postcolonial insurgencies that prevailed without foreign help. In this regard, Arreguin-Toft's assertion that external assistance to North Vietnam influenced the Vietnam War's outcome "only on the margins"—indeed, that it "hurt more than helped" Hanoi's war effort by encouraging disastrous escalation to positional warfare against U.S. forces[1]— is—there is no other word for it—preposterous. As we shall see, North Vietnam was completely dependent on China, the Soviet Union, and other Communist Bloc countries for all armaments, including small arms and small-arms ammunition. Additionally, thousands of Soviet technicians constructed and manned North Vietnam's sophisticated air defense system, while hundreds of thousands of Chinese troops operated and repaired North Vietnam's vital rail system. It is difficult to see how an *unarmed* North Vietnam could have translated its superior will and strategy into victory over the United States and its South Vietnamese allies.

The weaker side's possession of superior will and strategy is hardly a guarantee of success. Even the weaker side needs material resources. Substantial external assistance may be required to convert superior will and strategy into victory. A rebellion must have arms. Indeed, foreign help can alter the power relationship between weaker and stronger and thus distort the very meaning of the two terms. External assistance can come in various forms, ranging from simple political support, to the provision of money, to the supply of arms, military advice, and territorial sanctuaries, and finally to the introduction of foreign military forces. External assistance can also be intentional or unintentional. The former is self-evident: the provider's conscious aim is to help the recipient rebels. Less obvious is the fact that insurgencies can also be unintentionally assisted by *noninsurgent demands on the stronger side's military power*. Historically, most great powers have armed primarily against each other and only secondarily for imperial operations. When confronted simultaneously with great-power and insurgent threats, they will look first to secure themselves from the former and in so doing may compromise or even sacrifice their ability to defeat the latter. Unintentional external assistance unfortunately does not receive the treatment it deserves in the literature on insurgency, even though examples abound. Napoleon probably could have crushed the Spanish guerrilla but for much greater demands on French military power elsewhere in Europe, especially after his invasion of Russia. Indigenous resistance movements in Japanese-occupied East Asia profited immensely from the diversion of increasing amounts of Japan's military power to fighting the Americans in the Pacific. Similarly, post–World War II Jewish terrorism in Palestine struck at a British imperial presence so globally overstretched as to drive London to dump the entire issue of an Israeli state upon the United Nations.

It is also to be recognized that intentional external assistance may be available to the insurgent-besieged government side as well as the insurgent side. During the cold war the United States provided military assistance to a host of countries facing internal insurgent threats. In the case of South Vietnam, it intervened with massive force in 1965 to forestall an almost certain Communist defeat of the weak U.S. client regime in Saigon. Later in the cold war, the Soviet Union intervened in Afghanistan to preserve Communist rule in that country. In both cases strong outside powers intervened to save weak local clients from succumbing to strong insurgent enemies.

Great-power assistance to insurgencies against other great powers was hardly peculiar to the cold war. France intervened on the insurgent side in the American War of Independence; thirty years later, Britain intervened on the side of the

Spanish guerrilla against the French. As Machiavelli warned, "the prince who has more to fear from the people than from foreigners ought to build fortresses, but . . . the best possible fortress is—not to be hated by the people, because although you may hold the fortresses, yet they will not save you if the people hate you, for there will never be wanting foreigners to assist a people who have taken up arms against you."[2]

Consider the following cases of externally assisted insurgent victories: the American War of Independence (1775–83), the Spanish guerrilla against the French (1808–14), the Chinese Communist defeat of the Nationalist Government (1945–49), the French-Indochinese War (1946–54), the Vietnam War (1965–75), and the Soviet-Afghan War (1979–89). These cases are hardly exhaustive—six among history's hundreds, even thousands, of rebellions, but they illustrate the importance of foreign help, intentional and unintentional, to insurgent success.

American War of Independence

The American War of Independence turned decisively against the British only after the formation of the Franco-American military alliance of 1778, the subsequent infusion of massive French financial credits and munitions, and later, the dispatch to North America and its coastal waters of a powerful French army and fleet. French forces ashore and afloat sealed the fate of General Cornwallis's army at Yorktown, which in turn prompted the British to sue for peace.

Indeed, it is far from clear that the Americans and their French allies were the weaker side in the arena that counted: the Thirteen Colonies. Peak British military strength in the colonies never exceeded American strength, and though British army regulars always outnumbered Continental army regulars, American irregular forces dwarfed those of the few Loyalist militias the British attempted to raise. In the case of Yorktown the balance of forces was overwhelmingly favorable to the revolution: 38 French ships-of-the-line, plus 15,000 French sailors and marines, plus 7,800 French troops, plus 9,000 American troops (for a total of 31,000 men) versus only 8,500 British troops.[3] Thus the Franco-American side enjoyed an almost four-to-one advantage over the British in armed manpower as well as absolute naval control of the Chesapeake Bay upon which General Cornwallis's only hope of relief depended.

Even absent war with France, the difficulties of projecting and sustaining military power across 3,000 miles of often turbulent ocean in the pre-Industrial Age were formidable enough, especially against an American insurgency whose control of most of the colonial countryside (where the vast majority of the population resided) made it impossible for British forces to sustain themselves on indigenous fuel (wood and coal), forage (for horses and oxen), and foodstuffs, most of which had to be transported from Great Britain across waters swarming with American privateers.[4] (By 1781 there were about 450 privateers preying on British supply lines to North America.[5]) The British could take and hold such seaport cities as Boston, New York, Charleston, and Philadelphia. But they could move into the American interior only in great force, and even then they risked catastrophic defeat, as befell Gen. Sir John Burgoyne's army at Saratoga in 1777. The inherent difficulties of moving and supplying a large eighteenth-century regular army in the American wilderness prompted the Duke of Wellington to observe, "In such a country as America, very extensive, thinly peopled, and producing but little food in proportion to their extent, military operations by large bodies are impracticable, unless the party carrying them on has the uninterrupted use of a navigable river, or very extensive means of land transport, which such a country can rarely supply."[6]

It was, of course, the American victory at Saratoga that elicited the formal Treaty of Alliance with France and subsequent French naval and military intervention in North America. Even before Saratoga the French government had covertly provided the then huge expenditure of $8 million worth of arms, gunpowder, and equipment to the Americans through a dummy trading company, Roderigue Hortalez & Co.[7] As early as 1775, the French foreign minister, the Comte de Vergennes, who in 1763 predicted that the Americans would seek independence, had dispatched an agent to North America to meet with members of the Continental Congress and inform them that French assistance was secretly available. By the end of 1776, Congress's agent in France, Silas Deane, using French and Spanish money slipped to him by Vergennes, had ordered up and shipped to the colonies cargoes "indispensable to American forces fighting in the campaigns of 1777, especially troops charged with stopping Burgoyne"—cargoes that included 30,000 muskets, artillery, tents, 300,000 pounds of gunpowder, and 25,000 uniforms.[8] The Franco-American relationship was one of mutual self-interest: the American rebels desperately needed foreign assistance, most immediately French gunpowder, whereas the French saw in the American insurgency an opportunity to weaken an old enemy and avenge the loss of much of North America during the Seven Years' War (1756–63), also known in the United States as the French-Indian War.

Whether the British could have subdued the rebellious colonies even had France stayed out of the war can never be known. London almost certainly would have had to commit substantially more troops than it did. The British had the same problem in North America that the United States later had in Iraq: they never committed anywhere near the force necessary to seize control of the country. The British army (including Hessian mercenaries) never exceeded 35,000 men in a rebellious America containing about 3 million inhabitants.[9] (The number 35,000 also seems to have been the peak strength of American forces.[10]) Such a small British force was woefully inadequate to do more than hold selected ports and make occasional forays into the hostile American interior, where they faced constant attrition by American irregular forces and all too often the formidable combination of the regular Continental army supported by militias. Indeed, the British were unprepared to cope with the combination of conventional and unconventional warfare, and in the end, according to one assessment, it was "unconventional militia victories [in the countryside] that enabled Washington's conventional army to survive and ultimately to triumph. The British lost the war in the countryside."[11]

In fact America's predominantly agrarian society and the willingness of both Congress and the Continental army to flee the approach of British forces deprived the British of rebel geographical, economic, political, and military centers of gravity the loss of which could decide the war.

> [W]here was the center of gravity of the American rebellion? This loose confederation had no centralized administration to be overthrown by the occupation of a capital city, no common economic interest whose destruction would bring down the edifice. Was the center of gravity of the rebellion to be found in the Continental army? It was unassailable; for Washington's aim was to avoid or postpone decision, and he could do so by withdrawing into inaccessible country and impregnable positions.[12]

If there was a center of gravity in the Thirteen Colonies, it was arguably the "hearts and minds" of the American population, but absent a crushing British military victory, a rebellion that demanded the absolute objective of political independence could hardly be bought off by political concessions short of independence. A competitive political base might have been established had the British been in a position to protect Loyalist populations, which were strongest in the Carolinas and Virginia. But the British troops in America were simply too few in number to take and hold much inland territory; additionally, the dispersion of force required by a strategy of population protection would have invited defeat in detail. Thus most Loyalists were left at the mercy of Revolutionary activists, who controlled the militias and often employed them to terrorize Loyalist communities.[13] Revolutionary militia savagery was especially pronounced in the Southern colonies.

The British army also did not enjoy any significant technological advantage over the American rebels, who came to battle with firearms at least the equal of the smoothbore British Brown Bess musket and who captured sufficient artillery early on in the war (at Crown Point, Ticonderoga, and later, Saratoga) to dissolve any decisive British advantage. The effectiveness of British artillery was in any event limited against irregular forces and a Continental army that avoided stand-up fights. Local militias and the larger guerrilla bands such as those that operated in the Carolinas and Virginia under Andrew Pickens, Francis Marion, Thomas Sumter, and Daniel Morgan were essentially light infantry forces superbly suited for irregular warfare in the heavily forested colonial hinterland. They relied on individually aimed rather than volley fire, and those that possessed rifles had a significant range and accuracy advantage over British smoothbores. Irregulars were also more tactically mobile than regular units and often performed as skirmishers for such units. The British and Hessians had some light infantry units in North America (some Hessian units also had rifles), but they had no counterpart to the pervasive, indigenous local militias of the revolution.

What the British did have was contempt for Americans as soldiers—a common attitude of professionals toward amateurs, metropolitans toward colonials, regulars toward militias—a contempt that blinded them to the nature of the war they faced in the Thirteen Colonies. There, they confronted for the first time what Europe was to confront decades later in Revolutionary and Napoleonic France: a nation in arms. To be sure, as Piers Mackesy points out, the American nation in arms was essentially provincial and defensive whereas the French nation in arms was national and offensive.[14] But that did not make it any easier for the British to subdue. The British expected and sought a conventional, eighteenth-century-style, European war in North America but received instead a politically and militarily revolutionary war conducted by Americans who refused to fight the way the British wanted them to because they understood that to do so was to invite catastrophic defeat.

Further, the British government and army were not effectively organized to conduct a distant war against rebellious colonies. There was no single, central authority responsible for the war's overall conduct, and the critical function of supply was fragmented over a variety of agencies that were riddled with corruption and incompetence.[15] As for the army, which was small by European standards and lacked any professional staff, it was little more than a collection of regiments that in North America fought under divided command in campaigns that were all too often uncoordinated with one another or with the Royal Navy. Planning, such as it was, routinely ignored the logistical limits of an eighteenth-century European army operating in the American wilderness. For example, the campaign that ended in Saratoga, which was to have isolated New England from the rest of the rebellion via the conjunction of a southward advancing army from Montreal (Burgoyne's) and a northward advancing army from New York (Howe's), failed because Burgoyne was oblivious to the logistical difficulties involved and because Howe was never clearly informed of his role. Indeed, as characterized by the American military historian T. Harry Williams, the plan behind the campaign

> was so bad as to be almost unbelievable. The product of several minds, it emphasized unrealistic objectives, divided command, and separated armies. The blame for it must rest collectively on its architects, Lord George Germain in England, General Howe in America, and a new figure in the British command structure in America, General Sir John Burgoyne. No one of them had great strategic ability, but they might partially have overcome this lack if they had kept one another informed of their thinking. The most astonishing feature of planning . . . was the almost complete absence of communication among the planners.[16]

British strategy was also questionable. With few exceptions, Burgoyne, Howe, Clinton, and other British generals in North America concentrated on seizing territory rather than hunting down Washington and crushing his Continental army. If they believed that seizing cities like New York City and Philadelphia would compel Washington to come out and fight, it was because they failed to understand what Washington understood: namely, that for the weaker side to fight in the accepted manner of eighteenth-century European armies was to invite destruction at the hands of such an army. Washington wanted to duplicate such an army in America, but he recognized that his Continental army, which never numbered more than 20,000 men, was no a match for the much better trained and often numerically superior British professionals and Hessian mercenaries.

> Washington knew he had no reasonable hope of victory against the British army in open battle. At best he could wage defensive battles, judiciously withdraw after inflicting casualties, and wait to fight another day. With some good fortune (and poor British tactics) Washington might be able to fall upon isolated portions of the British force and inflict small defeats. Washington's objective had to be to buy time, raise the cost of the war to the British, and hope they would tire of the whole affair. The other American hope was for foreign help from France, Britain's traditional enemy and colonial rival.[17]

Neither the Continental army nor American irregulars, including militias in New England and the mid-Atlantic colonies and guerrilla bands in the southern colonies, were in a position to eject British forces from the Eastern seaboard, although irregulars could and did trap British detachments, and in the case of Saratoga even armies, that ventured too far into the hostile interior. After 1776 Washington, who learned from his operations in what is now greater New York City the dangers of positional warfare along the mid-Atlantic coast against a larger and professional army backed by naval supremacy, cunningly assumed the strategic defensive and "determined to win the war by not losing the Continental Army in battle, fighting only when conditions were extraordinarily advantageous." Observe military historians Allan Millet and Peter Maslowski, "This strategy entailed risks. Americans might interpret this as cowardice or weakness, and since defensive war meant protracted war, they might lose heart. But Washington believed he could be active enough to prevent excessive war weariness [and he believed that protracted war] would also fuel opposition to the conflict in England, as well as strengthen America's hand in European diplomacy."[18] The quality of Washington's appreciation of the war's military realities, the need to adapt strategy to those realities, and the relation of the desired strategy to favorable political outcomes found no counterpart on the British side.

French entry into the war greatly complicated what was thus already a very difficult fight for the British. The French supplied money, gunpowder (French gunpowder accounted for 90 percent of the total consumed by American forces during the war[19]), more artillery, and a professional army under the Comte de Rochambeau. They also provided an armada commanded by the Comte de Grasse, which decisively shifted the western Atlantic naval balance against Great Britain. Even more assistance was to come. French intervention in the war prompted Spain and the Netherlands to declare war on Britain in 1779 and 1780, respectively, though not as allies of the United States. These three naval powers brought a total of 180 ships-of-the-line into the fight against a Royal Navy diminished by almost two decades of budgetary neglect to only 120 ships-of-the-line.[20] Together with several hundred American privateers, the French, Spanish, and Dutch navies threatened not only Britain's transatlantic line of communications to America and its rich sugar empire in the Caribbean but also the security of Britain itself. For the first time in over a century, control over the maritime approaches to the British Isles themselves was seriously threatened by a naval coalition whose chief member also fielded the best army in Europe. (John Paul Jones was already raiding English seaports.) For Britain, with a much larger war now on its hands and the threat of invasion a very real possibility, the war in America overnight became a secondary theater of operations—indeed, a strategic liability. What had started out as a war to suppress a colonial rebellion had become a great-power war in which Great Britain was decidedly disadvantaged. The Americans thus became the beneficiaries of Britain's diplomatic isolation in Europe and of European balance-of-power considerations in Paris, Madrid, and The Hague. As Anthony James Joes observes,

> Without doubt, the most important consequence of the American victory at Saratoga and France's entry into the war . . . was that in the eyes of the London government, the major theater of combat was no longer the American colonies. French intervention would mean a naval war for control of the West Indies and India, but above all it raised the prospect of an invasion of the home islands. France was the dominant power on the

continent. Because Britain had no important allies in Europe, the French were free to contemplate a direct attack on the British Isles. And the eventual Spanish entry into the war further altered the [war's] strategic basis. . . . Now, with all her other worries, Britain would have to deal with a major threat to Gibraltar.[21]

The most dramatic impact of French intervention was the political concession London was now prepared to offer the Americans. With the war in America stalemated and relegated to the status of a strategic sideshow, and with Britain's lucrative and thinly defended West Indies possessions (especially Jamaica) now threatened by French naval power, London was ready to grant the colonies what amounted to complete self-rule within the British empire. To free British hands to fight France, the government of Lord North, with the assent of King George III, dispatched to the colonies in April 1778 a peace commission empowered to offer terms unthinkable before the colonial rebellion became a great-power war. The concessions included acceptance of Congress as the legal representative of the American people, removal of a standing British army in the colonies, the right of colonies to maintain their own military forces, and renunciation of parliamentary taxation of the colonies. The colonies were to remain within the empire and their trade was to be regulated by parliament; they would be prohibited from issuing their own coinage and possessing warships; and all American debts to British merchants would be honored. The Americans rejected London's concessions, insisting on, as a precondition for any negotiations, British military withdrawal from the colonies or recognition of independence.[22]

There was also growing domestic political opposition to the war. The Americans clearly recognized parliamentary opinion as Britain's key center of gravity, and Washington pursued a strategy aimed at coercing Britain out of the Thirteen Colonies via raising the costs of the war for parliament beyond the perceived benefits of continuing to wage it. King George III; Lord Frederick North, his chief minister; and Lord George Germain, minister for colonial affairs, insisted on a military solution because they believed that the rebellion was a personal affront to the monarch himself and because they labored under the illusion that the rebellion had little popular support and that terrorized Loyalist majorities were awaiting liberation. However, significant House of Commons opinion was against it from the start, favoring political conciliation rather than bloodshed.

The political struggle was as much over the king's prerogatives vis-à-vis parliament as it was over North American policy. Leading Whig luminaries, including such parliamentary giants as Edmund Burke, William Pitt the Elder (the architect of British victory in the Seven Years' War), William Pitt the Younger, and Charles Fox, believed the war was both a strategic mistake and a moral travesty. They warned that the enraged colonists could not be coerced into submission and that the war would invite French intervention. They also deplored the use of force, especially German mercenaries (hired to offset the shortage of British volunteers), against fellow Englishmen. In the wake of Saratoga, Pitt the Elder declared that "the conquest of English America is an impossibility. You cannot, I venture to say, you *cannot* conquer America." He went on to condemn the war against Americans as "unjust in its principles, impractical in its means, and ruinous in its consequences." Denouncing the employment of "mercenary sons of rapine and plunder," Pitt concluded, "If I were an American as I am an Englishman, while a foreign troop was landed in my country, I would never lay down my arms—never—never—never."[23] Four years later, just months before Yorktown, Pitt the Younger declared,

> I am persuaded, and I will affirm, that [this war] is a most accursed, wicked, barbarous, cruel, unnatural, unjust and most diabolical war. . . . The expense of it has been enormous, far beyond any former experience, and yet what has the British nation received in return? Nothing but a series of ineffective victories or severe defeats—victories . . . over our brethren whom we would trample down, or defeats which fill the lands with mourning.[24]

Even the British army's commander in chief, Lord Jeffrey Amherst, who had defeated the French in Canada during the Seven Years' War, opposed the war and refused to serve in America.[25]

Thus, even before Yorktown, the political balance in the House of Commons was shifting against the war. The combination of increased taxes and continued military stalemate made the war increasingly unpopular and fueled growing demands for greater parliamentary control over Treasury expenditure and an end to military operations in the Thirteen Colonies. Yorktown made the king's insistence on continued war untenable, and in February 1782 the House of Commons finally summoned a majority to end the war.

To sum up, even before France's intervention, the American side displayed a stronger will and superior strategy against its British adversary. Clearly, the rebels' strength of interest in the war's outcome was greater than that of the British. And in selecting a strategy of attritional irregular warfare against a conventional enemy Washington both denied the British a decisive military victory and promoted a steady erosion of parliamentary support for the war. In contrast, British strategy, if it can be so called, seemed to consist of seizing coastal and urban real estate in the hope of provoking the Continental army into exposing itself to destruction.

But to the advantages of strong will and better strategy must be added the American side's material superiority in the theater of operations. Great Britain was a far larger, and financially and militarily more powerful, state than the Thirteen Colonies, but the combination of distance and the intervention of France condemned it to be the weaker side in North America. Thus, within the theater of operations, the colonies were the stronger side, and assisted by massive external support, they won the war. Joes does not overstate the case that "There is probably no more clear-cut example of the importance of outside help to the success of an insurgency than the American War of Independence." Especially critical was the French navy, "which carried French troops to America as well as gold, clothing, and cannons to Washington's army [and] kept that specter of an invasion luridly before British eyes [and] interrupted the already quite tenuous system whereby the British supplied their forces in America."[26]

The Spanish Guerrilla

In his magisterial *On War*, Carl von Clausewitz devoted but a single, four-page chapter to what he called "general insurrection."[27] For Clausewitz, as for other contemporary observers of the Napoleonic Wars, war was almost exclusively armed struggle among sovereign states. The primary exception during the period was the savage popular uprising against the French occupation of Spain following Napoleon's placement of his brother Joseph on the Spanish throne in May 1808. The ferocity of the six-year insurrection was captured in the grisly etchings and paintings of Francisco Jose de Goya, whose depiction of the struggle remains arguably the greatest body of war art ever produced.[28]

The Spanish guerrilla of 1808–14 is important because the term "guerrilla" (small war) originates from it and because it was an insurgency conducted parallel to and in support of regular British, Spanish, and Portuguese army operations against the French on the Iberian Peninsula.[29] The Spanish rebellion against the French overthrow of the Spanish monarchy and occupation of Spain was a spontaneous national uprising that occurred within the context of a much larger great-power war in Europe in which Spain was a secondary theater of operations. The insurgency profited immensely from Napoleon's strategic overreaching elsewhere in Europe, most notably his disastrous defeat in Russia, as well as from the permanent presence on the Iberian Peninsula, beginning in 1808, of a British army under the command of Sir John Moore and his successor, Sir Arthur Wellesley (who later became the Duke of Wellington). Though neither the Spanish insurgents nor Wellington's army could have survived the full force of French military power on the Continent, they had to face only a portion of it, and they operated effectively to confront the French forces in Spain with the challenge of dealing simultaneously with regular and irregular military threats. The Spanish insurgents provided the British excellent intelligence on French forces, and the British in turn provided the insurgents direct and indirect military assistance.

In his chapter "The People in Arms," Clausewitz cautioned that, at least in Europe, even a general insurrection among an occupied population was most unlikely to drive the enemy out of the country.

> For an uprising by itself to produce such a [result] presupposes an occupied area of a size that, in Europe, does not exist outside Russia, or a disproportion between [the size of] the invading army and the size of the country that would never occur in practice. To be realistic, one must therefore think of general insurrection within the framework of a war conducted by the regular army, and coordinated in one all-encompassing plan.[30]

Clausewitz went on to list "the only conditions in which a general uprising can be effective":

1. The war must be fought in the interior of the country.
2. It must not be decided by a single stroke.
3. The theater of operations must be fairly large.
4. The national character must be suited to that type of war.
5. The country must be rough and inaccessible, because of mountains, or forests, marshes, or the local methods of cultivation.[31]

Spain satisfied all of these conditions. Insurgent bands, which by 1812 numbered at least 22 and contained no fewer than 38,000 guerrillas, operated primarily in the Spanish interior and understood the conflict to be a long, attritional
fight.[32] Iberia was a relatively spacious theater of operations and constituted one
of the most barren and poorly developed areas of Europe. "Approximately eighty
percent of Spain and Portugal was incapable of supporting an army for any length
of time, and certain districts—notably Estremadura and the borderlands between
the two countries—were deserts."[33] And the devoutly Catholic Spanish people,
especially the Castillians, were exceptionally tough, nationalistic, and warlike.
"Of all of Napoleon's enemies, the Spaniards were the most fanatical," contends
historian John R. Elting. "They were a hardy race . . . and expert haters, with a
once great military tradition and an even more pervasive tradition of revolt, civil
war, and disorder in general."[34] They were also enraged by exceptionally atro-
cious French behavior:

> Everywhere the French raped women of all conditions, including mi-
> nors, nuns, and expectant mothers. They pillaged and burned whole cit-
> ies. They made little effort to distinguish the peaceful from the resistant.
> Most disastrously for themselves, they looted and gutted cathedrals and
> churches, murdered priests, and committed public sacrilege of the gross-
> est sort.[35]

Men of the Church in fact played a major role in the insurgency, which consisted
of numerous, regionally based, and often British-supplied bands—numbering
anywhere from a few dozen to several thousand men—that operated in conjunction with one another as well as with the regular Spanish army and Wellington's
Anglo-Portuguese army. The Spanish rebels returned French savagery with their
own. Captured French soldiers were sawed in half, boiled or skinned alive, and
roasted over campfires; one guerrilla leader, a priest named Merino, specialized
in castrating captured French officers.[36]

The combination of British regular and Spanish insurgent forces confronted
the French with a dilemma they were never able to solve: the guerrilla threat
to their lines of communication to France compelled them to disperse their forces
to secure those lines, whereas force concentration was required to deal with
Wellington's army and the ever-present threat of a British naval descent on

Spanish ports. Though the French at one point had 345,000 troops on the Iberian Peninsula, they were never able to concentrate more than about 80,000 for offensive operations against Moore or Wellington, whose army numbered from 52,000 to 95,000 men; the remaining French forces were tied down by the general insurrection.[37] By one estimate, the French would have needed no fewer than 825,000 troops—substantially more than what Napoleon poured into his disastrous invasion of Russia—to have defeated both Wellington and Spanish resistance.[38]

Napoleon was clearly surprised by the eruption, ferocity, and duration of the Spanish guerrilla; he anticipated the loss of only 12,000 French lives to conquer the Iberian Peninsula.[39] Next to his invasion of Russia, his attempted dynastic coup d'etat in Madrid and subsequent occupation of Spain were his most egregious strategic blunders. Unencumbered by a general insurrection, the French probably could have conquered the entire Iberian Peninsula and in so doing denied the British the continental military entrée that Wellington exploited. But that was not to be. David Gates, an historian of the Peninsular War, concluded in his superb 1986 book, *The Spanish Ulcer*,

> An analysis of the factors that led to [Napoleon's] downfall reveals that the Peninsular conflict—the "Spanish ulcer" as he dubbed it—played a major role. What began as an opportunist gamble rapidly turned into a ruinous war of attrition that dragged on for six years. Napoleon's war in the Peninsula eventually came to mean for him what Vietnam was later to mean for the Americans, or, indeed, what Afghanistan currently represents for the Russians. Disregarding the age-old maxim that a simple military conquest does not in itself secure one's political aims, he made a fatal error by sending his troops into Spain, destroying any hope of winning popular backing for the government he sought to establish and, simultaneously, committing himself to a costly second front.[40]

The French lost an estimated 250,000 men in Spain, or over four times the toll of U.S. military dead in Vietnam, and at one time (1807–8) over one half of all French forces in Europe were deployed in Spain.[41] Though the Spanish guerrillas were smaller in number than any of the regular armies operating on the Iberian Peninsula, they exerted a disproportionate strategic influence of French fortunes in both Spain and Europe as a whole.

Chinese Communist Revolution

Students of guerrilla warfare commonly assert that the Chinese Communist Party (CCP) in 1945–49 achieved a rarity in insurgent warfare: victory without external assistance. By the end of World War II, Chiang Kai-shek's Nationalist Government, the Kuomintang (KMT), was certainly in a state of advanced political and military deterioration. The KMT's leadership was corrupt, its military forces poorly motivated, and its strategic objectives in China beyond its means to secure. In contrast to the KMT, the Chinese Communist Party was forging a strong and expanding political base in the countryside of north China and possessed, what in 1946 was designated the People's Liberation Army (PLA), a highly competent, disciplined, and motivated military force. By late 1948, entire KMT divisions complete with their commanders and equipment were defecting—not simply surrendering—to the PLA. In August 1949 the Truman administration issued a defense of its China policy in which it described the collapse of the KMT:

> The reasons for the failure of the Chinese National Government . . . do not stem from any inadequacy of American aid. Our military observers have reported that the Nationalist armies did not lose a single battle during the crucial year of 1948 through lack of arms or ammunition. The fact was that the decay which our observers had detected in Chunking [the KMT capital] early in the war had fatally sapped the powers of resistance of the Kuomintang. Its leaders had proved incapable of meeting the crisis confronting them, its troops had lost the will to fight, and its government had lost popular support. The Communists, on the other hand, through a ruthless discipline and fanatical zeal, attempted to sell themselves as guardians and liberators of the people. The Nationalist armies did not have to be defeated; they disintegrated. History has proved again and again that a regime without faith and an army without morale cannot survive the test of battle.[42]

The Nationalist army was not just demoralized. It was also venal and a terrible political liability in the countryside, where the great mass of China's people lived. According to a widely read history of guerrilla warfare,

> the army was . . . a conscript mass commanded by corrupt and, in general,

poorly trained and inefficient officers. Recruits were so miserably treated that in some areas a training death rate of 80 percent or more was the norm. Survivors fared badly. Division commanders received pay for their troops, passing on only what they judged fitting; unscrupulous commanders frequently sold unit rations; supplies, including arms and ammunition, disappeared into the vortex of greed to be sold to any buyers, Communists included. Armies lived off the countryside, robbing peasants and raping their women, human locusts as perverted as the Japanese enemy.[43]

In retrospect, it appears that nothing short of massive direct U.S. military intervention (if that) could have saved the KMT. Indeed, the Truman administration reached this conclusion no later than 1948 and was not prepared to intervene. The administration recognized the predominately political nature of the Communist threat and did not believe, as did Chiang Kai-shek, that the CCP could be militarily defeated absent major KMT political reform and concessions. The administration nevertheless provided substantial and economic military assistance to the KMT[44] and tried to broker a political settlement between the KMT and CCP, but neither side was prepared the make the necessary compromises.

The Communists almost certainly would have eventually defeated the KMT without intentional external assistance. Though KMT military forces enjoyed a numerical and technological superiority over the PLA until almost the very end, that superiority was more than offset by the PLA's superior will, leadership, and strategy. The claim of an externally unassisted PLA victory requires qualification, however, as it received critical unintentional assistance without which victory may have been elusive. First, though the People's Liberation Army was an exclusively internal Chinese creation, and though it emerged from World War II as a large and very powerful military and political force, beginning in 1946, it did receive, from departing Soviet forces in Manchuria, large quantities of Japanese weapons that the Soviets had taken from the surrendered Kwangtung Army. The question is whether these weapons made a critical or even significant contribution to the CCP's victory in 1949. Was China's internal military balance already irreversibly tipped in the Communists' favor? Second, the Soviet occupation of Manchuria from August 1945 to May 1946 established external Communist control over a strategically vital area where the CCP was politically and militarily weak. Soviet authorities in Manchuria permitted hundreds of thousands of CCP political cadre and PLA troops to enter Manchuria where, by the time the Soviets departed, they had established control of the countryside. The Soviets also looted much of Manchuria's industry, weakening the KMT to the CCP's advantage.

The role—obviously unintentional—of the Japanese army in Manchuria and China proper from 1931 to 1945 in paving the way for the CCP's victory also must be considered. Japan's seizure of Manchuria in 1931 deprived the KMT of China's industrial heartland, and Japan's seizure and occupation, from 1937 to 1945, of all of coastal and much of inland China opened the door for CCP political infiltration of rural areas now vacant of a KMT presence. (Japanese forces were concentrated in the cities and along strategic lines of communication.) Japanese aggression also excited Chinese nationalism on which the CCP was better able to capitalize than the KMT. Walter Laquer believes that the "two main causes of the Communist victory [in China] were the general disruption caused by the Japanese invasion and occupation and the superiority of Sino-Communism as a force rallying the masses. The Japanese victory destroyed the hold of the KMT. The nationalists had been weak even before 1937; subsequent military defeats accelerated and deepened the process of decomposition."[45] Bard E. O'Neill agrees:

> The Japanese occupation was fortuitous for Mao because it provided a nationalist appeal around which support could be rallied and also because it diverted the attention of the Kuomintang away from the Chinese Communist insurgents. Moreover, as the war dragged on, Mao's stature as a heroic nationalist was enhanced, while the dislocation and costs of the fighting further weakened Chiang Kai-shek's position. Indeed, there is reason to question whether Mao's strategy would have been successful against the Kuomintang if the Japanese had not invaded China.[46]

The Chinese civil war that erupted—or more accurately, reerupted—after World War II was an extension of fighting that broke out between the CCP and KMT in 1927 and continued until 1937, when the two sides formed a nominal united front against expanded Japanese aggression in China. During the late 1920s and 1930s Mao Tse-tung established a Communist political base and created a revolutionary guerrilla army in North China. During the Sino-Japanese War (1937–45), the KMT and CCP engaged in separate military actions against the Japanese but husbanded much of their strength for what both sides believed would be the inevitable resumption of civil war once the Americans had defeated the Japanese. Fortunately for the CCP, however, it was the KMT that bore the great brunt of Japanese aggression, losing many of its best military units. The Japanese regarded U.S.-supplied Nationalist forces as the primary military obstacle to fulfillment of their strategic objectives in the country; Communist guerrillas, in contrast, were treated as a nuisance.[47]

War resumed in earnest in mid-1946 between KMT forces numbering approximately 3 million men and PLA forces of approximately 600,000 regular troops and 400,000 irregulars. By the end of the year the KMT order of battle had dropped to 2.6 million whereas the PLA had gained an additional 100,000. By early February 1949 Nationalist forces had fallen to about 1 million troops, while the Communists fielded an estimated 1.6 million effectives.[48] Much of this dramatic shift in the military balance was a function of defections of entire KMT units, division-sized and even larger, to the Communist side, defections that also served to eliminate any significant technological advantage the KMT had initially enjoyed.

What was the Soviet role in the CCP's victory? Stalin initially refused to provide any help to Mao because he (Stalin) had reaffirmed Soviet recognition of the Nationalist Government in a treaty—the Treaty of Friendship and Alliance between the Republic of China and the USSR, signed on August 14, 1945—that also granted the Soviet Union extraterritorial rights in Manchuria.[49] Additionally, Stalin was suspicious of Mao's Communism and doubted the PLA's ability to defeat Chiang Kai-shek's armies. He believed that the KMT served Russia's strategic interests in the Far East better than a Chinese civil war during which the Communists would probably be defeated.[50]

Stalin soon changed his mind, however. The general hardening of relations with the United States, KMT foot-dragging on implementing the Treaty of Friendship and Alliance, the U.S. exclusion of any Soviet participation in the occupation and reconstruction of Japan, and the manifest unwillingness of the Truman administration to commit U.S. combat forces to China (an unwillingness shared by even the bitterest critics of the administration's China policy),[51] all combined to produce a change in Soviet policy.

The very presence of Soviet military forces in Manchuria not only denied

that region to the KMT, it also served to deter possible direct U.S. military intervention. The Truman administration had many good reasons to stay out of China's
civil war, and among them was the fear of provoking direct Soviet counter-inter-
vention. But Stalin's policy shift produced far more dramatic benefits to the CCP.
The first was the invitation to the CCP to send political cadres and PLA troops
into Manchuria; by February 1946 the latter numbered 319,000.[52] This permitted
Mao to bring the Communist revolution to Manchuria and the PLA to contest the
KMT's attempt to secure Manchuria for itself upon the departure of Soviet forces.
The second benefit was the transfer to the PLA of huge stocks of Japanese arms.
The Soviets had captured the Kwangtung Army's arsenal in Manchuria, which
contained weapons sufficient to equip a force of 600,000 to 700,000 men.[53] These
weapons, which included not just small arms but also artillery and tanks, permitted the PLA's rapid expansion in Manchuria and afforded it the capacity to launch
the kind of major conventional military operations that dominated the war from
then on. The third benefit was Soviet provision to the Chinese Communists of
considerable technical, medical, and other assistance, including restoration of
the Manchurian railroad network, which greatly facilitated the PLA's operational
mobility.[54]

But perhaps the greatest Soviet gift to the CCP was time:

> By the time the Red Army completed its withdrawal from Manchuria in
> 1946, the Chinese Communists, while still inferior to the Nationalists in
> strength of arms, had dispatched tens of thousands of troops and politi-
> cal cadres from North China [to Manchuria] and had begun the arduous
> task of organizing the countryside for revolutionary war. Without Soviet
> assistance, it would have been far more difficult for the CCP to mount a
> challenge to the Nationalists in Manchuria—an area where [because of
> Japanese control since 1931] the Party lacked support, experience, and
> local cadres.[55]

It is difficult to make the case that intentional Soviet assistance, significant
though it was, made the difference between the success or failure of the Chinese
Communist Revolution. Rather, eight years of war against the Japanese had de-
bilitated the KMT to the point where it could no longer compete effectively with
the CCP absent the kind of profound political and military reform that the

Americans urged upon the KMT leadership but that that leadership was unwilling or unable to undertake. Soviet assistance in Manchuria undoubtedly accelerated the military and political progress of the CCP, but by the end of World War II the KMT almost certainly was doomed. Perhaps direct U.S. military intervention might have made a difference, but that was never in the cards. The United States was recklessly demobilizing; Europe lay undefended; and the Truman administration believed there were no U.S. strategic interests in China worth a war. There was no public or congressional support for such a war; avoidance of war on the Asian mainland was a professional military injunction; and direct U.S. military intervention risked Soviet counter-intervention. Moreover, as Gen. George Marshall warned in early 1948, to intervene directly would mean that the United States would have

> to underwrite the Chinese Government's military effort, on a wide and probably constantly increasing scale, as well as the Chinese economy. The U.S. would have to be prepared virtually to take over the Chinese Government and administer its economic, military and governmental affairs. Strong Chinese sensibilities regarding infringement of China's sovereignty, the intense feeling of nationalism among all Chinese and the unavailability of qualified American personnel in the large numbers required argue strongly against attempting any such solution. It would be impossible to estimate the final cost of a course of action of this magnitude. It would certainly be a continuing operation for a long time to come. It would involve this Government in a continuing commitment from which it would practically be impossible to withdraw.[56]

The strategic reasoning behind Marshall's warning was impeccable, and it is tragic that such reasoning did not prevail in 1964–65, when the Johnson administration was considering direct military intervention in Vietnam, and in 2002–3, when the Bush administration was considering preventive war against Iraq. In Vietnam, the United States went to war on behalf of a South Vietnamese client as politically and militarily feckless as the KMT in the late 1940s. In Iraq, the United States achieved a swift conventional military victory only to provoke a tenacious insurgency that threatened strategic defeat of American purposes in that country. External assistance to the insurgent side is certainly no guarantee of success,

though victory seems improbable without it, but direct external military intervention on behalf of the government side may be automatic testimony to actual
insurgent status as the stronger side.

The Chinese Communists profited from both intentional Soviet and unintentional Japanese assistance. The KMT could not survive the combination of
internal insurgency and foreign invasion. Though the Japanese were hardly Mao's
ally, they could not have served the Communist cause better had they tried. When
the Spanish and the Dutch made war on Great Britain during the American War
of Independence, it was not their intention to assist the American rebels, but
assist they most certainly did by increasing the demands on already overtaxed
British sea power. The phenomenon of unintentional external assistance deserves
systematic inquiry.

French-Indochina War

In the French-Indochina War, the insurgent Vietminh were initially (1946–49)
isolated from outside assistance; they were short on military experience, poorly
armed, and incapable of mounting the kind of major military operations that
finally collapsed French political will in 1954. What turned the tide was the PLA's
victory in China in 1949 and the subsequent conversion of the Sino-Vietnamese
border into a conduit of major Chinese military assistance in the form of professional advisers and training teams, large quantities of small arms and military
gear, and most important, modern artillery captured from Nationalist armies.[57]
Chinese-supplied artillery enabled the Vietminh to crush the large French garrison at Dien Bien Phu, and the fall of Dien Bien Phu produced the French political concessions at the 1954 Geneva Conference that ended French rule in
Indochina and established Communist rule in what became North Vietnam.

In April 1950 the Chinese Communist Party's Central Military Commission ordered the establishment of a training school for Vietnamese officers in
China and the creation of a Chinese Military Advisory Group (CMAG) that supplied Chinese military advisers to the Vietminh army headquarters and down-
ward to divisional and regimental levels. Over the next five months China also
supplied the Vietminh with 14,000 rifles, 1,700 machine guns and recoilless rifles,
300 bazookas, 150 mortars, 60 artillery pieces, and large quantities of munitions,
medicine, communications gear, clothes, and food.[58] This assistance enabled the

Vietminh to clear the Chinese border areas of French forces and outposts, eliminating any obstacles to the passage of further assistance from China, and transformed the Chinese provinces bordering Vietnam into training and logistics sanctuaries for the Vietminh.[59] During 1951 and 1952, China provided the Vietminh an additional 58,000 rifles with 10 million rounds of ammunition, 5,200 machine guns, 600 mortars, 170 recoilless rifles, and at least 35 pieces of field artillery, and 50 light anti-aircraft guns. Chinese war matériel tonnage delivered monthly to the Vietminh increased as the war went on, from 250 tons during the first half of 1952, to 900 tons by early 1953, to 2,000 tons by mid-1953, to 4,000 tons by early 1954.[60] The Chinese effectively transformed the Vietminh from a collection of elusive bands of guerrillas into a powerful, conventional army. (Dien Bien Phu was an Asian Verdun—a thoroughly conventional fight involving frontal assaults on fortified defensive positions.)

> The massive aid in training and supplies [following the arrival of the PLA on the Vietnamese border] provided by the Chinese to the Viet Minh allowed the latter to entirely refit their army into a powerful force capable for the first time of engaging the French Expeditionary Corps in battle. With the onset of the rains in June 1950, the Viet Minh sent its battalions to Chinese training camps in the region of Wenshan, Long Tcheou, and Chingshi. The troops, without arms, crossed the border on foot and once in China were transported by truck. Clothed in new uniforms, they followed an intensive training course for three months under Chinese instructors. The Viet Minh used these troops to form an entirely new military organization. From 2,000 men, the Viet Minh regiments rose to 3,578 men. At all echelons, these regiments were henceforth supported by heavy equipment, signals, and headquarters units. Some 20,000 men were rotated through this training in 1950 alone.[61]

Chinese-supplied weapons and logistic support were crucial to the Communists' politically decisive victory at Dien Bien Phu. Though the French committed major errors in underestimating the Vietminh's fighting power and in choosing to fight at a place so distant from the center of their military strength in northern Vietnam (the Red River Delta), Dien Bien Phu, a remote place in the middle of mountainous jungles, was as much of a logistical challenge for the

Vietminh as it was for the French, and it was the logistical battle that determined the outcome of the siege. The PLA supplied Vietminh forces surrounding Dien Bien Phu from Chinese supply bases 600 miles away, moving supplies via 600 Soviet 2.5-ton trucks and thousands of specially configured bicycles, capable of carrying over 400 pounds, pushed on foot by porters; together these conveyances moved a total of almost 8,300 tons of weapons, ammunition, food, and other supplies to the Vietminh during the siege.[62]

Chinese-supplied artillery, including forty-eight superb U.S.-made 105-millimeter howitzers (captured from Nationalist Chinese forces in the late 1940s or from U.S. forces in Korea),[63] set up the French garrison for Vietminh infantry assault and defeated attempts to save the garrison through aerial resupply. Vietminh artillery not only defeated French artillery and inflicted heavy losses on French infantry, but also incapacitated the Dien Bien Phu airstrip and exacted a heavy toll on the meager French air force supporting the garrison. Especially effective were the four battalions' worth of Soviet 37-millimeter anti-aircraft guns, which, together with other artillery, shot down or destroyed on the ground 62 French aircraft and damaged another 167—extremely heavy losses for an air force that never had more than 75 combat aircraft and 100 supply and reconnaissance aircraft to support Dien Bien Phu.[64]

Though the loss of the Dien Bien Phu garrison hardly crippled French military power in Indochina (the French retained control of most of the populous and rice- and rubber-rich Red River and Mekong deltas), it capped eight years of a war that was never popular in France and that impeded the regeneration of French military strength in Europe.

Vietnam War

Donald Snow and Dennis Drew have noted the striking parallels between the American War of Independence and the Second Indochina War:

> The great irony and tragedy of the [American] revolutionary experience is in its parallels with the American morass in Southeast Asia 190 years later. As one sifts through the Revolution, the parallels draw closer and closer. . . . Great Britain was attempting to quell a rebellion far from home against a force and population largely hostile to it, just as the United States did in Vietnam. The war was also fought by an enemy who usually

refused to stand and fight in the accepted manner, preferring instead guer-rilla tactics. Moreover, the British had to fight two wars, one against the revolutionary militia guerrillas who attacked from ambush and who sup-pressed loyalist support (leading one British commander to refer to the activity as "the dirty little war of terror and murder") and the other against Washington's regular army. The parallels with the Vietcong and the North Vietnamese army are striking. Finally, public opinion turned against the British cause at home as success eluded them, just as American support waned for the struggle in Vietnam. The British problem in America was the American problem in Vietnam.[65]

Snow and Drew could have added that, as in the outcome of the American Revo-lution, external assistance was indispensable to the outcome of the Second Indochina War, which began with the formation of the National Liberation Front in South Vietnam in 1960 and ended with North Vietnam's conquest of South Vietnam in 1975. Though the nature of the war changed dramatically during those fifteen years, external assistance was a constant and critical factor for Communist forces in North and South Vietnam (as it was for the government and military forces of the Republic of Vietnam during its entire thirty-year existence).

Discussion of external assistance on the Communist side is complicated by dispute over what is to be considered external and what is not. The official U.S. view at the time was that the war was a case of external aggression by North Vietnam against South Vietnam, even though the war was predominately a civil war among Vietnamese and even though the 17th Parallel separating the two countries was intended by the signatories of the 1954 Geneva Convention that ended the First Indochina War to be a temporary line pending subsequent elec-tions to reunify all of Vietnam. This view renders all forms of material help mov-ing from North Vietnam into South Vietnam as foreign assistance. The Commu-nist view, shared by American opponents of U.S. intervention in the Vietnam War, was that the division of Vietnam was artificial, that the second Indochina War was simply a resumption of the first, and therefore that Vietnamese Commu-nists helping other Vietnamese Communists could hardly be considered foreign intervention. This view essentially restricted the definition of external assistance on the Communist side to that provided *to* North Vietnam by *other Communist states*, most notably China and the Soviet Union.

But even this restricted definition makes it impossible to argue that the Communist victory in South Vietnam was anything other than a triumph of foreign help. Indeed, the Communists could not have fought the war or won it the way they did without massive support from China and the Soviet Union. North Vietnam, a poor agrarian state, was dependent on outside assistance for virtually every item of military hardware, including small arms and small-arms ammunition. The magnitude of that dependence, moreover, grew as the war expanded in size and evolved from a largely self-sustaining insurgency in South Vietnam into a predominantly conventional war between the United States and North Vietnam throughout Indochina. Before the introduction of U.S. ground combat forces in the spring of 1965, which coincided with a counter-escalation by Hanoi in the form of regular People's Army of Vietnam (PAVN) units dispatched to the South, the war was largely a contest between U.S.-advised and supplied South Vietnamese forces and a growing insurgency that, while politically and militarily directed from Hanoi, was materially all but self-sufficient. The Vietcong fed itself off the countryside and armed itself with homemade, captured, and cached weapons and munitions,[66] and—being a completely foot-mobile force—it had little need for gasoline or other petroleum products.

The PAVN presence in the South in early 1965 consisted of three regiments of the 325th Division, which, because it was dispersed over many provinces, could do little more than stiffen the Vietcong. The division's 7,800 personnel constituted less than 4 percent of estimated Communist strength in the South, the rest consisting of 194,000 Vietcong main-force troops, self-defense militia, and armed political cadre.[67] Even by late 1967, on the eve of the Tet Offensive, PAVN troops in South Vietnam numbered 55,000 compared to the Vietcong's 245,000; and of the Communist forces' total daily supply requirement of 380 tons, all but 34 tons, or less than 1 percent of the daily 5,700 tons North Vietnam imported from the Soviet Union, China, and other foreign suppliers, were being raised from within South Vietnam.[68] The Ho Chi Minh Trail was at this point a jungle path along which occasional man-pushed bicycle portage moved.

At this point, then, the insurgency in South Vietnam was predominately indigenous and largely self-sustaining, which made it a very poor candidate for strangulation via attempted U.S. interdiction of what northern assistance it did receive. This explains in part why at least the interdiction component of Operation Rolling Thunder (1965–68) was a failure.

The nature of the war, however, began to change in the wake of the Tet Offensive of January–April 1968. Tet was a massive Vietcong assault on South Vietnam's cities and towns in which the attackers suffered large and irreparable manpower losses because they attempted to take and hold positions against overwhelming U.S. firepower. The offensive shocked an American public that had been led by the Johnson administration to believe that the United States was winning the war in South Vietnam[69] and forced the administration to reconsider U.S. war aims in Vietnam. Tet was, however, a military disaster for the Vietcong and the beginning of the end of the insurgency as the Communists' preferred means of victory in South Vietnam. Indeed, by 1971 the insurgency had been substantially reduced and effectively contained by a combination of military action, ruthless counterterrorism, land reform, and major improvements in economic infrastructure and agricultural productivity.[70] But this success counted for little strategically because by then the original insurgency had been replaced by a large and superbly armed conventional North Vietnamese army as the primary threat to South Vietnam's survival. This army, not the Vietcong, brought South Vietnam down in 1975. South Vietnam was conquered by a military force that had, especially after 1968, access to massive logistical support from China and huge quantities of sophisticated weaponry from the Soviet Union.

During the period from the defeat of the Tet Offensive to the spring of 1972, the intensity of the war declined because of Vietcong losses, the unilateral withdrawal of most U.S. ground combat forces (though not airpower) from South Vietnam, the suspension (by President Johnson in late October 1968) of U.S. combat operations against North Vietnam, and the preoccupation of Hanoi with creating a conventional military force that could conquer South Vietnam via open invasion rather than covert infiltration. The PAVN took over the brunt of the war for the Communist side, whereas a rearmed and expanded South Vietnamese army replaced the departing U.S. ground forces on the non-Communist side. Thus Lewis Sorley's book, *A Better War: The Unexamined Victories and the Final Tragedy of America's Last Years in Vietnam*, misses the point: Defeating the southern insurgency did not matter by 1973 because the U.S. military's evacuation of Indochina—the result of collapsed American political will for which the insurgency could take primary credit—left South Vietnam open to inevitable, and inevitably successful, North Vietnamese conventional military assault.[71]

In 1972 and again in 1975 Hanoi attempted to conquer South Vietnam by conventional military means. It failed in the first attempt but succeeded in the second, but in neither case would a conventional military choice have been available as a substitute for the failed insurgent option but for massive Chinese and Soviet assistance. Such assistance, which began before 1965 and lasted over a decade, included huge quantities of war matériel and the use of hundreds of thousands of Chinese troops and Soviet advisers. It enabled Communist forces to undertake offensive operations in South Vietnam, to offer punishing resistance to U.S. air attacks on North Vietnam, and to impose heavy penalties on U.S. attack and transport helicopter operations throughout Indochina. (Between 1962 and 1973 the United States lost a total of 8,588 fixed-wing aircraft and helicopters throughout Indochina.[72])

Hanoi profited immensely during the 1960s from the growing Sino-Soviet ideological dispute and rivalry for power and influence in decolonizing Asia and Africa. Neither Moscow nor Beijing could afford to be seen as less than thoroughly committed to the Communist cause, and they accordingly met almost every supply request Hanoi made. China was North Vietnam's primary military supplier through the Tet Offensive. As the war became more conventional, and as Hanoi increasingly sided with Moscow in the Sino-Soviet struggle, Chinese assistance waned but was more than replaced by Soviet and Eastern European arms deliveries.[73]

As early as 1958, however, China, at the request of Hanoi, supplied the PAVN with 50,000 Soviet-designed AK-47 rifles even before this weapon was delivered to the PLA; another 90,000 rifles were provided in 1962.[74] In August 1964, shortly after the Gulf of Tonkin incident, China sent approximately 15 MiG-15 and MiG-17 fighter aircraft to North Vietnam, agreed to train Vietnamese pilots, and began to construct new airfields designed to serve as sanctuary repair and maintenance facilities for North Vietnamese aircraft on the Chinese side of the Sino-Vietnamese border.[75] In May 1965, as the United States ratcheted up air attacks on North Vietnam, Beijing decided that the PLA should assume responsibility for road and rail repair and construction in North Vietnam, and beginning in June, not just Chinese railroad and engineering units but also Chinese anti-aircraft artillery, surface-to-air missile (SAM), minesweeping, and logistic units began flowing into North Vietnam. Chinese troops assumed responsibility for North Vietnam's air defense above the 21st Parallel, built highways in northwest Vietnam, operated and maintained two rail supply lines between China and Hanoi, and constructed fortifications along the northeast coast and in the Red River delta.[76] All told, some 320,000 Chinese troops served in North Vietnam between June 1965 and March 1968, peaking at 170,000 in 1967.[77] They were arguably decisive in maintaining North Vietnam's logistical infrastructure against U.S. air attack. Their presence also freed up PAVN manpower for operations in South Vietnam.

From 1964 to the end of the war in 1975 China supplied North Vietnam the following quantities of selected military items: 1,923,000 small arms; 64,530 artillery pieces (including mortars); 1,707,000 artillery shells; 30,300 radio transmitters; 560 tanks; 150 naval vessels; 160 aircraft; 15,770 wheeled military vehicles; and 11,400,000 sets of uniforms.[78] With respect to artillery, including anti-aircraft systems and mortars, China delivered more to the PAVN during the Vietnam War than it did to the PLA.[79] China also supplied North Vietnam with massive quantities of foodstuffs.

In addition to its military and manpower largesse toward North Vietnam, China's very presence north of Hanoi served to limit U.S. military action against North Vietnam. China's brutal surprise attack on U.S. forces in Korea in November 1950 deprived the United States of a quick and conclusive victory in North Korea and transformed the Korean War into a protracted conflict that permanently damaged the presidency of Harry Truman. President Lyndon Johnson, who rightly took the Chinese threat of war seriously,[80] was determined to avoid any action against North Vietnam that might provoke Chinese intervention. In his view and that of U.S. Army leaders, this ruled out an invasion of North Vietnam and mandated significant restrictions on bombing (e.g., no mining of Haiphong, North Vietnam's main port; no bombing close to the Sino-Vietnamese border; and no attacks on surface-to-air missile sites except in response to missile launches). More important, Johnson's preoccupation with possible Chinese intervention also dictated a gradually escalating application of U.S. airpower. "In the final analysis," observes historian Guenter Lewy, "Chinese deterrence was the main impediment to a more effective air campaign against North Vietnam. . . . The decision for gradualism . . . was made primarily because of fear of Chinese intervention."[81] Yet Beijing-induced gradualism, which included deliberate bombing pauses, greatly assisted North Vietnam by giving the Vietnamese Communists time to adjust to the U.S. bombing and take active and passive measures to contain its effects, and in so doing contributed significantly to North Vietnam's eventual victory.

Soviet assistance to North Vietnam began in earnest in 1965 and continued until the end of the war a decade later. The Soviets provided both vast quantities of nonmilitary items such as medical supplies, machine tools, industrial and tele-communications equipment, trucks, iron ore, and nonferrous metals as well as highly advanced military hardware such as fighter aircraft, main battle and light amphibious tanks, and the integrated air defense system installed in the greater Hanoi-Haiphong area that inflicted such a heavy toll on U.S. aircraft and air crew. The Soviets dispatched thousands of technical advisers to North Vietnam and schooled thousands of North Vietnamese soldiers and officers in Soviet military colleges, where they trained for service in the air force and antiaircraft units.[82]

According to one source, during the years 1965–72 the Soviets provided North Vietnam the following quantities of selected items: 340 aircraft; 711 pieces of field artillery; 132,000 cases of artillery ammunition; 90 SAM batteries; 165 radars; 131,000 small arms; 946 tons of food; and 53 tons of medical supplies.[83] These figures do not include material sent from 1972 to 1975, much of which was employed to construct the massive logistical infrastructure running from North Vietnam to South Vietnam via Laos to support the final and victorious PAVN offensive of 1975. That infrastructure, which included three diesel fuel pipelines and their associated pumping stations and storage sites (to support the 400 Soviet T-54 tanks and thousands of trucks involved in the offensive) and 12,000 miles of road (by 1971 an average of over 1,400 tons of matériel was moving down the Ho Chi Minh Trail every day), was testimony to the war's long journey from a largely self-sustaining insurgency in South Vietnam.[84] In contemporary dollar terms the total value of Soviet assistance to North Vietnam from 1965 to 1975 has been estimated at $4.45 billion.[85]

None of this is to ignore the Vietnamese Communists' possession of a superior political will vis-à-vis the Americans and the South Vietnamese; though southern forces had a considerable paper-strength advantage over the attacking PAVN forces in 1975, they were demoralized and poorly led.[86] Nor is it to ignore the Vietnamese Communists' possession of a superior strategy—protracted irregular warfare against the Americans and conventional invasion against militarily isolated South Vietnam. But even together, superior will and strategy could not deliver military victory for a state that produced no war matériel.

In his introduction to the English-language edition of the official Vietnamese Communist history of the war, William Duiker, the preeminent American historian of Vietnamese Communism, concludes that "It is difficult to imagine Hanoi's stunning victory without the firm support of its fraternal allies, who will not be pleased at the lack of gratitude expressed here."[87] It is no less difficult to dispute Duiker's conclusion.

Soviet-Afghan War

The Soviets had their Vietnam in Afghanistan, where insurgent mujahideen profited significantly, perhaps decisively, from U.S. and other external assistance, including thousands of Arab volunteers, funneled through friendly Pakistan. Especially important was the U.S. provision of Stinger surface-to-air missiles, which greatly reduced the effectiveness of the Soviet heliborne operations that formed the backbone of Soviet tactical mobility in Afghanistan.

Prospects for Soviet success in Afghanistan were problematic from the start. According to the Russian General Staff assessment of Soviet operations in Afghanistan, first published in English in 2002, the 1979 decision to invade the country was a hasty one that completely ignored Afghanistan's history of fierce resistance to foreign invaders.

> When the highest leaders of the USSR sent its forces into this war, they did not consider the historic, religious, and national peculiarities of Afghanistan. After the entry, these peculiarities proved to be the most important factors as they foreordained the long and very difficult nature of the conflict. Now it is completely clear that it was an impetuous decision to send Soviet forces into this land. It is now clear that the Afghans, whose history includes many centuries of warfare with various warring groups, could not see these armed strangers as anything but armed invaders. And since these strangers were not Muslim, a religious factor was added to the national enmity. Both of these factors were sufficient to trigger a large mass resistance among the people, which various warriors throughout history had been unable to overcome and which Soviet forces met when they arrived in Afghanistan.[88]

In addition to unintentionally provoking war with a "nation in arms," invading Soviet forces proved to be completely ill-suited for counterinsurgency operations, which may explain the reported opposition to the invasion of Marshal Nikolai

Ograkov and his successor as chief of the General Staff, Marshal Sergei Akhromev.[89] Observe the translators and editors of *The Soviet-Afghan War: How a Superpower Fought and Lost: The Russian General Staff*:

> The Soviets [had] designed their armed forces to fight large-scale, high-tempo offensive operations exploiting nuclear strikes on the northern European plain and China. In this type of war, massed Soviet air and artillery fire would blast gaps through enemy positional defenses. Soviet armored columns would dash through these gaps and move deep within enemy territory. In this type of war, tactical predictability was preferred to tactical agility. The war would be won on the operational level. Soviet force structure, weaponry, tactics, and support infrastructure were all designed to support this operational vision. These were all inappropriate for a long counterinsurgency effort in Afghanistan.[90]

Further reducing the chances of success was the low density of Soviet forces in Afghanistan. Moscow seemed determined to limit its military liability in Afghanistan even at the cost of a conclusive military decision there. The unexpected insurgency, misplaced confidence in the forces of the Soviet-backed Afghan Communist government (the Democratic Republic of Afghanistan, or DRA), and—after 1985—the growing willingness of a new Soviet political leadership (Mikhail Gorbachev) to liquidate imperial burdens no longer affordable combined to preclude the kind of open-ended escalation of the war to which the United States had fallen victim in the 1960s in Indochina. In contrast to an American peak strength in South Vietnam of 550,000 troops, Soviet force deployments in Afghanistan, a country five times the size of South Vietnam, varied from 90,000 to 120,000 troops.[91] This relative force scarcity deprived the Soviets of any chance of controlling the countryside; most Soviet troops were deployed in Afghanistan's major cities and along the lines of communication between as well as those linking the Soviet Union to Afghanistan. Throughout the war the Soviets relied heavily on DRA forces, which never numbered more than 300,000 and were plagued by constant desertions and defections. The Soviet military commitment in Afghanistan, though sufficient to prevent a mujahideen victory over the DRA, "was insufficient to achieve Soviet long-term objectives of quelling the insurgency movement and stabilizing the situation within the country."[92] The Soviets committed the cardinal strategic sin of committing *under*whelming force—a sin the United States seems to have later repeated in Iraq.

Soviet defeat was hardly inevitable, however. Though the Soviet invasion outraged most Afghans and though invading Soviet military forces were dismally unprepared for counterinsurgency, the Afghan resistance suffered serious weaknesses, and the Soviet military leadership in Afghanistan displayed an impressive tactical and operational adaptability to warfighting conditions in that primitive country. Also, the Soviet Union was not a modern democracy constrained by moral and other considerations in using force.

The Afghan resistance, which by 1985 fielded an estimated 150,000 fighters, was not a unified, centrally directed enterprise, but rather a constellation of 200 to 300 guerrilla groups formed around seven major factions, among which not only tribal chieftains but also nationalist and Islamist objectives competed.[93] Such fragmentation simultaneously forfeited maximum military effectiveness against the Soviets and permitted them to employ a divide-and-rule strategy. The resistance also did not have an effective counter to changes in Soviet strategy and tactics. In 1982–83 the Soviets began putting tactically remote mujahideen base camps at grave risk via the employment of heliborne assaults of highly trained *spetznaz* (special forces) units supported by very effective use of helicopter gunships and attack aircraft.[94] The Soviets also launched a systematic assault on the mujahideen's supporting population base via the "deliberate destruction of buildings, irrigation systems, crops and orchards as well as the deliberate targeting of noncombatants to sow terror and 'cleanse' disputed valleys."[95] Barbarism against the Afghan people, which included employment of small anti-personnel mines disguised as toys for children to pick up, weakened the resistance by depopulating much of the countryside and generated enormous refugee flows both within Afghanistan and out of Afghanistan—mostly to Pakistan. Coupled with heliborne *spetznaz* strikes on increasingly vulnerable mujahideen bases, the Soviets by 1985–86 had effectively stalemated the war and might have gone on to win it but for the impossibility of isolating the Afghan resistance from external assistance.

The literature on the Soviet-Afghan War is virtually unanimous in affirming the decisiveness of foreign help in defeating the Soviets in Afghanistan. Even Arreguin-Toft, whose strategic interaction thesis devalues external assistance to weak actors as a predictor of asymmetric war outcomes, concedes that "the mujahideen gained increasing advantages from the arms they received through Iran and Pakistan, and these increased the costs of conquest and occupation to the Soviet Union and its DRA client." Indeed, "the arrival of U.S.-made Stinger SAMs dramatically shifted the balance of power in Afghanistan" by eliminating deadly mujahideen vulnerability to Soviet heliborne infantry and helicopter gunships.[96] (One wonders how the course of U.S. intervention in Vietnam would have been affected by the Communist introduction of such missiles early in the war.) The Russian General Staff assessment dryly observes that "use of helicopters was severely limited by the introduction of the man-portable Stinger air defense missile. This appreciably decreased the results of operations and combat which frequently did not achieve their projected goals." With the mujahideen in possession of missiles that gave them the ability "to hit an aircraft out to a distance of 4,800 meters and up to 2,000 meters in elevation," the "Soviet command had to severely limit the employment of helicopters, especially during daylight."[97] According to another assessment,

> The Stingers transformed the war immediately. According to a U.S. Army study after the war, 340 of them were fired in combat, and 269 aircraft were downed. Even if the figures include some exaggeration, there can be no doubt that the weapon's effectiveness forced [a] shift in Soviet tactics. Soviet combat aircraft . . . had to fly higher to avoid risks; Soviet ground troops began deriding the pilots as "cosmonauts" because they flew so high. Soviet supply flights were grounded or inhibited. The resistance learned to lie in wait for aircraft along known routes and to set traps by staging ground ambushes that drew in close-support aircraft. They regained almost unrestricted movement for their own forces and supplies on the ground.[98]

The U.S. decision to introduce Stingers into the war, reluctantly made in April 1986,[99] must be seen within the context of an antecedent and much richer menu of external assistance to the Afghan resistance. The Stingers came on the heels of years of previous U.S. arms and other aid to the mujahideen, all of it funneled through Pakistan's Inter-Services Intelligence (ISI) organization. Indeed, Pakistan served as both a sanctuary for the Afghan resistance and an umbilical cord of foreign assistance. ISI operatives trained and equipped Afghan resistance fighters as well as facilitated the movement into Afghanistan of thousands of volunteer fighters from Saudi Arabia and other Arab states. Iran also assisted key elements of the resistance. By the end of the war, the anti-Soviet fight in Afghanistan had become an impressive international war.

———————

It is, of course, impossible in any of these cases to determine with certitude whether external assistance was decisive or even whether it contributed more to the weaker side's victory than superior insurgent will and strategy. To argue that an insurgency could not have won without foreign help is not to claim that external assistance was the decisive factor. Such assistance may be a precondition for victory—the weaker side naturally seeks it (with as few strings attached as possible). But it cannot redeem a weak will or bad strategy. Fighting power is a mélange of measurables (e.g., troop strengths, weapon counts, sortie rates) and intangibles (e.g., generalship, organizational quality, morale). It seems reasonable to conclude that no amount of outside assistance can redeem the fortunes of a weak-willed and strategically incompetent insurgency. It seems no less reasonable to conclude that highly motivated and skilled insurgents can be defeated if denied access to external assistance and if confronted by a stronger side pursuing a strategy of barbarism against the insurgency's civilian population base, or conversely, a strategy that combines effective grievance redress and discrete use of force. In this way, conventional militaries defeated the insurgencies of the Boers in South Africa, the Aguinaldo insurgents and Hukbalahaps in the Philippines, the Communists in Malaya, and the National Liberation Front in Algeria. In each of these cases the insurgents received little or no external military assistance either because such assistance was unavailable from the start or because the government side, the stronger side in each case, successfully halted external assistance already under way. In the cases of the Boers, Aguinaldo insurgents, and Algerian rebels, the stronger side arguably resorted to barbarism, whereas in the cases of the Filipino and Malayan Communists, the stronger side combined grievance redress and discrete force.

Geography and politics conspired to deny the Boers, Aguinaldo insurgents, Huks, and Malayan Communists outside assistance. The Boers were fighting in the South African interior and a hemisphere away from Germany, where sympathy existed for the Boers but not for intervention. Though the Boers had purchased excellent German rifles and some German and French field guns before the outbreak of hostilities, the British, by virtue of their command of the sea, quickly shut down further access to external assistance. The British eventually committed a total of 450,000 troops against the Boers, whose own numbers peaked at about 87,000.[100] Against such odds, and subjected to ruthless British destruction of their farms, livestock, crops, foodstuffs, and forage, the completely horse-mounted Boers capitulated. The Aguinaldo rebellion had no potential external sponsor and was in any event operating on a remote island. The Huks, operating on the same island, were no less isolated and were effectively crushed by 1954—long before the Soviet Union began actively supporting Communist insurgencies in the third world. The Chinese Communists, exhausted from the Korean War and preoccupied with consolidating their own revolution at home and assisting the Vietminh in French-Indochina, provided no help.

The Algerian War (1954–62) offers a more interesting, if more complicated case. At great cost, the insurgent *Front de Liberation Nationale* (FLN) won politically but lost militarily, and it lost militarily because of ruthless French counterinsurgency methods and French success in shutting off access to external material assistance. The French army had learned much from its defeat in Indochina, where it was never in a position to isolate the Vietminh from external assistance, and in Algeria it faced a smaller and much less politically formidable enemy than the Vietminh. The peak strength of the FLN's military arm, the *Armee de Liberation Nationale* (ALN), never exceeded 40,000, including regulars, auxiliaries, and irregulars, and it is testimony to the FLN's limited political appeal within Algeria that five times that number of Algerians fought on the French side.[101] The FLN, which was governed by a fractious collective leadership, lacked not only a charismatic, Ho Chi Minh-like, single authoritative leader, but also any political program for the impoverished rural masses of the country. Unlike the Vietnamese Communists, who promised land and as well as national liberation to the peasantry, the FLN promised national but no social liberation.

Even had the FLN enjoyed a larger popular base, which its heavy reliance on urban terrorism worked against, it confronted a massive French military presence and a skilled and barbarously effective counterinsurgent strategy. French forces in Algeria peaked at 500,000, including at least 200,000 mobilized reservists, in 1960, by which time there were only a few thousand ALN fighters still operating inside Algeria (the bulk of the ALN was ensconced on the other side of the Tunisian border).[102] French forces always maintained at least a 10:1 numerical advantage over the insurgency inside Algeria. They moreover made widespread use of torture, collective punishments, and forcible population relocations to extract intelligence, terrorize potential FLN supporters, and isolate vulnerable communities from FLN penetration. In 1957, in the face of a massive FLN terrorist campaign launched in Algiers, the French government transferred civil authority in Algiers to the military, which proceeded to crush the FLN in Algiers. In what became known as the Battle of Algiers, elite parachute units under Gen. Jacques Massu brutally broke an FLN-sponsored general strike (by threatening to destroy shops on the spot unless shop owners opened them) and then brutally rooted out the FLN infrastructure through mass arrests and torture.[103]

But what really killed any chance of an FLN military win was the French success in physically isolating the insurgency from external material assistance. During the first two years of the insurgency the FLN suffered an acute shortage of weapons; it armed itself largely with weapons captured from government security and police forces. This situation changed dramatically when France granted neighboring Morocco and Tunisia independence in March 1956. From then on those two countries became conduits of external Arab military assistance to the FLN. Tunisia also became a sanctuary for ALN forces; indeed, as the war got worse for the FLN inside Algeria, Tunisia became the ALN's main operating base. It encamped on the Tunisian side of the Algerian-Tunisian border, trained and armed its forces there, and then launched raids into Algeria.

The French could have responded by invading western Tunisia but chose instead to erect a barrier over 200 miles long stretching along the Tunisian border from the Mediterranean to the empty Sahara, where crossings could be detected. The barrier consisted of an eight-foot electric fence charged with 5,000 volts and flanked on both sides by fifty-yard belts of ground seeded with antipersonnel mines and backed up with thick, World War I–style barbed wire entanglements. (A similar barrier was constructed along the Moroccan-Algerian border.) Completed in September 1957 and known as the Morice line (after French Defense Minister Andre Morice), the barrier was defended by 80,000 troops who constantly patrolled the line and had immediate on-call artillery available to shell any insurgent infiltration.[104] The border area was also cleared, through relocation, of populations potentially sympathetic to the insurgency. By the end of April 1958, an estimated 6,000 insurgents and 4,300 weapons had been lost in attempts to cross the line into Algeria, and the ALN made no more significant attempts to breach it.[105] From then on, the ALN strength inside Algeria steadily declined even as it expanded in Tunisia. Together with naval control of the Algerian coastline, the French had achieved in Algeria what they had failed to achieve—as would later the Americans—in Indochina: isolation of the insurgents from external assistance. The effects of this isolation, coupled with stepped up French counterinsurgency operations inside Algeria, were militarily decisive:

> The French strategy had a devastating impact on the Algerian insurgents. Whole FLN and ALN formations were hunted down in their previous sanctuaries—the night and the mountains. The units of the nationalist movement became younger, less experienced, badly supplied, and often short-lived. Their morale, critical for a prolonged campaign, was deeply shattered. Local FLN commanders inside Algeria began to realize the magnitude of the damage inflicted by the French force, even before 1959. Algerian communities rejected the FLN authority more vigorously than before, its forces' efforts to extract money failed more frequently, and the organization's overall revenues diminished accordingly. The exiled nationalist leadership was confronted by the hard-pressed leaders of the forces inside Algeria who bluntly questioned its motives and objectives as well as prospects of success in the struggle.[106]

Yet three years later France granted Algeria its independence. How did this come about? Here is a summary of what happened: Though the French had virtually won the military war by the end of 1959, French behavior in Algeria, especially the open and widespread use of torture, had profoundly alienated most international and much of French elite opinion. Additionally, the war, deeply unpopular among conscripted troops, was placing increasing economic and military strains on France. Worse still was the political crisis in France. The Fourth Republic, proclaimed in 1946, had by 1958 become an unworkable instrument of government; plagued by a weak executive and a fractious legislative system based on proportional representation of a multiplicity of parties, it could not survive the domestic political crisis over Algeria. The French army's leadership in Algeria was profoundly contemptuous and suspicious of the Fourth Republic, whose political parties were deeply divided over the issue of Algerian independence. In mid-April the last of the republic's twenty-eight coalition governments fell, leaving France without a government for more than five weeks. In May, Gen. Raoul Salan, the commander of French forces in Algeria, sent a telegram to the General Staff in Paris threatening direct army intervention to prevent any civilian government from abandoning French sovereignty over Algeria. The situation was temporarily saved by Charles de Gaulle, who agreed to form a new government on condition that he be permitted to rule by decree for six months as well as granted a mandate to draft a new constitution and submit it to the country for a vote.

French army leaders in Algeria assumed that de Gaulle supported a French Algeria. However, by September 1959, even with the insurgency being beaten to a pulp, de Gaulle had concluded that self-determination for Algeria was the minimum solution for relieving France of a strategic albatross that was polarizing the French army and depriving France of the power and influence in Europe that de Gaulle wished to resurrect. This put him on a collision course with the French military leadership in Algeria. His public offer of self-determination provoked military leadership and elite parachute units into a revolt, which de Gaulle suppressed via a January 29, 1960, radio broadcast that appealed to the honor of France and ordered all officers and men in Algeria in loyal units—the vast majority—to disobey any orders by rebel officers. Dissident army leaders and their followers subsequently went underground and formed a terrorist organization, the *Organisation Armee Secrete*, or OAS, that sought to thwart Algerian independence through violence, including terrorist strikes in metropolitan France and repeated attempts to assassinate de Gaulle.

The Algerian War provoked a political crisis in France that threatened civil war and brought down coalition governments as well as the Fourth Republic itself. That republic was replaced in 1959 by the Fifth Republic, led by President Charles de Gaulle, who engineered a final settlement of the war in 1962 that ceded to Algeria full and complete independence against the backdrop of horrendous OAS terrorist attacks against FLN targets and in France itself. During the three years separating de Gaulle's public offer of self-determination and the final settlement of the war, the fact that the FLN insurgency had been effectively deprived of any chance of military success, and indeed was on the run from superior French forces and strategy, made no difference in the war's political outcome, which was determined by political events in France, not counterinsurgent military events in Algeria. In this way the FLN, which was far more successful in mobilizing support abroad than in Algeria, managed to snatch political victory from the jaws of military defeat.

Even had the French home front not collapsed, it is difficult to see how France could have held onto Algeria. Foreign occupations can fail even if the insurgent side is denied external assistance. The French pursued a purely military brand of counterinsurgency in Algeria; indeed, the French believed that the insurgency was inherently illegitimate because they believed French rule in Algeria was inherently legitimate. They rejected the possibility that Algerians might have nationalist aspirations independent of union with France. Counterinsurgency was not a political challenge, but rather a question of proper military and propaganda techniques. "Tactical competence does not magically enable the counterinsurgent to manufacture an adequate political story," observes British strategist Colin Gray.

> Modern [counterinsurgency] war, French-style, could work tactically and operationally in Algeria, but never strategically. The reason was that the French military effort, no matter how tactically excellent and intellectually sophisticated, was always politically hollow. The French had, and could promise, no political idea with a potent appeal to the Moslem populace. The [counterinsurgency] force must work in support of a credible, publicly attractive political vision. That vision cannot be imposed from outside the society.[107]

The vitality of external assistance to insurgent *military* success is nowhere better illustrated than in Britain's defeat of the post–World War II Communist insurgency in Malaya. At no time during the Malayan Emergency (as the British officially termed it) of 1948–60 did the Malayan Races Liberation Army (MRLA), the military arm of the Malayan Communist Party (MCP), have access to external military assistance. In his comparison of the Malayan Emergency to the Vietnam War, Sir Robert Thompson, who served as secretary for defense in Malaya from 1957 to 1961 and later as head of the British Advisory Mission to South Vietnam, concluded that among the many counterinsurgent differences separating the two wars, "perhaps the greatest advantage of all was that Malaya was completely isolated from outside communist support" by virtue of "having only a 150-mile frontier with friendly Thailand in the north (with whom there was a border agreement under which Malayan police forces could operate across the border) and a 1,000-mile sea coast which could easily be patrolled."[108] There was, in Malaya, no equivalent of North Vietnam and the Ho Chi Minh Trail. Like the Boer commandos in South Africa, the MRLA was militarily on its own; indeed, the Communist insurgents in Malaya were much more poorly prepared for war than their Boer counterparts, who had modern rifles and artillery, and who, as a completely mounted force, enjoyed a substantial tactical mobility advantage over British forces.

The insurgents in Malaya, a country largely of city dwellers rather than peasants, were also ethnically and politically isolated. The war in Vietnam had no ethnic dimension; it was waged on both sides almost entirely by Vietnamese, who accounted for over 80 percent of the country's total population. In contrast, 90 percent of the MCP and MRLA were Chinese, who represented less than 40 percent of Malaya's total population (the insurgents were actually a minority within a minority, drawn as they were from the Chinese community's impoverished rural dwellers); as such, Malayan insurgents were readily identifiable from the country's Malays and Indians, who constituted 60 percent of Malaya's population. Compounding the insurgents' military and ethnic isolation was eventual British success in addressing insurgent economic and political grievances, which involved resettling over 400,000 Chinese squatters, estate workers, and villagers into "New Villages" that provided security, education, employment, and basic economic and political rights to their inhabitants. This initiative, combined with a politically and militarily integrated counterinsurgency program and exceptionally discriminate use of force, essentially stripped the MCP of any chance of success. No less important was the MCP's failure to convert the war into a nationalist, anticolonial struggle. From the outset of the emergency the British were committed to Malaya's eventual independence (which was granted in 1957), but they were not about to turn the country over the MCP. Following considerable fits and starts and after implementing far-reaching economic, social, and political reforms, and profiting from a Korean War–induced boom in the Malayan economy, the British finally met the challenge of "convincing the Chinese population that their future was in an independent Malaya rather than one subordinate to the Chinese Communists."[109]

The MCP/MRLA's military, ethnic, and political isolation combined to limit the size and lethality of the insurgency. The MRLA's strength peaked at 8,000 in 1951, and throughout the entire twelve-year-long emergency (which was essentially over by the end of 1957 though not officially terminated until 1960), the MRLA inflicted only 1,865 deaths on government security forces at a cost of 6,698 dead to itself.[110] Had the MRLA had even a fraction of the access to external support enjoyed by the Vietnamese Communists in Vietnam, the cost of the war could have been politically intolerable to Britain. (As it was, the war in Malaya never became a significant domestic political issue in Britain, as later did the Algerian War in France and the Vietnam War in the United States.)

One has difficulty finding a successful, externally unassisted insurgency, except in those cases of exceptionally weak or disintegrating governments—for example, the Russian Czarist government in 1918 and Cuba's Batista government in 1959. Bard O'Neill contends, with respect to many cold war insurgencies,

> Unless governments are utterly incompetent, devoid of political will, and lacking resources, insurgent organizations normally must obtain outside assistance if they are to succeed. Even when substantial popular support is forthcoming, the ability to effectively combat government military forces usually requires various kinds of outside help, largely because beleaguered governments are themselves beneficiaries of external assistance, which in some cases compensates for their lack of popularity.[111]

The scarcity of victories by isolated weaker sides underscores the vitality of foreign assistance, and there is probably no better example than the American Civil War. The Union at the outset of the war was the much stronger side in virtually every quantitative index: it had an eight-to-one advantage in draftable (i.e., white) manpower, a six-to-one advantage in financial resources and industrial production, a four-to-one advantage in railroad track mileage, and an overwhelming superiority in commercial maritime and naval power, including a latent capacity to gain control of the inland waterways that bounded and bisected the Confederacy.[112] Nor was the North burdened by a large and potentially rebellious slave population; indeed, whereas Confederate ideology precluded military service for blacks, at least until the very end of the war, a total of 190,000 blacks—9 percent of all those who wore the federal uniform—performed service in the Union army or navy.[113] In Abraham Lincoln, the Union also had an even greater superiority in political leadership; and in Ulysses S. Grant and William Tecumseh Sherman, the Union—albeit belatedly—had military leadership that, like Lincoln, appreciated the war at the strategic level (in contrast to Robert E. Lee, whose vision of the war was confined to his own theater of operations) and understood the operational and strategic opportunities afforded by the North's manpower and industrial superiority. Above all, the North's leadership understood the strategic opportunities that flowed from the capacity to control the waters that surrounded the Confederacy on all sides in the form of oceans and rivers and provided a commons upon which to move and protect land forces.

Under these circumstances, the operational virtuosity of Lee and his Army of Northern Virginia, though greatly assisted until 1864 by an Army of the Potomac commanded by generals varyingly timid (McClellan), mediocre (Pope, Hooker, Meade), or incompetent (Burnside), could only retard the Confederacy's inevitable strategic defeat. The Confederate leadership's cardinal mistake was to embrace a conventional military strategy against a conventionally preponderant foe, thus violating Arreguin-Toft's injunction against the weaker actor selecting the same strategy as the stronger actor. "If strong and weak actors use a strategy representing the same strategic approach—direct against direct, or indirect against indirect—strong actors should win." On the other hand, if "strong and weak actors employ strategies representing opposite strategic approaches—direct against indirect or indirect against direct—weak actors are much more likely to win."[114]

If this analysis is correct, then the South had only two hopes for victory: to reduce the unfavorable material odds via external assistance or, failing that, to adopt an indirect strategy of guerrilla warfare. Unfortunately, prospects for foreign help in the form of British and French diplomatic recognition of the Confederacy were problematic from the beginning. By late summer of 1862, French Emperor Napoleon III favored recognition, but only if Britain would follow suit. In Britain, however, political opinion was divided: upper-class conservatives favored recognition, whereas the middle and working classes opposed it. The government itself was also divided: Lord Russell, the foreign secretary, wanted to recognize the Confederacy, whereas Lord Palmerston, the prime minister, was most reluctant because he believed recognition would lead to war with the United States. In the end, it all boiled down to whether the South could convincingly demonstrate that it could defend its declared independence. In this regard, Lee's defeat at Antietam in September 1862 and Lincoln's subsequent issuance of the

Emancipation Proclamation, which committed the Union to the abolition of slavery, fatally weakened Confederate prospects for foreign intervention.[115] As for the option of guerrilla warfare, it was beyond the imagination of the leading Confederate generals, who saw themselves as soldiers in the European tradition of regular combat. Senior Confederate political or military leaders believed that Southern society and culture bred superior political will and military skill, and they were in any event hardly disposed to embracing a strategy that threatened to destroy the South's neo-feudal social order. (The very example of guerrilla warfare could inspire slave insurrections—the nightmare of the white South.) Anthony James Joes argues that the Confederate failure to turn to guerrilla warfare after Appomattox was attributable to (1) extreme war exhaustion; (2) widespread misgivings within the South over secession; (3) popular resentment of conscription and forced requisitions; (4) bitter factionalism within the Confederacy's political leadership; (5) moral disquiet over the institution of slavery; and (6) Lincoln's "malice toward none" approach to the defeated South.[116]

Antietam, not Gettysburg, was the strategically decisive battle of the war because it ended any real prospect of foreign intervention and because it permitted Lincoln to issue the Emancipation Proclamation, which openly transformed the war from an arcane dispute over the relationship between the individual states to the Union into a moral crusade against slavery. Absent external intervention, the South was probably doomed to defeat as long as Lincoln's genius, assisted by timely Union victories, could sustain sufficient northern support for his war policies.

It is natural for an insurgency—the weaker side—to seek foreign help. Though that help may come with unwanted conditions and advice, it can reduce, even eliminate, the insurgency's material inferiority. The availability of external assistance, however, does not excuse an insurgent leadership from surmounting the challenges of crafting effective strategy and maintaining morale and motivation, which foreign help can dramatically boost—as did the French Alliance of 1778 for the American rebel leadership.

3

The Iraqi Insurgency:

Vietnam Perspectives

John Mueller, an expert on war and American public opinion, observed in late 2005 that

> In Iraq, as they did in Vietnam, U.S. troops face an armed opposition that is dedicated, resourceful, capable of replenishing its ranks, and seemingly determined to fight as long as necessary. In Vietnam, the hope was that after suffering enough punishment, the enemy would reach its "breaking point" and then fade away or seek accommodation. Great punishment was inflicted, but the enemy never broke; instead, it was the United States that faded away after signing a face-saving agreement. Whether the insurgents in Iraq have the same determination and fortitude remains to be seen. The signs thus far, however, are not encouraging: the insurgency does not appear to be weakening.[1]

An examination of past insurgencies reveals that the combination of a stronger political will, a superior strategy, and external assistance can be a potent formula for insurgent success. Conversely, for the counterinsurgent side, the combination of a weaker political will and an inferior strategy can be a recipe for defeat. What of the present insurgency in Iraq? Does it possess a superior political will and strategy? Is it receiving foreign assistance, and if so, what kind and will that assistance make the difference between victory and defeat? And what

can be said of U.S. political will and strategy in Iraq? Can it stay the domestic
political course, or will it end up as it did in Vietnam, being militarily frustrated
into a political defeat? Indeed, are there meaningful military and political comparisons between the Vietnam War and Iraq War, and if so, what do they tell
about U.S. prospects in Iraq?

It is of course profoundly premature to draw anything other than the most
tentative conclusions about an insurgency whose outcome cannot be known, although as we shall see, comparisons with Vietnam, which do not and are not intended to suggest the inevitability of defeat in Iraq, provide useful perspectives on
the Iraq War. Many facts about the situation in Iraq are already known, and these
can be analyzed using conclusions from the previous discussion of why the strong
lose and more specifically why great powers lose to overseas insurgencies.

Characteristics of the Iraqi Insurgency

First, the United States is clearly the stronger side in the Iraq War. It is not only
the most powerful state in the world; it also enjoys conventional military supremacy in Iraq as well as a large numerical troop advantage over the insurgents.

Second, the Iraqi insurgency differs from the familiar Maoist model in
several key respects: it is predominately communally based, urban-centered, decentralized, and heavily invested in terrorism.[2] The Chinese and Vietnamese insurgencies were class-based, rural-centered, highly centralized, and comparatively
selective in the employment of terror. They also had explicit, comprehensive, and
revolutionary objectives: to liberate their countries from foreign power and influence and to establish a new political and social order. The Iraqi insurgency has no
explicit political program and no evident social program other than—and here
one must rely on inference based on the targets of insurgent violence—effecting
the departure of U.S. forces and preventing the emergence of a new, U.S.-backed
ethnically proportional Iraqi political order in which the Sunni Arab minority would
be deprived of its traditional political dominance of Iraqi politics.[3]

A reliable determination of the insurgency's objectives beyond these apparent general negative aims seems impossible because of the insurgency's structure
and composition. It is a loose confederation of groups, organizations, and individuals with competing agendas in Iraq: a Baathist underground seeking to re-
store Baathist, or at least Sunni Arab, rule; Baathist mercenaries recruited from
freed criminal populations and unemployed army veterans; traditional Iraqi

nationalists aroused by the humiliation of foreign occupation and the cultural offensiveness of initial U.S. counterinsurgency tactics; al Qaeda and other jihadist elements seeking to use the war in Iraq as an opportunity to humiliate the United States and further the cause of driving the United States out of the Middle East and establishing a Muslim caliphate; and groups and individuals seeking to advance the national interests of neighboring states in Iraq. Iraqi insurgency expert Ahmed Hashim believes that four key values—"nationalism, honor, revenge, and pride"—motivate the insurgency, and he counts no fewer than eighteen insurgent groups, eleven of them nationalist/tribal oriented and seven religious-oriented.[4]

President George W. Bush has declared that the "enemy in Iraq is a combination of rejectionists, Saddamists, and terrorists." The rejectionists, "by far the largest group, . . . are ordinary Iraqis, mostly Sunni Arabs, who miss the privileged status they had under the regime of Saddam Hussein—and they reject an Iraq in which they are no longer the dominant group." They fear, above all, vengeful Shiite hegemony. The Saddamists are smaller in number "but more determined." They are "former regime loyalists who held positions of power under Saddam Hussein—people who still harbor dreams of returning to power." The third group "is the smallest, but the most lethal: terrorists affiliated with or inspired by al Qaeda. Many are foreigners who are coming to fight freedom's progress in Iraq," and they were led by a brutal Jordanian-born, Sunni Arab terrorist named Abu Musab al-Zarqawi—al Qaeda's chief of operations in Iraq—who had pledged his allegiance to Osama bin Laden. "Their objective is to drive the United States . . . out of Iraq, and use the vacuum that would be created by an American retreat to gain control of that country."[5] Another group might include ordinary Iraqis simply alienated by foreign invasion and occupation.

Third, the Iraqi insurgency seems significantly bounded by ethnicity and geography, despite some limited and sporadic cooperation between Sunni insurgents and Shiite radicals led by Muqtada al-Sadr. The Chinese and Vietnamese Communist insurgencies were waged in ethnically homogenous countries and had nationwide appeal. In Iraq, a country of politically profound ethnic and sectarian divisions, the insurgency is confined largely to the Sunni Arab community and the four provinces where they are the dominant population; Iraq's fourteen other provinces, though hardly free of violence, do not seem vulnerable to significant insurgent encroachment. Iraq's Sunni Kurdish and Shia Arab populations, which dominate the northern and southern provinces, respectively, and together constitute 75–80 percent of Iraq's total population, were victims of centuries of Sunni Arab rule culminating in the murderous tyranny of Saddam Hussein and as such are immune to significant Sunni Arab insurgent recruitment. To be sure, within the Kurdish and Shia communities there are significant political, tribal, and other divisions. So far, however, the Sunni Arab insurgents have not successfully exploited these divisions to the insurgency's strategic benefit. Hashim observes that given the absence of Kurdish and significant Shia participation in the insurgency, the insurgency can hardly be called a war of national liberation. "More accurately, the insurgency may be about liberation for the Sunnis, but they are only one community and a minority."[6]

Complicating matters is al-Zarqawi, who has directed attacks against Shia leaders and other Shia targets with the apparent objective of fomenting a Sunni-Shia civil war. Such a war would prevent the formation of a united Iraqi front based on nationalist objectives.[7] Though "[al-]Zarqawi and his band of foreign fighters are not Iraqi and are widely despised," they have attempted to exploit "the anger and frustration felt by Iraq's Sunni Arabs."[8] Al-Zarqawi's continued attacks on Shia targets, however, have offended even the leadership of al Qaeda, who for tactical reasons oppose Muslim divisions in the presence of a hated "crusader" occupation of Iraq.[9] Thus even within the terrorist "wing" of the Iraqi insurgency (the other two wings being the rejectionists and the Saddamists), there are sharp divisions over strategy. Al-Zarqawi's formal alliance with Osama bin Laden in December 2004 was a marriage of convenience; bin Laden, in no position to take charge in Iraq, essentially franchised the most effective Islamist terrorist organization operating in Iraq.[10] But al-Zarqawi's suicide terrorism against Iraqis has sparked increasing intra-insurgency violence. Many non-jihadist Iraqi insurgents have been repelled by the intervention of foreign terrorists in Iraq, and by January 2006 there were increasing reports that a war was raging inside the Iraqi insurgency between indigenous Iraqi fighters and foreign jihadists.[11]

These significant differences between the Iraqi insurgency and the Maoist model should not obscure Iraqi insurgent reliance on the same strategy that worked for the Chinese and Vietnamese Communists: protracted irregular warfare aimed at weakening the stronger side's political will. As such, the war in Iraq fits Andrew Mack's model of an asymmetric conflict between a stronger side fighting a limited war and the weaker side waging a total war; the war can never be as important to the United States as it is to the Iraqis, who are fighting to determine their future. The Americans can always go home; the Iraqi insurgents, excepting the small minority of foreign fighters, *are* home. What remains to be determined in Iraq is the strategic outcome of Ivan Arreguin-Toft's model of strategic interaction between the Americans and the insurgents and of Gil Merom's model of democracies' fundamental distaste for protracted counterinsurgency.

External Assistance

None of this means that the Iraqi insurgents are destined to win—far from it. Among other things—and this is the fourth fact of the Iraq War pertinent to this discussion—the insurgents have not enjoyed external assistance, intentional and unintentional, remotely approaching that from which the Chinese and Vietnamese Communists profited so handsomely. Foreign arms, expertise, and fighters are crossing Iraq's porous borders, and clearly, all of Iraq's neighbors have vital strategic interests in the outcome of the Iraq War and in Iraq's political future. That said, there are several observations to make about the Iraqi insurgency and external assistance.

The first is that pre-insurgency Iraq was full of weapons, munitions, and men with prior military service. Saddam Hussein's Iraq was armed to the teeth, and virtually every able-bodied Iraqi male was trained in the use of small arms. Thus the Iraqi insurgency did not have to invest significant time and energy, as did Communist insurgencies in East Asia, scrounging up operationally significant quantities of weapons and training recruits from scratch. From the start the Iraqi insurgents had ready access to weapons and munitions inside Iraq; they did not have to seek out foreign sources of supply. According to one assessment, "Iraqi civilians may have gained control of 7 million–8 million small arms."[12] The Iraqi insurgency also has, in former Baathist operatives, a considerable body of technical and engineering expertise, which together with jihadist volunteers, has permitted it to develop and perfect the two most potent weapons of the insurgency: improvised explosive devices (IEDs), employed primarily as roadside bombs against U.S. forces and other military targets; and suicide car bombs, employed against softer and mainly Iraqi targets. Loretta Napoleoni contends that Saddam Hussein

had anticipated the possibility that a full-fledged resistance against Coalition forces would take place in Iraq and made sure that the country was
awash with weapons before the official war began. He lifted the gun
control law that was in place and distributed small arms to the population and various militias. He hoped Iraqis would mount a Somali-like
resistance against Coalition forces, along the lines of the lynching in
Fallujah.[13]

Though other assessments dispute the claim that Saddam planned an insurgent
war in anticipation of conventional defeat,[14] it really does not matter in the end
whether he did or not; an insurgency erupted anyway.

Second, to the extent that the insurgency receives foreign assistance, it seems
to be coming largely in the form of money and individual technical experts and
volunteer jihadists or small groups of such people. For the insurgents in Iraq,
there is no analogy to the kind of massive external assistance of the kind that
France supplied the American War of Independence and that the Soviet Union
and Communist China supplied the Vietnamese Communists in their war against
the Americans. Instead, external aid comes mostly in the form of individual foreigners, including Iranian agents, who volunteer money or enter Iraq to participate in the insurgency themselves. Foreigners (non-Iraqis) represent but a small
percentage of total Iraqi insurgent strength—estimated between 4 and 10 percent.[15] However, to the extent that they represent the great majority of suicide
bombers in Iraq, their contribution is disproportional to their numbers. Two studies released in 2005, one sponsored by the Saudi government, the other a separate
Israeli assessment, shed considerable light on who the foreign fighters are and
why they came to Iraq. The Saudi study, based on interrogations of almost 300
Saudis captured while trying to enter Iraq and on additional case studies of more
than three dozen others who blew themselves up in suicide attacks, found that
almost all had been radicalized by the Iraq War itself; few had any prior history of
involvement in terrorism. The Israeli study, based on profiles of 154 foreign fighters killed in Iraq, reached the same conclusion; it also found that the majority—61
percent—of suicide bombers were Saudis, with Syrians and Kuwaitis accounting
for another 25 percent.[16] Like the Soviets' invasion of Afghanistan before it, the
Anglo-Americans' invasion of Iraq has sparked an explosion of radical Islamist
violence. One study shows that Saudi jihadists in Iraq

were motivated by revulsion at the idea of an Arab land being occupied by a non-Arab country. These feelings were intensified by the images of the occupation they see on television and the Internet—many of which come from sources intensely hostile to the US and the war in Iraq, and which repeat or manipulate "worst case" images. The catalyst most cited was Abu Ghraib, though images from Guantanamo Bay were mentioned.[17]

Another assessment concludes,

American-occupied Iraq is both the catalyst and incubator for the birth and evolution of the third generation of Salafi-jihadists. Without the Iraq theater, the entire al-Qaeda-inspired global jihad movement would be faced with critical ideological and recruitment problems. It is compellingly clear that the American occupation of Iraq, with its associated human rights abuses such as the Abu Ghraib scandal, has played a major role in driving young men to join al-Qaeda and affiliated organizations. . . . As long as the United States remains in Iraq as an increasingly unpopular occupation force, more young people will be drawn to radical Islamists movements.[18]

The most notorious and deadly jihadist organization is al-Zarqawi's al Qaeda in the Land of the Two Rivers. Al-Zarqawi and his network are "largely the product of the invasion and occupation of Iraq"[19] and seek to destroy the American political experiment in Iraq and convert the country, or at least part of it, into a base of operations aimed at destroying secular regimes throughout the Middle East (as well as such "apostate" religious regimes as the Saudi monarchy) preparatory to the reestablishment of a Muslim caliphate. Beyond the foreign jihadists are Syria and Iran, which have critical strategic interests at play in Iraq as well as borders with Iraq that are highly porous—conduits, in the case of Iran, for the infiltration of political operatives and ordnance expertise (in the form of experts and sophisticated explosive devices) into the Shia areas of southern Iraq and, in the case of Syria, for the infiltration of insurgent volunteers and the exfiltration of insurgent groups back into Syria to gain sanctuary from U.S. military sweeps in western Iraq. Most foreign fighters enter Iraq through Syria, which has neither the will nor the resources to seal its 380-mile border with Iraq. Millions of tourists,

hundreds of thousands of them Saudis, visit Syria annually, and there is no way to
prevent jihadists posing as tourists from infiltrating from Syria into Iraq.[20] Jihadists
radicalized by Saudi clerics are also entering Iraq across the Saudi border.

A clear and comprehensive picture of the role of foreign help in the Iraqi
insurgency nevertheless remains elusive because there remains as yet no clear
and comprehensive picture of the insurgency itself—its size, composition, leadership, organization, popular base, military and political objectives, and foreign
linkages. There is moreover no clear separation of insurgent and sectarian violence. Sunni Arab extremists attack Shia as well as U.S. and reconstruction targets, and most Shia violence is directed against Sunni targets. Enough is known,
however, about insurgent-U.S. strategic interaction, U.S. objectives in Iraq, the
political and military performance of the nascent U.S.-sponsored Iraqi government, and the play of the Iraqi insurgency on American opinion to frame the
questions pertinent to assessing prospects for the stronger side's (i.e., America's)
military and political success.

The Vietnam Lens

The historical instruction of the Vietnam War can greatly assist framing those
questions because the military and political challenges America faced in Vietnam were similar to those it confronts today in Iraq: crafting and implementing a
counterinsurgent strategy superior to the insurgents' strategy; fostering the creation of a politically legitimate indigenous government; and building professionally competent military and police forces to assume the security burden upon the
departure of U.S. forces. Above all is the challenge of sustaining sufficient domestic political support in the United States during the years of war and reconstruction. That the United States failed to accomplish these tasks in Vietnam
does not mean that it is doomed to fail in Iraq. What it does mean is that the
United States will have to do a much better job in Iraq than it did in Vietnam
under conditions in Iraq that arguably are both less and more favorable than
those of Vietnam.

The Vietnam comparison also recommends itself simply because critics of
the Bush administration's decision to invade Iraq and its handling of events in
post-Baathist Iraq have repeatedly invoked the Vietnam analogy to "prove" their
case. Whereas the administration invoked the Munich analogy to justify its
decision to overthrow Saddam Hussein—an Arab Hitler whose appeasement

only invited a war later on with a nuclear-armed Iraq (or so the argument went)—opponents of the war contended that the United States was stepping into a political-military quagmire from which it would be very difficult to extract U.S. forces and American prestige.[21]

What can the experience in Vietnam teach about prospects for success in Iraq? Comparing a finished war to one still in progress is analytically risky. We know how the Vietnam War turned out, although there remains considerable disagreement over why it turned out the way it did. But no one knows how the Iraq War is going to end, much less why. We nonetheless have enough war experience—four years of war going on five—to make solid preliminary judgments on differences and similarities and to draw insights from both.

Differences

First, the differences—and they are numerous and significant, especially in the military realm.[22] Take, for example, the enemy. The United States faced a far more powerful enemy in Vietnam than it has so far in Iraq. In the Vietcong (VC) and the regular People's Army of Vietnam (PAVN), the United States confronted Communist forces that totaled, on the eve of the Tet Offensive, approximately 700,000–800,000 troops—250,000–300,000 VC and PAVN soldiers in South Vietnam backed by 550,000–600,000 PAVN regulars in North Vietnam. Both VC and PAVN forces operated at battalion and sometimes (for the PAVN) division strength and lived in the field. Beginning in 1966, Communist forces in the South benefited increasingly from external Soviet and Chinese assistance funneled through North Vietnam and then sent down the Ho Chi Minh Trail. Communist strength in both Vietnams peaked at almost one million in 1973, a year after the last U.S. combat forces were withdrawn from South Vietnam.[23]

U.S. intelligence had an accurate picture of the Vietnamese Communist order of battle, which was a familiar, Soviet-model, hierarchical one with numbered units and tables of organization and equipment. Documentary and defector intelligence was plentiful; indeed, just a year after the United States began committing ground combat forces to South Vietnam, Douglas Pike, a U.S. government expert on the Vietnamese Communists, published a remarkably detailed profile, *Viet Cong: The Organization and Techniques of the National Liberation Front of South Vietnam*.[24] The senior Communist leadership—Ho Chi Minh, Vo Nguyen Giap, Pham Van Dong—were international figures, having led the

Vietminh to victory over the French in 1954 and (in the case of Ho Chi Minh and Pham Van Dong) participated in the highly publicized Geneva Conference of that same year.

Published estimates of Iraqi insurgent strength since mid-2004 have ranged from 20,000 to 40,000, with most estimates pointing to 20,000, though it is not clear what these estimates include.[25] In late July 2005 a former top U.S. Army general who headed repeated Pentagon assessments of enemy strength declared that U.S. and Iraqi forces had killed or captured more than 50,000 insurgents in the preceding seven months, a number that would be hard to reconcile with a base force of 40,000, and certainly 20,000, unless one presumes for the insurgency remarkable powers of regeneration.[26] Even at 40,000-strong the insurgency pales in numerical comparison to the VC alone, to say nothing of the PAVN.

Yet if the Iraqi insurgency is much smaller than Communist forces in Vietnam, so too are the counterinsurgent forces it faces. U.S. forces in South Vietnam peaked in 1969 at 543,000 personnel—or over three times the 160,000-peak strength of U.S. forces in Iraq during the period of counterinsurgent operations. U.S. forces in South Vietnam were of course buttressed by South Vietnamese army and regional and provincial security forces, which fielded a total of 820,000 personnel in 1968, a number that rose to over one million by 1972.[27] In contrast, the paper strength of Iraqi forces recruited and trained by the end of 2005 was about 200,000, although their reliability and level of training and equipment was the subject of much critical commentary.

The Iraqi insurgency's size must also be seen in the context of its relative opaqueness. It does not present a familiar hierarchical order of battle and identifiable field formations. As noted, it is largely an urban insurgency waged by what appears to be a loose coalition of disparate groups with competing agendas, and because it is centered among a sectarian minority (the Sunni Arab community) it operates at a distinct strategic disadvantage compared to its Vietnamese Communist counterpart. Vietnam's ethnic homogeneity and the Communist insurgency's national breadth and appeal made a Communist victory quite imaginable. Such is not the case in Iraq; there are no imaginable circumstances under which the country's Kurdish and Shia communities would accept a return of Sunni Arab rule in any political guise. The insurgency, as a largely Sunni Arab enterprise, has little appeal to the hearts and minds of the Sunni Kurds or the Shia Arabs, and as an insurgency that employs much more terrorism—and spectacularly indiscriminate terrorism to boot—than the Vietnamese Communists, it has already alienated the hearts and minds even of many Sunni Arabs. Indeed, by the end of 2005 there was growing evidence of sharp differences between Baathist insurgent groups and al-Zarqawi's terrorist organization. Baathist groups reportedly were increasingly alienated by al-Zarqawi's extreme tactics, whereas al-Zarqawi was apparently dismayed by Sunni Arab "defections" to the U.S.-supported political process, defections evident in large Sunni Arab voter turnout in the parliamentary elections of December 15, 2005.[28]

It is testimony to the Iraqi insurgency's relative military weakness and the effectiveness of U.S. force protection techniques and technologies that the insurgency has failed to inflict casualty rates on U.S. forces remotely approaching those the United States incurred in Vietnam. The U.S. force presence in Iraq is of course considerably smaller than it was in Vietnam. Against a presence in Iraq ranging between one-quarter and one-third that in Vietnam, the Iraqi insurgency has been able to inflict but about one-tenth the U.S. casualties of their Vietnamese counterparts. During the eight years of major U.S. combat operations during the Vietnam War (1965–72), the United States suffered a total of 55,750 dead and 292,000 wounded, which translate into loss rates of 6,968 dead/36,600 wounded per year, 134/703 per week, and 19/100 per day. These loss rates are well below those sustained in World War I (108 dead per day) and World War II (305 per day) but considerably above those of the Gulf War (7 dead per day) and—so far—the present conflict in Iraq.[29] As of November 28, 2005, or 985 days after the launching of Operation Iraqi Freedom (OIF), U.S. forces had posted losses of 2,108 dead and 15,804 wounded. These losses translated into 779 dead/5,840 wounded per year, 15/112 per week, and 2.1/15 per day.[30]

The military dimensions of the Iraq War bear little comparison to those of the Vietnam War, which was a much larger conflict against a much more powerful enemy. That said, the United States faces in Iraq the same two daunting political challenges it failed to surmount in Vietnam: fostering the creation and survival of a legitimate indigenous government and sustaining American domestic political support for the war.

It is not altogether clear how U.S. casualties figure into insurgent strategy because we do not have a clear picture of the insurgency's precise political and military objectives. It is, however, reasonable to conclude that the insurgency targets Americans in Iraq (civilian as well as military personnel) for the purpose of driving the United States out of that country via destroying American public support for "staying the course." This has been a strategy common to all irregular enemies of the United States since the beginning of the Vietnam War, and it seems to have worked in Vietnam, Lebanon, and Somalia, if not (so far) in Iraq or the Middle East as a whole. The insurgents in Iraq have neither achieved a single spectacular attack on Americans like the 1983 truck bomb attack on U.S. Marine Corps forces in Lebanon nor managed to inflict anywhere near "Vietnam" casualty rates on U.S. forces. They have, however, fought U.S. forces to a stalemate and continue to conduct daily attacks on American, Iraqi, and reconstruction targets; indeed, insurgent attacks on coalition troops, Iraqi security forces, and Iraqi civilians actually increased—by 29 percent—from 2004 to 2005.[31] In so doing they have, assisted by other factors, significantly weakened U.S. public and congressional support for the war (a topic discussed below).

U.S. strategy against the Iraqi insurgency appears to be a combination of expeditiously moving Iraq toward political self-government, arming and training Iraqi army and police forces to assume the primary security burden, thereby permitting a U.S. military withdrawal, and in the interim trying to defeat the insurgency militarily. The United States is also seeking to exploit differences between insurgent Iraqi nationalists and al-Zarqawi and his organization. Al-Zarqawi had no popular base inside Iraq, and his exceptional brutality tars the entire insurgency with illegitimacy. This could encourage nationalist insurgents to isolate the jihadists by joining a political process increasingly legitimized by sequential elections. The Sunni Arab price for abandoning the insurgency, however, may be a U.S. withdrawal from Iraq, or at least a declared timetable for withdrawal—a course of action the Bush administration so far has adamantly rejected.

The United States faces exceptionally difficult challenges in Iraq. As a 2005 U.S. Army War College study warned,

> to be successful in Iraq, the United States must help empower a functioning and unified Iraqi government, support the effort to build an indigenous security force to protect that government and the Iraqi public, and help to prevent a breakdown in those intercommunal relations necessary to foster power-sharing and avoid civil war. The U.S. government must also do this in a time frame that is acceptable to both Iraqis and U.S. public opinion. Furthermore, these tasks must be accomplished while

coping with an ongoing and highly adaptive insurgency. The deeply challenging and multidimensional nature of this effort leaves little latitude
for mistakes by the Iraqi government or in future U.S. dealings with Iraq.[32]

The situation is complicated by the likelihood that the insurgency will per-
sist, perhaps unabated and for years, after the United States transfers the main
burden of Iraq's internal defense to indigenous security forces. Early administration hopes that U.S. forces would be able to defeat the insurgency before departing Iraq proved unfounded. Former Secretary of Defense Donald Rumsfeld
observed in June 2005 that the insurgency could last "10, 12, 15 years," meaning
that "it is going to be a problem for the people of Iraq." He did not explain how
newly trained and relatively poorly equipped Iraqi security forces were going to
defeat an insurgency that far more powerful U.S. forces could not.[33]

From the beginning U.S. strategy has been seriously hampered by what critics across the political spectrum agree are several interrelated errors: an insistence on providing for only a small invasion force that ignored potential demands
for policing post-Baathist Iraq; lack of planning for post-Baathist Iraq; failure to
consider that destroying the Baathist regime could also collapse the Iraqi state
(the two were virtually synonymous), producing a "catastrophic success"; and
failure to anticipate the likelihood of an extended U.S. occupation of Iraq and
insurgent resistance to it.[34] All of these errors stemmed from unfounded official
optimism about the military and political potential of OIF, an optimism that Francis
Fukuyama attributes to the belief, based on the way the cold war ended, that "totalitarian states were hollow at the core and would crumble with a small push from
outside," and an assumption that "democracy was a kind of default condition to
which societies reverted once the heavy lifting of coercive regime change occurred, rather than a long-term process of institution-building and reform."[35]
Indeed, it is far from clear that war proponents fully grasped the extraordinary
ambitiousness of U.S. objectives in Iraq. In South Vietnam, the U.S. objective
was regime *preservation*. In the 1960s the United States was the counterrevolu-
tionary power in Southeast Asia; it sought to preserve the non-Communist status
quo in South Vietnam by containing the expansion of Communism south of the
17th Parallel that separated the Communist North from South Vietnam. The United
States wanted to stop the dominoes from falling to Communism, and it was per-
fectly prepared to back non-Communist dictatorships such as the Ngo Dinh Diem
regime (1955–63) in Saigon to accomplish its objectives.

In 2003 the United States was the revolutionary power in the Middle East by virtue of the Bush administration's proclaimed intention to democratize Iraq for the purpose of providing an inspirational model for the rest of the Arab world. The *National Strategy for Victory in Iraq* declares long-term victory in Iraq as an "Iraq that is peaceful, stable, democratic, and secure, where Iraqis have the institutions and resources they need to govern themselves justly and provide security for their country."[36] The United States wants to *start* Middle Eastern dominoes falling to democracy. It remains to be seen whether the United States can implant democracy in Iraq and whether the effect of a democratic Iraq would be to undermine autocracy elsewhere in the Arab world. The objective of establishing a stable democracy in a country of deep ethnic/sectarian divisions that has experienced only autocracy, however, sets the standard of political success so high that anything less than a stable and democratic outcome will call into further question the wisdom of a war that was marketed in the first instance on the basis of bogus intelligence and optimistic assumptions. Establishment of genuine democratic governance in Iraq will certainly be impeded by continuing insurgent and sectarian violence that U.S. forces and their much weaker Iraqi counterparts have been unable to suppress.

Which brings us to one of the most remarked upon issues of the war: force size. Critics, again across the political spectrum, believe that from the insurgency's very inception the United States has failed to field enough force—specifically, that Secretary of Defense Donald Rumsfeld invited post-Baathist disorder and insurgent violence in Iraq by insisting on conducting the invasion and occupation with "transformed" U.S. ground forces that were too small to establish order and suppress residual irregular resistance. Indeed, Michael R. Gordon and Bernard C. Trainor, authors of the most comprehensive assessment to date of the planning and implementation of the U.S. invasion of Iraq, contend that the insurgency was in large measure a function of counterinsurgent force scarcity:

> Though some degree of opposition was unavoidable, the virulent insurgency that emerged was not inevitable but was aided by military and political blunders in Washington. Having failed to prepare for post-combat burdens, undertaken the war with minimal acceptable forces, and cancelled the deployment of badly needed reinforcements, the Bush administration compounded the problem by disbanding the Iraqi army, putting more than 300,000 armed men on the streets.[37]

Though it is not altogether clear that a U.S. force twice or even three times the size of the one that invaded and occupied Iraq could have established order or crushed the insurgency,[38] it is clear that U.S. forces have not been sufficiently strong either to protect threatened populations or to impose on the insurgency a combat loss rate beyond its ability to replace. Indeed, U.S. forces appear to have been far more focused on killing and capturing insurgents than on securing populations.[39] Though these two fundamental approaches to counterinsurgency are hardly mutually exclusive, pursuit of a "body count" strategy is doomed to failure against an enemy willing and able to replace his losses. This was true of Communist forces in Vietnam, and—so far—appears to be true of the Iraqi insurgency. The alternative strategy of population protection, however, traditionally has required prodigious amounts of manpower in the form of very high government-to-insurgent force ratios and great strategic patience—commodities that are not available to the United States in Iraq.

With the appearance of growing Iraqi military and police forces, however, the possibility of a population strategy has emerged. Indeed, by December 2005 there was evidence of a deliberate shift from search-and-destroy to a clear-and-hold strategy.[40] Under this new approach U.S. forces would clear specified areas of insurgents and then turn the areas over to Iraqi forces for policing and pacification. The object would be to create secure zones for Iraqi civilians and to prevent insurgent forces from establishing their own sanctuaries. Clear and hold reflects a belated, perhaps too belated, recognition of the bankruptcy of a strategy of simply killing members of an insurgent force that is more than capable of replacing its losses; it also constitutes a huge bet on the ability of Iraqi forces to secure "cleared" populations.

These observations do not mean the Iraqi insurgency is destined to win in Iraq; in neither force size nor political appeal nor external support is the Iraqi insurgency nearly as impressive as the Vietnamese Communists. It is indeed quite possible that both the insurgency and the United States could fail in Iraq. The outcome of the present conflict in Iraq could be another Lebanon, a degeneration into civil war in which both the insurgency and the United States would lose any pretense of control over events in Iraq and in which the primary beneficiaries would be secessionist forces in Kurdish and Shia Iraq. This could mean the disintegration of the Iraqi state itself for the second time since the launching of OIF, only this time it would be permanent because the glue of the American force presence would be absent.

Similarities

This brings us to the real parallels between the Iraq and Vietnam wars. Though on the purely military side of the ledger there are few meaningful comparisons between Iraq and Vietnam (beyond the obvious that both pit the United States against a cunning and tenacious irregular adversary), the nonmilitary side of the ledger, especially the political challenges facing the United States, bulges with instruction and warning. Specifically:

1. Can the United States foster the creation in Iraq of a politically legitimate government capable of commanding the loyalty of most Iraqis?
2. Can the United States create in Iraq a politically reliable, professionally competent, and incorruptible Iraqi military capable of assuming the primary burden of counterinsurgency and external security?
3. Can the United States stay the domestic political course—in other words, can the George W. Bush administration and its successors sustain sufficient public and congressional support to achieve declared U.S. objectives in Iraq?

The United States failed to surmount these three great challenges during the Vietnam War. It was driven out of Indochina by collapsed public and congressional support for continued involvement in the war, and it left behind in South Vietnam a politically and militarily weak client regime that stood little chance against the inevitable Communist onslaught. Notwithstanding a lavish, twenty-year political and military investment in the preservation of an independent, non-Communist South Vietnam, the Saigon regime proved a house of cards, disintegrating after but two months of fighting in 1975.

What happened? The conservative historiography of the war argues that the United States abandoned a gallant ally in terminal distress. In fact, that ally was politically and militarily unsalvageable absent a major U.S. ground and air combat presence and its repeated employment against Vietnamese Communist assaults. In 1965 the United States went to war on behalf of an exceptionally feeble client state against an enemy as skilled and tenacious as any in America's history. Nowhere else could the United States have picked the combination of so feckless an ally and so formidable an insurgent foe.

The United States supported the Republic of Vietnam (RVN) from its inception in 1955 as a bulwark against further Communist expansion in Southeast

Asia, and it is fair to say that but for U.S. political sponsorship and economic and military largesse, the anti-Communist regime of Ngo Dinh Diem and its successors could have been neither created nor sustained. Indeed, the RVN's impending military collapse in 1965 prompted major U.S. combat intervention, and the absence of that intervention a decade later doomed the U.S. cold war client state. The United States embraced state-building in South Vietnam for two decades. It fostered, advised, and funded governmental institutions and activities across the board; it equipped and trained the RVN armed forces (RVNAF) and security services; it financed the RVN's war costs and subsidized its economy; and it attempted to guide the RVN toward adoption of democratic institutions. In the end, however, state-building failed. Why? The obvious answer is because of the RVN's military defeat in 1975. But this begs the question, why was the RVN defeated so quickly, surprising even the Communists, who expected their final offensive to take two, even three years?[41] Why did the RVNAF, well-equipped and numerically strong, disintegrate in less than two months, with senior officers fleeing ahead of their men? Why did the RVNAF, which for all practical purposes *was* the South Vietnamese state by virtue of its monopoly of RVN political and administrative authority, fail to fight effectively for the non-Communist order it represented?

It is easy to blame the United States, and many have. In the wake of the Tet Offensive, the United States reduced its principal war aim from securing an independent, non-Communist South Vietnam to seeking an honorable withdrawal; it then proceeded unilaterally to withdraw its ground combat troops from the fight, and in 1973 signed a treaty with North Vietnam that barred the return of U.S. forces while leaving undisturbed PAVN forces inside South Vietnam.[42] During this same period of "Vietnamization," the United States also funded the RVNAF's expansion and modernization well beyond the RVN's capacity to man and maintain it. And when the final Communist offensive was launched in 1975, the United States refused to reenter the war or even to provide the material assistance (mostly ammunition, spare parts, and replacement equipment) Saigon desperately requested in the wake of the RVNAF's abandonment of massive quantities of weapons and equipment in its pell-mell retreat from the Central Highlands.

None of this excuses the RVN from the primary share of responsibility for its own demise. In its life-and-death struggle with North Vietnam, the RVN was crippled from the start by three main weaknesses that no amount of American intervention could offset: professional military inferiority, rampant corruption, and lack of political legitimacy. Joseph Buttinger, a renowned scholar of Vietnamese history and society, concluded in the wake of South Vietnam's destruction that

> The swift and dramatic collapse of the South Vietnamese army and the Saigon regime was not the result of an overwhelming attack by superior military forces. It came about because of the degree of moral disintegration the South Vietnamese army had reached by 1975. This in turn reflected the degree of moral and political decay to which South Vietnamese society had sunk after years of increasing political terror, mass misery and corruption. Moral disintegration alone can explain why an army three times the size and possessing more than five times the equipment of the enemy could be as rapidly defeated as the ARVN [Army of the Republic of Vietnam] was between March 10 and April 30, 1975.[43]

Cao Van Vien, the RVNAF's last chief of staff, described a domino doomed to fall by 1975:

> South Vietnam was approaching political and economic bankruptcy. National unity no longer existed; no one was able to rally the people behind the national cause. Riddled by corruption and . . . ineptitude and dereliction, the government hardly responded to the needs of a public which had gradually lost confidence in it. . . . Under these conditions, the South Vietnamese social fabric gradually disintegrated, influenced in part by mistrust, divisiveness, uncertainty, and defeatism until the whole nation appeared to resemble a rotten fruit ready to fall at the first passing breeze.[44]

Vien could have gone on to observe that South Vietnam was never a national state, that it was the southern half of the larger Vietnamese nation. Indeed, as an ad hoc creation of U.S. cold war diplomacy the RVN was as artificial a state as was Iraq when it was created after World War I. There was a powerful Vietnamese nationalism but hardly *South* Vietnamese nationalism.

From its inception in 1955 until its collapse twenty years later, the RVN's leadership failed to create a military establishment of sufficient integrity and competence to give as good as it got from the PAVN and Vietcong. The RVNAF enjoyed a numerical and firepower advantage over its Communist foe, but it suffered—before, during, and after the war's Americanization—a decided inferiority in the intangibles, such as political will and strategy, that comprised genuine fighting power. Most RVNAF units were poorly led and motivated, and in great contrast to both Communist and U.S. combat forces, they did not seek contact with the enemy. Most of the RVNAF was also corrupt, from the chicken-stealing private to the kickback-taking province chief, and, by most accounts, thoroughly penetrated by Communist agents.[45] A 1967 State Department assessment of the ARVN concluded that it suffered from poor leadership, poor morale, poor relations with the population, and

> low operational capabilities including poor coordination, tactical rigidity, overdependence on air and artillery support arising in part from inadequate firepower, overdependence on vehicular convoy, unwillingness to remain in the field at night or over long periods, and lack of aggressiveness.[46]

The sources of the ARVN's professional incapacity were evident to close observers. At the center of that incapacity was a highly politicized and venal senior officer corps and a soldiery whose high desertion rates reflected at bottom an understandable unwillingness to die for "leaders" who cared only for themselves. Both Diem and his military successors elevated political loyalty over professional competence as the key to promotion and other rewards. Key ARVN units were withheld from combat to protect the government from the ever-present threat of a coup d'etat, and generals who displayed too much professional skill were usually posted far away from Saigon. Additionally, military promotions and such important administrative offices as province chieftainships were more often than not offered to the highest politically acceptable bidder.

There was also widespread theft of American military and economic aid. Stealing became obscenely profitable in a relatively small and poor country suddenly flooded with American wealth, and it was certainly easier and much safer than fighting the enemy, which, after all, the Americans had volunteered to take care of anyway. Black market operations trafficking in U.S. goods stolen or bribed away from vast U.S. and RVN warehouses were a major feature of RVNAF corruption. Anything could be had for the right price on the teeming black market, including U.S. arms, ammunition, military radios, and medicine. Communist agents plied the market, especially for items, such as medicines, in short supply among Communist field forces. No wonder that the professional attractiveness of combat command that was paramount in other armies was notable for its absence in the ARVN, where the lure of material gain was well-nigh irresistible. The National Military Academy in Dalat (South Vietnam's West Point) graduated officers who wanted staff rather than line billets; in one 1966 class, every graduating officer expressed preference for assignment to a division headquarters rather than an infantry company.[47]

A postwar survey of exiled South Vietnamese military officers and civilian leaders revealed that "corruption was considered more than a problem that could have been solved by the firing of a few generals or civilians. It was regarded by many respondents as a fundamental ill that was largely responsible for the ultimate collapse of South Vietnam."[48] Stuart Herrington argues that the venality was so pervasive that purging the corrupt would have "decimated the officer corps. . . . To have attempted to cut out the cancer would have killed the patient."[49]

The ultimate corruption—and testimony to Vietnamization's innate futility—was moral: the ARVN's unwillingness to seek battle with the Communists. Vietnamization armed and trained, but it could not create superior, combative leadership.[50] The ARVN undoubtedly recognized the Communists' superior fighting power, which, as Anthony James Joes points out, stemmed in no small measure from (1) presentation of an attractive political program of "expel the foreigner, give land to the peasants, and unite the nation"; (2) a totalitarian political system that disciplined, controlled, and directed society far more effectively than possible in South Vietnam; and (3) a "military doctrine and fielded armed forces well-suited to both the aims and the territory for which they were fighting."[51] The South Vietnamese military also hoped, after 1965, and probably believed, that the Americans would win the war for them. However, even when it became apparent that the Americans were going to leave without having done so, the RVN, preoccupied with internal politics and rotted with corruption, proved incapable of endowing its officer corps or soldiery with the ingredients necessary to become competitive with the PAVN. The ARVN lacked what the Communist side had: superb discipline and a powerful and unifying patriotism capable of eliciting a willingness to sacrifice one's life on behalf of a larger cause. "The South

Vietnamese soldier, in the end," concludes Guenter Lewy, "did not feel he was part of a political community worth the supreme sacrifice; he saw no reason to die for the [government]. The country lacked a political leadership which could inspire a sense of trust, purpose, and self-confidence."[52]

At bottom, the RVN was unsustainable because it failed to achieve the measure of political legitimacy necessary to compete with the Communists. William J. Duiker, the leading American historian of Vietnamese Communism, argues persuasively that the most important factor underlying the RVN's defeat was the Communist Party's "successful effort to persuade millions of Vietnamese in both North and South that it was the sole legitimate representative of Vietnamese nationalism and national independence." This success was personified in the charismatic Ho Chi Minh, whose public personality, "embodying the qualities of virtue, integrity, dedication, and revolutionary asceticism, transcended issues of party and ideology and came to represent . . . the struggle for independence and self-realization of the Vietnamese nation."[53]

In Vietnam, anti-Communism was always burdened by its initial association with detested French colonial rule (many senior RVNAF leaders had fought on the French side during the First Indochina War) and by its antipathy to the powerful Vietnamese nationalist sentiment mobilized by Ho Chi Minh against both the French and their American successors. Additionally, as the Americans assumed ever-greater responsibility for the anti-Communist struggle, the more they compromised the RVN's claim to even a pretense of national legitimacy. The situation became acute with the Americanization of the war beginning in 1965. The deployment of over 500,000 U.S. troops to South Vietnam, observes Timothy J. Lomperis,

> made it difficult for the Saigon government to hold on to its claims of traditional legitimacy, and correspondingly easy for the Communists to depict themselves as champions against yet another foreign intervenor and to link themselves with all the heroes of the past who had fought against the intrusions of outsiders. If the Americans thought they were very different from Frenchmen, they did not appear to be to the villagers.[54]

All this points very strongly to the conclusion that the RVN, sponsored and sustained in the wake of what was intended to be a temporary division of Vietnam, was little more than an artifact of U.S. cold war diplomacy and in its short life failed to achieve the political legitimacy necessary to survive without a powerful U.S. military presence. "We are so powerful that Hanoi is simply unable to defeat us militarily," wrote Henry Kissinger in 1969. "By its own efforts, Hanoi cannot force the withdrawal of American forces from South Vietnam. Unfortunately, our military strength has no political corollary; we have been unable . . . to create a political structure that could survive the withdrawal of American forces from Vietnam."[55] Concludes George Herring, the preeminent American historian of the Vietnam War,

> Originally created by the French, the Saigon regime could never overcome its origins as a puppet government. Political fragmentation, the lack of able and farsighted leaders, and a tired and corrupt elite which could not adjust to the revolution that swept Vietnam after 1945 afforded a perilously weak basis for nationhood. Given these harsh realities, the American effort to create a bastion of anticommunism south of the seventeenth parallel was probably doomed from the start.[56]

The fact remains, however, that notwithstanding the issue of South Vietnamese governmental legitimacy, the United States was unable to defeat the Communist insurgency militarily. Additionally, the United States discounted the political dimension of the war; it failed to understand the depth of the RVN's legitimacy deficit and accordingly made an insufficient effort to construct a better non-Communist alternative.

In Iraq, as in Vietnam, political success for the United States will require the creation of a government regarded as legitimate by the great majority of the country's inhabitants, and security forces capable of protecting the new political order. Moreover, in Iraq, as in Vietnam, America's time is limited; the United States cannot indefinitely wage a large-scale protracted war against a militarily irregular enemy that seems immune to decisive defeat. Indeed, in Iraq, as in Vietnam, the United States may be compelled to lower its central war aim. U.S. Army War College analysts W. Andrew Terrill and Conrad C. Crane observe that

> U.S. vital interests . . . never demanded a democratic state in Iraq before 2003, and it remains uncertain if Iraq is going to be democratized as a result of a foreign presence in that country. Clearly, the successful

consolidation of governmental authority will depend upon the degree to which most Iraqis make supporting and defending the new government a continuing priority. If they do not, it becomes important to ask if the United States can live with less than a Western-style democracy in Iraq and, if so, how much less? Furthermore, if a more modest set of goals becomes inevitable, what is the best way to implement them without abandoning the establishment of full Iraqi democracy in the long term after the departure of all or most U.S. troops?[57]

Terrill and Crane later note that a "friendly but undemocratic Iraq that does not engage in massive human rights violations would look very similar to an array of current U.S. allies in the region, and this outcome, in most cases, would still be better than a sustained and bloody civil war should these two alternatives become the only available choices."[58]

The United States intervened in Vietnam believing that it could win the war and thereby preserve an independent, non-Communist Vietnam. The protracted and bloody military stalemate, however, reduced America's strategic aim to "peace with honor," a euphemism for military withdrawal capped by a "peace" treaty that left South Vietnam as militarily dependent on the United States as it had been in 1965 but without any realistic prospect of American reentry into the war in the event of another Communist assault. The Bush administration invaded Iraq believing it could gain a quick and decisive military victory that would somehow automatically translate into the creation of a stable and democratic political order that would permit an early withdrawal of most U.S. military forces. It accomplished the relatively easy mission of defeating the Baathist regime's conventional military resistance but failed to anticipate or—so far—to defeat the continuing insurgency in Iraq. The administration also failed to discover any weapons of mass destruction in Iraq or proof of a collaborative relationship between the Baathist regime and al Qaeda, much less any Iraqi connection to the 9/11 attacks.

These failures are hardly redeemed by over four years of costly counterinsurgent warfare and maddeningly slow progress in Iraq's economic reconstruction: as of January 2006, oil and electricity production remained below prewar levels, as did the percentage of Iraqis with access to potable water and sewage service.[59] The U.S. performance in Iraq has weakened public and congressional support for the war and heightened White House emphasis on a strategy of "standing down" U.S. forces as Iraqi forces are "stood up" to replace them. Though the White House rejects artificial timetables for U.S. troop withdrawals, the intensifying focus on substituting newly trained and equipped Iraqi forces for U.S. forces is as much a strategy of withdrawal as Nixon's strategy of "Vietnamization." It is not clear whether the stand-down strategy represents a reduction of U.S. objectives in Iraq; on one hand, the administration continues to speak of Iraq's democratization as a vehicle for political revolution throughout the Arab world. On the other hand, the administration has been unable to staunch rising domestic political pressures to reduce U.S. forces in Iraq, pressures that could force the administration to settle for something less than a democratic or even stable Iraq. Nor is it clear, assuming the emergence of a legitimate government in Iraq capable of shouldering the primary burden of internal security, what the long-term U.S.-Iraqi military relationship will be. The treaty that ended U.S. military involvement in the Vietnam War prohibited both the reintroduction of U.S. combat forces and the retention of U.S. bases in South Vietnam. A residual U.S. force presence in Iraq would be problematic: it could be essential in assisting the new Iraqi government in containing or defeating remaining insurgent violence and in providing a guarantee of Iraq's security against its neighbors; on the other hand, it could attract terrorist assault as well as undermine the government's political legitimacy.

Can the United States succeed in Iraq where it failed in Vietnam? Any attempt to address this question must acknowledge the great differences separating South Vietnam in the 1960s and Iraq forty years later. The two cases present different societies, cultures, histories, and enemies. Analysis also must not be misled by false analogies to American state-building success in Germany and Japan after World War II. Among other things, the United States entered Germany and Japan with overwhelming force, precluding any postwar resistance; and in Japan, the Emperor Hirohito himself legitimized General Douglas MacArthur's rule. The United States was also able to maintain an internationally supported military presence in Japan and Germany for years during which democratic institutions could be created and nurtured.

Unique Challenges in Iraq

The central task of creating a politically legitimate government was inhibited from the start by the unexpected collapse of the Iraqi state and the daunting challenge of reconciling to minority political status a Sunni Arab community that had dominated indigenous Iraqi politics for centuries—under the Ottomans, British, and Baathists. The unusual artificiality of the Iraqi state also works against achieving national legitimacy. Like the former Yugoslavia, Iraq was cobbled together after World War I from the remnants of a disintegrated empire; congregated within its boundaries were ethnic/sectarian communities with long histories of mutual antagonism and no shared interest in forming a common state in which they could be excluded from power. As in Yugoslavia, these conditions encouraged strong authoritarian rule from the center, and when that strong rule was removed, in Yugoslavia by Tito's death and in Iraq by the U.S. invasion, the state disintegrated. Indeed, some observers believe that the United States is on a fool's errand in Iraq—that in removing the Baathist regime it has shattered a Humpty-Dumpty and should accept the inevitability of Iraq's devolution into separate Shia, Sunni, and Kurdish successor states. In her assessment of the Iraqi insurgency and Abu Musab al-Zarqawi's role in it, Loretta Napoleoni concludes,

> Far from following the classic model of insurgency and counterinsurgency of the Cold War era, Iraq resembles more and more the outburst of violence that plagued the Balkans in the 1990s. As in Yugoslavia, in Iraq a cluster of ethnic groups, deeply suspicious of each other, have been kept inside the borders of the same country by a strong dictatorship which used secular, socialist values to homogenize the country. The removal of the dictator unleashed forces that had been simmering for decades. The infiltration of jihadist groups and their targeting of Shi'ites acted as a catalyst to set off the "Balkanization" of Iraq. This may well be [al-]Zarqawi's terrifying legacy.[60]

Stephen Biddle argues that the United States has fundamentally misread the nature of the war in Iraq, mistaking a communal civil war "featuring opposing subnational groups divided along ethnic and sectarian lines" for a "people's war" driven by "nationalist passions."[61]

Iraq's relative newness as a state and its deep ethnic/sectarian divisions make it very different from Vietnam, an old state populated overwhelmingly by ethnic Vietnamese and having no politically significant ethnic/sectarian divisions.[62] Indeed, as Arreguin-Toft notes of Vietnam's long history of resistance to foreign invaders, the "Vietnamese people were therefore effective 'nationalists' hundreds if not thousands of years before the rise of nationalism in Europe."[63]

Given Iraq's history and makeup, the goal of a unitary *and* democratic *and* stable Iraq seems very ambitious. That said, there is a political process at work in Iraq that on December 15, 2005, brought to Iraqis the makings of their first demo- cratically elected parliament and in May 2006 the formation of a new govern- ment under Prime Minister Nuri al-Maliki. Indeed, any objective observer could not fail to be impressed by the countless Iraqis, including Sunni Arabs, who turned out to vote in the face of terrorist violence targeted against them and the democratic process. Free and fair elections generate legitimacy, though they are of course but one component of democratic governance and are certainly no guarantee of liberal democracy in which minority civil rights and liberties are protected. In fact, the December elections revealed an unsettling pattern: "very few people voted as Iraqis; most voted as Shiites, Sunnis or Kurds."[64] Though Sunni Arabs turned out in large numbers, the biggest winners were the Shia reli- gious parties whose politicians have won the ministries and whose militias have won the streets of southeastern Iraq since 2004. With the Kurds retaining control of northern Iraq, the December elections portend some measure of theocratic rule in Baghdad and the solidification of Iraqi national disunity, not unity. More- over, continued insurgent violence could provoke a civil war—al-Zarqawi's avowed objective—that could demolish prospects for a national democracy; in- deed, if there is one shared interest between insurgent Baathist remnants and al Qaeda–inspired terrorists it is the visceral totalitarian fear and hatred of the very idea of democracy. Thus the course of the insurgency and the course of political events in Iraq are intertwined.

Containing or defeating the insurgency will require not only political suc- cess but also military success, and the latter will depend ultimately on Iraqi forces, not U.S. forces whose time in Iraq is politically limited. Can the United States create Iraqi military and police forces that can handle the insurgency? The great difference here between Iraq and Vietnam is that Iraqi forces face no inevitable battle with an equivalent of the powerful PAVN. There is little prospect of the insurgency transitioning from irregular to conventional warfare, as the Vietnam- ese Communists did, or, given its limited ethnic and geographical base, of the insurgency becoming national in scope. This makes the insurgent threat in Iraq much more containable than the Communist threat in Vietnam. A Communist takeover of South Vietnam was always quite imaginable; an insurgent takeover of Iraq is much less so. More imaginable is Iraq's disintegration.

It is of course far too early to determine the professional worth (or loyalty to the new constitutional system) of the Iraqi military and police forces, now being trained to assume the primary responsibility for Iraq's security. They remain under de facto American leadership and are being raised and maintained separately from political authority—a major difference from South Vietnam, where, after the overthrow of the Diem regime in 1963, the military leadership became the country's civil authority. Though there is no specific reason to believe that the new Iraqi military leadership will become as corrupted and professionally ineffective as South Vietnam's, venality and mediocrity are not uncommon among third world military establishments. For this and other reasons, the formation of growing numbers of new Iraqi army battalions should not be taken as the most important metric of "Iraqization" of the war; on the eve of South Vietnam's abrupt military collapse in 1975, ARVN and supporting territorial forces numbered over one million strong. Quality will be more important than quantity in determining Iraqi military effectiveness, and quality is always harder to measure than quantity. Terrill and Crane rightly warn,

> One of the most serious threats to U.S. goals in Iraq is the danger of unrealistic optimism about the capabilities and élan of the Iraqi security forces, and especially those units that have not been tested in combat. Such wishful thinking, if acted upon, could cause the Iraqi military to be given too much responsibility and then collapse in the face of enemy opposition which they are not prepared to address. The United States does not have the time or resources to build and then rebuild the Iraqi security force after a series of collapses.[65]

President Bush has acknowledged initial mistakes in training Iraqi forces. Aside from time lost as the administration woke up to the fact that it had a genuine and enduring insurgency on its hands in Iraq,[66] the Iraqi Civil Defense Corps (now merged with the regular army), which the United States originally set up to handle Iraq's internal defense, "did not have sufficient firepower or training" to deal with an insurgent enemy "armed with machine guns, rocket-propelled grenades, and mortars." This imbalance produced several instances of "Iraqi forces running from the fight."[67] These deficiencies are presumably being remedied, although one independent assessment concluded in December 2005 that "the readiness of many Iraqi units is low, their loyalty and morale are questionable, regional and ethnic divisions are sharp, [and] their overall numbers overstate their real effectiveness." While acknowledging that "the training and numbers are getting better," the

> problems created by the insurgency are getting worse—and getting worse faster than the Iraqi forces are improving. Measured against what it would take to leave Iraqis fully in charge of their own security, the United States and the Iraqi government are losing ground. Absent a dramatic change— in the insurgency, in American efforts, in resolving political differences in Iraq—America's options will grow worse, not better, as time goes on.[68]

The administration, however, is not talking about leaving Iraqis fully in charge of their own security, at least in the near future. The plan is to reduce U.S. forces' exposure to insurgent attacks by progressively turning the counter-insurgency war over to the Iraqis. As Iraqi security forces are stood up, U.S. forces will be withdrawn from the cities to heavily fortified bases from which they will police Iraq's borders and provide Iraqi forces combat support and combat-service support. The United States is thus embarking on a strategy that envisages two partial military withdrawals: a withdrawal from the centers of insurgent violence *within* Iraq and a withdrawal *from* Iraq. The *National Strategy for Victory in Iraq* declares,

> As Iraqis take on more responsibility for security, Coalition forces will increasingly move to supporting roles in most areas. The mission of our forces will change—from conducting operations and keeping the peace, to more specialized operations targeted at the most vicious terrorist and leadership networks.
>
> As security conditions improve and as Iraqi Security Forces become increasingly capable of securing their own country, our forces will increasingly move out of the cities, reduce the number of bases from which we operate, and conduct fewer patrols and convoy missions.[69]

On December 22, 2005, Secretary of Defense Donald Rumsfeld announced plans to reduce the U.S. baseline force of 138,000 in Iraq by 7,000 troops by withholding the planned rotational deployment to Iraq of two U.S.-based Army brigades.[70] His announcement signaled the possible beginning of incremental withdrawals preferably tied to the course of military and political events in Iraq, although withdrawals, once begun, and given the unpopularity of the Iraq War in the United States, could develop an irresistible momentum of their own. As of early summer 2006, no brigade-sized reductions had been undertaken and the administration remained noncommittal over prospects for U.S. troop withdrawals prior to the November 2006 congressional elections. Indeed, in late May the Pentagon announced it was reinforcing U.S. deployments to Iraq with a Kuwait-based, 3,500-member armored brigade.[71]

Hovering over the entire American political and military enterprise in Iraq is time. The American war effort in Vietnam failed because it became unsustainable at home. Though the United States was militarily unbeatable in Vietnam—as it is in Iraq today—it lacked the political stakes in the war that the Vietnamese Communists did. In the end, the Vietnam War boiled down to a contest of political wills, as has the war in Iraq. President Bush is correct in his assessment that the insurgents hope to break America's will to "stay the course" in Iraq. In his major Iraq policy speech at the U.S. Naval Academy on November 30, 2005, he declared that the insurgents' aim was "to shake our will to achieve their objectives. They will fail. America's will is strong." He rejected setting an artificial deadline to withdraw U.S. forces from Iraq because "it would send a message across the world that America is weak and an unreliable ally. Setting an artificial deadline to withdraw would also send a signal to our enemies—that if they wait long enough, America will cut and run and abandon its friends."[72]

The Vietnamese Communists understood that the Americans had to be beaten politically because they could not be beaten militarily, although they could be denied decisive military victory. General Vo Nguyen Giap told journalist Stanley Karnow in 1990 that

> We were not strong enough to drive out a half-million American troops, but that wasn't our aim. Our intention was to break the will of the American Government to continue the war. Westmoreland was wrong to expect that his superior firepower would grind us down. If we had [attempted to pit our material inferiority directly against your superiority], we could have been defeated in two hours.[73]

The turning point was the Tet Offensive, a military defeat for the Communists but a political shock for the United States; Tet, for all to see, popped the balloon of official optimism on the war. For the preceding half year, Johnson administration spokesmen, in a White House–orchestrated campaign, declared that the corner had been turned in Vietnam, that the Communists were in irreversible retreat, and that the end of the war was in sight. The size and the savagery of the Communist assault, which inflicted the highest weekly and monthly U.S. manpower loss rates of the war, belied these claims and suggested the prospect of an endless military stalemate, of more and more American bloodshed without convincing progress toward the declared U.S. objective of saving South Vietnam.[74]

War Costs

Large public and congressional majorities, as well as editorial opinion of such mainstream liberal newspapers as the *Washington Post* and *New York Times*, supported U.S. military intervention in the Vietnam War, and support for staying the course in Vietnam remained strong, notwithstanding rising casualties and a growing domestic antiwar movement, as long as the United States, however slowly, seemed to be winning the war.[75] Underlying this support were levels of trust in the competence and integrity of the U.S. government, especially on matters of war and peace, a trust that diminished as the war continued and opposition to the war within America's opinion-making elite increased. By March 1969, a year after the Tet Offensive and four years after the deployment of U.S. ground combat forces to Vietnam, U.S. battle deaths equaled those of the highly unpopular three-year Korean War, and nearly two out of three Americans polled said they would have opposed U.S. entry into the Vietnam War had they known what it would cost in American lives.[76]

Studies of the Vietnam and other American wars of the twentieth century reveal that, contrary to the post–Vietnam War conventional wisdom that profound casualty aversion dominates all other considerations in determining war and peace decisions, most Americans are influenced by such pragmatic considerations as perceived stakes at hand and benefits of intervention, chances of success, possible and actual costs, alterations in initial and subsequent expectations, and elite opinion.[77] U.S. political and military leaders may have convinced themselves that the American public is intolerant of casualties;[78] in fact, however, "support for U.S. military operations and the willingness to tolerate casualties are based on a sensible weighing of benefits and costs that is influenced heavily by consensus (or its absence) among political leaders."[79] Writing on the matter of casualties two decades after the fall of Saigon but with the Vietnam War clearly in mind, Richard K. Betts observed,

> There is no clear evidence that Americans will not tolerate many body bags in the course of intervention where vital interests are not at stake. What is crucial for maintaining public support is not casualties per se, but casualties in an *inconclusive* war, casualties that the public sees as being suffered indefinitely, for no clear, good, or achievable purpose.[80]

This was certainly the situation that confronted the Nixon administration when it took office in 1969 and explains the administration's decision to launch a unilateral, incremental withdrawal of U.S. forces from South Vietnam absent any political concessions from the Communists. From April 1969 to December 1972, U.S. military personnel in Vietnam dropped from 543,000 to 24,000, with American military dead during those same years falling from 9,377 to 300.[81] The strength of the domestic political imperative was evident in Nixon's determination to proceed with a unilateral pullout even though he clearly understood that a shrinking U.S. force presence reduced his bargaining leverage with the Communists.

As of early June 2006 U.S. casualties in Iraq totaled over 2,400 dead and 18,000 wounded. All but 138 of the dead and 550 of the wounded were incurred after President Bush declared the termination of major combat operations on May 1, 2003. Moreover, U.S. casualties have been steady; they have not decreased as Iraq takes apparent steps toward representative government, as important insurgent leaders are killed or captured, or even as newly formed Iraqi units began assuming a larger share of the counterinsurgency effort. Though varying from month to month, for the duration of the war casualties have registered a remarkably stable average of a little over two dead and fifteen wounded per day. Though low by Vietnam standards, public and congressional tolerance for casualties in protracted and seemingly indecisive conflicts is lower today—by virtue of the Vietnam experience—than it was in the 1960s. In the case of Iraq, moreover, tolerance for casualties almost certainly has been weakened by the revelation that Saddam Hussein's multiple WMD threats and collaboration with al Qaeda—the primary official rationales for war—were figments of the administration's imagination.

There is the matter of treasure as well as blood. The dollar costs of the war have been far greater than expected. A detailed and objective estimate of Iraq War costs published by January 2006 by two economists at Harvard University's John F. Kennedy School of Government noted that before the war Deputy Secretary of Defense Paul Wolfowitz claimed that resurgent oil production would finance Iraq's reconstruction, and that Secretary of Defense Donald Rumsfeld and Office of Management and Budget Director Mitch Daniels estimated that total war costs would range from $50 to $60 billion. This estimate neither included indirect costs nor anticipated the possibility of a "postwar" insurgency. The study also noted that, as of January 2006, the United States had already spent $251 billion on the war and that military operations in Iraq might continue until 2010 or even 2015. Depending upon assumptions about the war's duration and future U.S. troop levels and casualties in Iraq, and factoring in such indirect war expenses as additional Veterans Administration costs, veterans' health expenditures and disability payments, demobilization costs, replacement costs of military hardware lost or rapidly depreciated in Iraq, and—last but hardly least—interest payments on the additional debt incurred by financing a war entirely on borrowed money, the study concluded that the true total cost of the Iraq War will range from $1.026 to $2.239 *trillion*.[82] If even the lower estimate is correct, it is still testimony to yet another gross prewar miscalculation about the course, cost, and consequences of the decision to invade Iraq.

Public Opinion

The combination of failed predictions, casualties, protracted and apparently stalemated hostilities, spiraling war costs, and rising public suspicion that the administration mistakenly or even willfully led the country into an unnecessary war has had a telling effect on public support for the war. The Gallup Organization polling data from the beginning of Operation Iraqi Freedom through the end of November 2005 reveals a dramatic drop in public support for the war—a drop more precipitous than those registered during the Korean and Vietnam wars, the only other two American wars since 1945 involving sustained ground combat and the loss of more than 300 U.S. dead.[83] In response to the question, "All in all, do you think it was worth going to war in Iraq, or not?" only 38 percent of those polled in November 2005 responded in the affirmative—down from a high of 73 percent in April 2003. Sixty percent said it was not worth going to war—up from a low of 23 percent in April 2003. In April 2003, the war appeared to be heading toward a decisive conclusion with low American casualties and there was a widespread expectation that the decision for war would be vindicated by the discovery of Iraqi weapons of mass destruction and of evidence of Iraqi–al Qaeda collaboration.

In response to the somewhat differently worded question, "In view of the developments since we first sent our troops to Iraq, do you think the United States made a mistake in sending troops to Iraq, or not?" 54 percent replied that it was a mistake and 45 percent responded that it was not a mistake. In July 2003, only 27 percent believed it was a mistake and 72 said it was not. These changes in opinion are further reflected in responses to the question, "In general, how would you say things are going for the U.S. in Iraq—very well, moderately well, moderately badly, or very badly?" In early May 2003, 86 percent of those polled believed things were going very or moderately well and only 13 percent said that things were going very or moderately badly. By October 2005, 57 percent believed things were going badly and 42 percent said they were going well. Perhaps most ominously for the administration, by late October 2005, 53 percent of those polled believed that "the Bush administration deliberately misled the American public about whether Iraq had weapons of mass destruction"—up from 31 percent following President Bush's announcement in early May 2003 that major U.S. combat operations had ended.[84] Polls have also revealed an emerging majority who do not believe the Iraq War has made the United States any safer—a major and continuing claim of the Bush administration. A *Washington Post/ABC* poll taken in early June 2005 disclosed that 52 percent of respondents believed the "war in Iraq has not contributed to the long-term security of the United States."[85] The following month, a CNN/*USA Today*/Gallup Poll found that 57 percent of respondents believed the Iraq War had actually made the United States "less safe from terrorism."[86]

American public attitudes toward the Iraq War remained remarkably consistent during the first half of 2006. An absolute majority of Americans continued to believe that the war was not worth the cost, that the Bush administration had deliberately misled the public on the issue of Iraqi WMD, and that the White House was mishandling the war.[87]

Not surprisingly, declining public support for the war has generated increasing sentiment for pulling U.S. troops out of Iraq. By mid-November 2005,

19 percent of those polled favored an immediate withdrawal and another 33 percent supported withdrawal within twelve months; 38 percent favored eventual withdrawal, taking as many years as necessary to turn control of the war over to the Iraqis. Only 7 percent favored sending more troops. Sentiment for withdrawing all troops regardless of consequences rose from 14 percent in August 2003 to 30 percent in September 2005, but leveled off in the following months.

If the experience of the Truman and Johnson administrations during the Korean and Vietnam wars, respectively, is any guide, these negative opinion trends will be irreversible to any significant degree, absent some kind of dramatic success or turn of events that is difficult to imagine. As John Mueller observed in late 2005,

> it is difficult to see what a spate of good news would look like at this point. A clear-cut victory, like the one scored by George H. W. Bush in the Gulf in 1991, is hugely unlikely—and the glow even of that faded quickly as Saddam continued to hold forth in Iraq. From the start of the current Iraq war, the invading forces were too small to establish order, and some of the early administrative policies proved fatally misguided. In effect, the United States created an instant failed state, and clambering out of that condition would be difficult in the best of circumstances. If the worst violence diminishes, and Iraq thereby ceases to be quite so much of a *bloody* mess, the war will attract less attention. But there is still likely to be plenty of official and unofficial corruption, sporadic vigilantism, police misconduct, militia feuding, political backstabbing, economic travail, regional separatism, government incompetence, rampant criminality, religious conflict, and posturing by political entrepreneurs spouting anti-American and anti-Israeli rhetoric. Under such conditions, the American venture in Iraq is unlikely to be seen as a great victory by those now in opposition, over half of whom profess to be not merely dissatisfied with the war, but angry over it.[88]

Conclusions

The Iraq War fits Andrew Mack's paradigm of a metropolitan power waging a limited war against an insurgency waging a total war. The asymmetry in stakes, and therefore in political will to fight to decisive victory, works to the insurgency's advantage against its materially stronger enemy. The war also supports Ivan Arreguin-Toft's thesis of strategic interaction as the best predictor of asymmetric war's outcomes; the Iraqi insurgents have chosen the classic strategy of protracted irregular warfare (with such relatively modern features as suicide bombing attacks) to break America's political will to continue the war. The war is also friendly to Gil Merom's model of a democracy waging a nasty counterinsurgent war against a foreign insurgency in which the brutality necessary to prevail may not be within domestic political reach of those running the war. The Iraq War as yet, however, vindicates none of these paradigms. It is an unfinished war and will likely remain so for years to come.

Against clear signs of weakening American public and congressional will must be placed the inherently self-limiting prospects of the Iraqi insurgency imposed by its composition and the local circumstances in which it operates. As a decentralized, networked coalition of groups with competing agendas in Iraq, it lacks the cohesion and discipline of the Vietnamese Communist movement. Moreover, its most highly visible though not main component, the foreign jihadists and their Iraqi supporters fighting under the rubric and inspiration of Abu Musab al-Zarqawi's terrorist network, has little political traction within Iraq because of excessive reliance on indiscriminate terrorism and because of an agenda that would sacrifice Iraqi national interests for broader Islamist objectives. The insurgency's narrow, Sunni Arab base also forfeits chances of achieving a national victory; it can disrupt, intimidate, destroy, perhaps even plunge Iraq into civil war, but it cannot take over the country as a whole. Nor does the insurgency have an analog to North Vietnam—a powerful regular military ally with access to large quantities of great power war matériel and techno-military expertise. The Vietnamese insurgency in South Vietnam could always call upon the PAVN; the Iraqi insurgency has no like partner or any real prospect of shifting from irregular to regular military operations.

The limitations of the Iraqi insurgency do not necessarily translate into an American counterinsurgent success, however. As the stronger side, the United States brings to the fight in Iraq the potential for political failure rooted in the paradigms of Mack, Arreguin-Toft, and Merom. Also working against the United States, however, are a national way of war that divorces war from politics and a professional military aversion to counterinsurgency.

So will the United States win or lose in Iraq? No one can say for sure, but what we do know so far is not encouraging: domestic American public support for the war is declining; sectarian violence in Iraq is rising; and competent and uncorrupted Iraqi military and police forces able to "stand up" to the task of securing peace, law, and order in Iraq seem a distant hope.

Epilogue

Events in the United States and Iraq since the manuscript for this book was first submitted for publication in early summer 2006 reinforce this chapter's analysis. In the November 7, 2006, congressional elections, which were widely regarded as a referendum on the Bush administration's handling of the Iraq War, the Democrats recaptured both houses of Congress. Shortly thereafter, President Bush, whose public approval ratings had plummeted to new lows, asked for Donald Rumsfeld's resignation as secretary of defense and replaced him with former CIA Director Robert Gates, who testified before Congress that the United States was "not winning" in Iraq. President Bush himself acknowledged that things were not going as well as he had expected in Iraq, and by mid-January 2007 he had announced his support for two initiatives his former secretary of defense had strongly resisted: a significant escalation in U.S. troop strength in Iraq to suppress sectarian violence in Baghdad and a permanent increase in the authorized personnel strengths of the U.S. Army and Marine Corps. Both supporters and critics regarded the surge, which was accompanied by a turnover of U.S. military leadership in Iraq and the Middle East, as a desperate, last-ditch effort to salvage American policy in Iraq.

In Iraq, meanwhile, insurgent and sectarian violence continued unabated, notwithstanding the deaths of al-Zarqawi and Saddam Hussein; the U.S.-backed government on Nuri al-Maliki remained unwilling or unable to quell escalating Shiite militia attacks on Sunni Arab targets and ethnic cleansing of Sunni Arabs living in Shiite neighborhoods in Baghdad. In January 2007, as the United States approached its fifth year of fighting in Iraq (surpassing the duration of U.S. participation in World War II), the toll of U.S. military dead in Iraq crossed the 3,000 mark.

4

The American Way:
War Without Politics

In 2003, shortly after President George W. Bush declared the termination of major U.S. combat operations in Iraq, the neo-imperialist Max Boot declared that the American victory was "one of the signal achievements in military history." Operation Iraqi Freedom (OIF), even when placed beside the stunning German blitzkrieg against France in 1940, he said, made "such fabled generals as Erwin Rommel and Heinz Guderian seem positively incompetent by comparison." Boot conceded that Iraqi forces "were not all that formidable to begin with," that they were demoralized, poorly trained, badly equipped, and incompetently led, all of which would seem to argue against OIF as a signal achievement in military history and Tommy Franks as the twenty-first century's American Heinz Guderian. Boot nonetheless asserted that the United States had perfected a new way of war relying on "speed, maneuver, flexibility, and surprise" to achieve "quick victory with minimal casualties"[1]—a fair description, it would seem, of the German victory of 1940. Curiously, the gushing Boot mentioned neither OIF's failure to deliver the U.S. political objective in Iraq nor the insurgency that was beginning to erupt in that country. (Three years after the launching of OIF, Boot lamented the "horrifying and inexplicable failure to undertake adequate preparation for the running of Iraq after the fall of Saddam Hussein" and declared that the "most criticized aspect of this failure—and rightly so—was not sending enough troops to control a population of 25 million." He then proposed "a thorough spring cleaning at the Department of Defense."[2])

This book so far has focused on factors that analysts regard as common to many, perhaps most, stronger-side defeats by materially weaker adversaries. But, of course, no two stronger sides are alike: each has its own history, culture, and way of war. Are there distinctive aspects of America's history, culture, and way of war that further disadvantage a democratic United States in wars against a materially weaker irregular foe with superior will and strategy? I believe there are at least two. The first is the American tendency to separate war and politics—to view military victory as an end in itself, ignoring war's function as an instrument of policy. The second is the U.S. military's profound aversion to counterinsurgency. Both combine to form a recipe for politically sterile uses of force, especially in limited wars involving protracted hostilities against weaker irregular opponents.

Much has been written about America's strategic culture and way of war. Both derive from a variety of factors, including national political culture, geography, historical military experience, and comparative strategic advantages and preferences. Particular factors shaping America's strategic culture include geographic isolation from Europe, success in subjugating a vast continental wilderness, hemispheric domination, an ideology of democratic expansionism and national exceptionalism, and a persistent isolationist impulse. These and other factors, argued the highly respected British strategist Colin S. Gray in an exceptionally insightful 2005 essay, have produced a strategic culture—more specifically, an "American way of war"—having twelve specific characteristics:

1. *Apolitical*: Americans are wont to regard war and peace as sharply distinctive conditions. The U.S. military has a long history of waging war for the goal of victory, paying scant regard to the consequences of the course of its operations for the character of the peace that will follow.

2. *Astrategic*: Strategy is, or should be, the bridge that connects military power with policy. When Americans wage war as a largely autonomous activity, leaving worry about peace and its politics to some later day, the strategy bridge has broken down.

3. *Ahistorical*: America is a future-oriented, still somewhat "new" country, one that has a founding ideology of faith in, and hope for, and commitment to, human betterment. It is only to be expected, therefore, that Americans should be less than highly respectful of what they might otherwise allow history to teach them. A defense community led by the historically disrespectful and ill educated is all but condemned to find itself surprised by events for which some historical understanding could have prepared them.

4. *Problem-Solving, Optimistic*: Holding to an optimistic public culture characterized by the belief that problems can be solved, the American way in war is not easily discouraged or deflected once it is exercised with serious intent to succeed. . . . The problem-solving faith, the penchant for the "engineering fix," has the inevitable consequences of leading U.S. policy, including its use of armed force, to attempt the impossible. Conditions are often misread as problems. Conditions have to be endured . . . , whereas problems, by definition, can be solved.

5. *Culturally Ignorant*: American public ideology, with its emphasis on political and moral uniqueness, manifest destiny, divine mission even, married to the multidimensional sense of national greatness . . . has not inclined Americans to be respectful of the beliefs, habits, and behaviors of other cultures. . . . [T]he American way of war has suffered from the self-inflicted damage caused by a failure to understand the enemy of the day.

6. *Technologically Dependent*: The exploitation of machinery is the American way of war. . . . America is the land of technological marvels and of extraordinary technology dependency. It was so from early in the nineteenth century, when a shortage of skilled craftsmen . . . obliged Americans to invent and use machines as substitutes for human skill and muscle. Necessity bred preference, and the choice of mechanical solutions assumed a cultural significance that has endured. American soldiers say that the human being matters most, but in practice the American way of war, past, present, and prospectively future, is quintessentially and uniquely technologically dependent.

7. *Firepower Focused*: It has long been the American way in warfare to send metal in harm's way in place of vulnerable flesh. This admirable expression of the country's machine mindedness undoubtedly is the single most characteristic feature of American war making at the sharp end. Needless to say, perhaps, a devotion to firepower, while highly desirable in itself, cannot help but encourage the U.S. armed forces to rely on it even when other modes of military behavior would be more suitable. In irregular conflicts in particular, heavy and sometimes seemingly indiscriminate, certainly disproportionate, resorting to firepower solutions readily becomes self-defeating.

8. *Large-Scale*: As a large rich country, for the better part of two hundred years the United States has waged its many wars regular and irregular, domestic and foreign, as one would expect of a society that is amply endowed materially. Poor societies are obliged to wage war frugally. They have no choice other than to attempt to fight smarter than rich enemies. The United States has been blessed with wealth in all its forms. Inevitably, the U.S. armed forces, once mobilized and equipped, have fought a rich person's war. They could hardly do otherwise.

9. *Profoundly Regular*: Few, if any, armies have been equally competent in the conduct of regular and irregular warfare. . . . As institutions, however, the U.S. armed forces have not been friendly either to irregular warfare or to those in its ranks who were would-be practitioners and advocates of what was regarded as the sideshow of insurgency. American soldiers . . . overwhelmingly have been very regular in their view of, approach to, and skill in warfare. They have always been prepared nearly exclusively for "real war," which is to say combat against a tolerably symmetrical, regular enemy.

10. *Impatient*: Americans have approached warfare as a regrettable occasional evil that has to be concluded as decisively and rapidly as possible. That partially moral perspective has not always sat well with the requirements of a politically effective use of force. For example, an important reason why [the U.S. military command in Vietnam] was not impressed by the promise of dedicated techniques of counterinsurgency in Vietnam was the undeniable fact that such a style of warfare would take far too long to show major results.

11. *Logistically Excellent*: The whole of American history is a testimony to the need to conquer distance. With few exceptions, Americans at war have been exceptionally able logisticians. With a continental-size interior and an effectively insular geographic location, such ability has been mandatory if the country was to wage war at all, let alone wage it effectively. . . . A large logistical footprint, and none come larger than the

American, requires a great deal of guarding, helps isolate American troops from local people and their culture, and generally tends to grow, as it were, organically in what has been called, pejoratively, the "logistical snowball."

12. *Sensitivity to Casualties*: In common with the Roman Empire, the American guardian of world order is much averse to suffering a high rate of military casualties. . . . Both superstates had and have armies that are small, too small in the opinion of many, relative to their responsibilities. Moreover, well-trained professional soldiers, volunteers all, are expensive to raise, train, and retain, and are difficult to replace. Beyond the issue of cost-effectiveness, however, lies the claim that American society has become so sensitive to casualties that the domestic context for U.S. military action is no longer tolerant of bloody adventures in muscular imperial governance.[3]

How do these strategic cultural attributes manifest themselves in how Americans approach the use of force? Thomas G. Mahnken contends that America's geography, history, society, and comparative advantages have produced an approach to war at the strategic level characterized by "a strong and long-standing predilection for waging war for far-reaching objectives" (Americans "have been uncomfortable with wars fought for limited political aims") and "a preference for the direct approach . . . over the indirect" ("The U.S. military has throughout its history sought to close with and destroy the enemy at the earliest opportunity"). At the operational and tactical levels of war, these strategic preferences translate into "a lavish use of firepower," which among other things "saves American lives," and more specifically and recently, "growing reliance on high-technology weapons," especially those delivered from the air.[4]

Permeating the entire fabric of America's strategic culture and approach to war, especially the aversion to fighting for limited political purposes, is an unwillingness to accept war as a continuation of politics. Clausewitz repeatedly reminded his readers that "the only source of war is politics—the intercourse of governments and peoples" and warned that "it is apt to be assumed that war suspends that intercourse and replaces it by a wholly different condition, ruled by no law but its own." War, he repeated, "is simply a continuation of political intercourse, with the addition of other means." Most Americans, however, do not

accept the wartime subordination of military operations to political considerations even though, as Clausewitz pointed out, "Subordinating the political point
of view to the military would be absurd, for it is policy that creates war. Policy is
the guiding intelligence and war only the instrument, not vice versa."[5]

Gen. Douglas MacArthur spoke for most Americans when he declared, in an
address to a Joint Session of Congress on April 19, 1951, "Once war is forced
upon us, there is no other alternative than to apply every available means to bring
it to a swift end. War's very object is victory, not prolonged indecision. In war
there is no substitute for victory."[6] MacArthur had just been fired as commander
of UN forces in Korea because he had publicly challenged President Truman to
widen the Korean War by bombing and blockading mainland China, a course of
action Truman and the Joint Chiefs of Staff opposed. They did not want an open-
ended war with China at a time when Europe remained defenseless against a Soviet attack. MacArthur, however, rejected the very idea of politically restricted
military operations. War was, for him, a substitute for policy, not its continuation.

This view underpins the conventional wisdom in the United States regarding the failed prosecution of the Vietnam War. Meddling politicians and Defense
Department civilians, it is said, snatched defeat from the jaws of victory; if they
had just gotten out of the way and let the military professionals do their job, the
United States would have won the war. One need look no farther than the Gulf
War of 1991, so this reasoning goes, to see what happens when the civilians
stand aside or no farther than Bosnia and Kosovo to see what happens when they
resume their interference.

Conventional wisdom conveniently overlooks the reality that limited war
necessarily entails restrictions on the use of force (and the Gulf War was no
exception); otherwise, it would not be limited war. Military means are proportional to the political objective sought; thermonuclear weapons are not used against
insurgency.[7] Letting MacArthur attack mainland China would have involved use
of force excessive to the limited objective of restoring South Korea's territorial
integrity. Even in OIF, the object of which was the overthrow of a hostile regime
via invasion of its homeland, extensive restrictions were placed on ground force
size and aerial targeting.

Perhaps worse still, conventional wisdom is dangerously narcissistic. It
completely ignores the enemy, assuming that what *we* do determines success or
failure. It assumes that only the United States can defeat the United States, an

outlook that set the United States up for failure in Vietnam and for surprise in Iraq. Custer may have been a fool, but the Sioux did, after all, have something to do with his defeat along the Little Big Horn.

Military victory is a beginning, not an end. Approaching war as an apolitical enterprise encourages fatal inattention to the challenges of converting military wins into political successes. It thwarts recognition that insurgencies are first and foremost political struggles that cannot be defeated by military means alone—indeed, that effective counterinsurgency entails the greatest discretion in the use of force. Pursuit of military victory for its own sake also discourages thinking about and planning for the second and by far the most difficult half of wars for regime change: establishing a viable replacement for the destroyed regime. War's object is, after all, a better peace. There can be no other justification for war. "Military conflict has two dimensions," observe former presidential national security advisers Samuel Berger and Brent Scowcroft, "winning wars and winning the peace. We excel in the first, but without an equal focus on the second, combat victories can be lost."[8]

The U.S. military's aversion to counterinsurgency (the Marine Corps is the prominent exception) is a function of sixty years of preoccupation with high-technology conventional warfare against other states and accelerated substitution of machines for combat manpower, most notably aerial standoff precision firepower for large ground forces. Indeed, evidence mounts of growing alienation between the kind of war the United States prepares to fight and the kinds of war it has actually fought in recent decades and will likely fight in the future. To put it another way, U.S. military force posture appears increasingly at odds with the emerging strategic environment. Hostile great powers, once the predominant threats to American security, have been supplanted by rogue states, failed states, and non-state actors—all of them pursuing asymmetrical strategies to offset U.S. military strengths. This new threat environment places a premium on what, until recently, the Defense Department termed "military operations other than war" (MOOTW)—operations other than the powerful conventional force-on-force missions for which the U.S. military is optimized. Such operations include peace enforcement, counterinsurgency, stability, and state-building. For British strategist Lawrence Freedman,

It is hard to imagine contingencies in which the United States would seek to defeat the army of another major power, or indeed circumstances in which another major power would knowingly try to defeat the United States in conventional battle. This does not mean that future inter-state wars are impossible, with or without the United States, or that they might not take on the form of classical conventional warfare. It does, nonetheless, put a large question mark against the notion of a true revolution in military affairs because of the unlikelihood that all serious powers as well as aspirants will structure their armed forces in similar ways to prepare for some rather standardized encounters. . . .

Those who are almost bound to lose wars fought on Western terms have every incentive to adopt alternative strategies that play to their advantages. These could be found in geography (short supply lines and opportunities for urban warfare), a threshold of pain (a readiness to accept casualties), patience (leading to frustration in Western capitals) and even a relative lack of humanitarian scruples (allowing the war to extend into civil society).[9]

The Iraq War, like the Vietnam War before it, has exposed the limits of conventional military power in unconventional settings. OIF achieved a quick victory over Iraqi conventional military resistance, such as it was, but did not secure decisive political success. An especially vicious and seemingly ineradicable insurgency arose, in part because coalition forces did not seize full control of the country and impose the security necessary for Iraq's peaceful economic and political reconstruction. The Office of the Secretary of Defense, encouraged by the easy American win over the Taliban in Afghanistan, was determined to demonstrate that minimum force was sufficient to topple the Baathist regime in Iraq. Francis Fukuyama believes that

> the success of American military technology during the 1990s created the illusion that military victory would always be as clean and cheap as the Gulf or Kosovo wars. The Iraq War has already demonstrated the limits of this form of light, mobile warfare: it can defeat virtually any existing conventional military force, but it provides no special advantages in fighting a prolonged insurgency. [Precision-guided munitions] cannot distinguish between insurgents and noncombatants or help soldiers speak Arabic. Indeed, the very model of a professional, all-volunteer military that was

established in Vietnam's waning days works only for short, high-intensity wars. If the United States were serious about regime change and the use of its military to promote political goals in countries around the world, it would need a military different in many ways from the one [it now has].[10]

Gordon and Trainor also note the "profound and irreconcilable tensions between Rumsfeld's push to enact his principles of transformation by beginning the attack with a lean force and the administration's rationale for the war, disarming Iraq and preventing WMD from falling into the wrong hands." The "surprising contradiction" between means and ends was that the

> United States did not have nearly enough troops to secure the hundreds of suspected WMD sites that had supposedly been identified in Iraq or to secure the nation's long, porous borders. Had the Iraqis possessed WMD and terrorist groups been prevalent in Iraq as the Bush administration so loudly asserted, U.S. forces might well have failed to prevent the WMD from being spirited out of the country and falling into the hands of the dark forces the administration had declared war against.[11]

OIF followed not only three decades of determined U.S. Army disinterest in the counterinsurgency mission but also over a decade of steady cuts in active-duty U.S. ground forces, especially Army infantry.[12] Most MOOTW, however, including counterinsurgency, are inherently manpower intensive and rely heavily on special skills—human intelligence, civil affairs, police, public health, foreign language, foreign force training, psychological warfare—that are secondary, even marginal, to the prosecution of conventional warfare. Forces capable of achieving swift conventional military victory thus may be quantitatively and qualitatively unsuited for post-victory tasks of the kind that the United States has encountered in Iraq. U.S. Army counterinsurgency expert Robert Cassidy argues that

> Great power militaries do not innovate well. This is particularly true when the required innovations and adaptations lie outside the scope of the conventional war focus. In other words, great powers do not "win" small wars because they are great powers: their militaries must maintain a central competence in symmetric warfare to preserve their great power status

vis-à-vis other great powers; and their militaries must be large organizations. These two characteristics combine to create a formidable competence on the plains of Europe or in the deserts of Iraq. However, these two traits do not produce institutions and cultures that often exhibit a propensity for counter-guerrilla warfare.[13]

Antulio Echevarria, director of research at the U.S. Army War College's Strategic Studies Institute, believes the United States "is geared to fight wars as if they were battles, and thus confuses the winning of campaigns . . . with the winning of wars." He further contends that "the characteristics of the U.S. style of warfare—speed, jointness, knowledge, and precision—are better suited for strike operations than for translating such operations into strategic successes."[14] Strategic analyst David Lonsdale observes that America's strategic culture stresses "technological fixes to strategic problems" and "the increasing removal of humans from the sharp end of war," resulting in postmodern warfare "in which precise, distant bombardment dispenses with the need to deploy ground forces in a combat role and thereby relegates them to a constabulary function." He warns that "these notions are not only astrategic and ignore the paradoxical logic of strategy; they also implicitly rely on unrealistically effective operations, and thereby seemingly ignore the presence of friction."[15]

Former West Point professor Frederick W. Kagan also believes that the primary culprit in delivering politically sterile victories is the Pentagon's conception of war. The reason "the United States [has] been so successful in recent wars [but] encountered so much difficulty in securing its political aims after the shooting stopped," he argues, "lies partly in a 'vision of war' that see[s] the enemy as a target set and believe[s] that when all or most targets have been hit, he will inevitably surrender and American goals will be achieved." Unfortunately, this vision ignores the importance of "how, exactly, one defeats the enemy and what the enemy's country looks like at the moment the bullets stop flying." For Kagan, the "entire thrust of the current program of military transformation of the U.S. armed forces . . . aims at the implementation and perfection of this target set mentality."[16]

But target destruction is insufficient and perhaps counterproductive in circumstances where the United States is seeking regime change in a manner that gains the support of the defeated populace for the new government. Such circumstances require large numbers of properly trained ground troops for purposes of securing population centers and infrastructure, maintaining order, providing humanitarian relief, and facilitating revived delivery of such fundamental services as electrical power and potable water. Kagan continues,

> It is not enough to consider simply how to pound the enemy into submission with stand-off forces. . . . To effect regime change, U.S. forces must be positively in control of the enemy's territory and population as rapidly and continuously as possible. That control cannot be achieved by machines, still less by bombs. Only human beings interacting with human beings can achieve it. The only hope for success in the extension of politics that is war is to restore the human element to the transformation equation.[17]

Infatuation with the perfection of military means can cause the user to ignore the political purpose on behalf of which those means are being employed. Did the Pentagon simply lose sight of the main political objective in Iraq, which was not the destruction of Iraqi military forces but rather the establishment of the requisite security environment for Iraq's successful reconstruction? To be sure, the former was a precondition for the latter, but was the latter an especially, perhaps impossibly, tall order for a military "obsessed with stupendous deeds of fire and movement rather than the political function that war must serve"?[18]

Accelerated military speed may in fact be strategically counterproductive. "The focus on high-intensity conflict means that the United States is winning wars faster and with fewer casualties," observe Berger and Scowcroft. "But that 'transformation' has had an unintended consequence. Rapid victory collapses the enemy but does not destroy it. Adversaries can go underground to regroup, creating a need for more troops for longer periods of time after combat ends."[19] Colin Gray contends that though "the transformational push may well succeed and be highly impressive in its military-technical accomplishments, it is likely to miss the most vital marks." Why?

> There are a number of reasons for this harsh judgment. First, high-tech transformation will have only modest value, because war is a duel and all of America's foes out to 2020 will be significantly asymmetrical. The

most intelligent among them, as well as the geographically more fortu-
nate and the luckier, will pursue ways of war that do not test U.S. strengths.
Second, the military potential of this transformation, as with all past trans-
formations, is being undercut by unstoppable processes of diffusion which
spread technology and ideas. Third, the transformation being sought appears to be oblivious to the fact . . . that there is more to war than warfare.
War is about the peace it will shape. It is not obvious that the current
process of military transformation will prove vitally useful in helping to
improve America's strategic performance. Specifically, the country needs
to approach the waging of war as political behavior for political purposes. Sometimes one is moved to the despairing conclusion that
Clausewitz wrote in vain, for all the influence he has had on the American way of war.[20]

None of the foregoing is to argue against continued conventional military
perfection. U.S. conventional military primacy is inherently desirable because it
deters enemy attack in kind and effectively eliminates conventional warfare as a
means of settling disputes with the United States. These are no mean accomplishments. Conventional primacy also enables the United States to crush the
conventionally weak and incompetent, like the Taliban in Afghanistan and the
Baathist government in Iraq. Primacy, at least of the kind sought by Pentagon
transformationists, also permits increasing substitution of technology for blood,
which in turn has reduced U.S. casualty rates to historic lows and arguably increased public tolerance for the use of force overseas (a very mixed blessing, to
be sure).

The same primacy that has yielded conventional deterrence, however, has
pushed America's enemies into greater reliance on irregular warfare responses
that expose the limits of conventional primacy. It has also, argues one critic,
bewitched the Pentagon. Though wars of "flesh, faith, and cities" now predomi-
nate, the Pentagon remains mesmerized by the notion "that machines can replace
human beings on the battlefield," contends Ralph Peters, "[w]e are seduced by
what we can do, whereas our enemies focus on what they must do. We have
fallen so deeply in love with the means we have devised for waging conceptual
wars that we are blind to their marginal relevance in actual wars."[21]

The language and recommendations of the Defense Department's much-
awaited *Quadrennial Defense Review* (QDR) of February 2006 hardly demolish

the reality of a growing disconnect between U.S. force planning and the evolving global strategic environment.[22] The QDR formally acknowledges what has been self-evident for fifteen years—namely, that "irregular warfare has emerged as the dominant form of warfare confronting the United States."[23] The QDR also calls for heightened service-wide investment in foreign language training and cultural awareness as well as expanded special operations forces, which can have considerable utility in counterinsurgency operations but are tasked to perform other missions as well, "especially long-duration, indirect and clandestine operations in politically sensitive environments and denied areas."[24] But the QDR calls for no increases in overall U.S. ground force levels and stands pat on all major cold war legacy weapons systems; though it makes occasional passing references to the war in Iraq, it is obsessed with technology and future war. Four years of war against a deadly unconventional enemy have not affected the maintenance of every conventional weapons system in the pipeline. "The new QDR reflects a concerted effort by the Pentagon to return to its pre-9/11 course," laments Frederick W. Kagan, "focusing on long-term dangers as though the wars in Iraq and Afghanistan had never happened, as if America's ground forces were not badly overstretched, as if the nation were not really at war."[25] The QDR leaves U.S. forces organized, trained, and equipped largely for traditional warfare, and as such represents a major if predictable victory of entrenched service preferences and contractor interests. "Despite Rumsfeld's own bold talk of major structural changes in the defense budget (now coming in at $500 billion), more than a decade of discussion of a less platform-centered approach to warfare, and a stress on lighter forces more appropriate to contemporary conditions, the U.S. defense budget is still dominated by platforms," notes Lawrence Freedman. "Rumsfeld has been no more successful than his predecessors in turning the services away from the 'big ticket' systems of aircraft, warships and armoured vehicles that would only really be necessary in the event of a major war against a far more substantial enemy than can currently be identified."[26]

For most Americans, war and politics are two mutually exclusive enterprises. Politics cease when war starts and resume when war ends. This reduces the object of war to military victory for virtually its own sake, which in turn encourages politically sterile wars.

5

The American Way:

Search and Destroy

The American strategic analyst Carnes Lord, writing in the early 1990s, warned against the Pentagon's unpreparedness for what in the professional jargon of the day was termed "low intensity conflict." Noting that "the record of U.S. involvement in contingency operations as well as protracted revolutionary warfare in the less developed world is spotty at best, with serious flaws apparent even in victory," Lord went on to educate his readers:

> What distinguishes low intensity conflict from other forms of conflict is not the scale of violence as such but the fact that violence is embedded in a political context that directly shapes and constrains it. . . . Low intensity warfare is distinguished from other warfare by the extent to which politics dictates not merely strategy but military operations and even tactics. In low intensity warfare, non-military instrumentalities of national power may have an equal or even greater role to play than military forces. What this means in practice is either that military forces must perform essentially non-military functions, or else that special means must be devised to coordinate and integrate military forces with non-military agencies of government.[1]

Lord went on to observe that the United States was peculiarly ill-suited to deal with low-intensity wars because of the national tendency "to view war and peace as sharply delineated activities" and because "the American national security establishment as a whole is not structured in a way that facilitates coordination between the armed forces and other agencies of government."[2]

The policy question is not whether the United States should continue to maintain its hard-won and indispensable conventional primacy, but whether, given the evolving strategic environment, it should create ground (and supporting air) forces dedicated to performing operations other than war, including counterinsurgency. Extant army forces and tactical doctrines are hardly optimized for the counterinsurgent mission, which demands the utmost restraint and discrimination in the application of force. Firepower is the instrument of last rather than first resort. There is no big enemy to close with and destroy, but rather the presence of threatened civilian populations that must be protected in ways that minimize collateral damage. Conventional ground force preparation for counterinsurgency and other MOOTW requires major doctrinal and training deprogramming of conventional military habits and reprogramming with the alien tactics, doctrines, and heavy political oversight of MOOTW. Needless to say, forces so reprogrammed—commonly manpower-intensive and relatively low on firepower—will not be optimized for big, high-tech conventional conflicts.

In his *Insurgency in Iraq: An Historical Perspective*, counterinsurgency expert Ian F. Beckett argues that

> the essentials of counterinsurgency . . . have remained fairly constant . . . since 1945 [and include] first, a recognition of the need for a political rather than a purely military response to insurgency; second, a need for coordination of the civil and military response; third, a need for the coordination of intelligence; fourth, a need to separate the insurgents from the population; fifth, a need for the appropriate use of military force, which generally means the minimum necessary in any given situation; and, last, the need to implement long-term reform to address grievances that led to support for the insurgency in the first place.[3]

These essentials are not easily mastered by the conventional warriors. "Thinking about regular warfare offers strategists a sort of comfort zone, where conflict will be governed by familiar principles and sets understood requirements for the development of capabilities, doctrine and training," observes Freedman.

Irregular warfare, by contrast, is unfamiliar and perplexing, lacking obvious boundaries. The range of forms it can take is disorienting, taking in guerrilla struggle, warlord rivalries and gangsterism, inter-communal violence and mass-casualty terrorism. The standards of victory can be equally confusing, especially when (as is usually the case) no culminating point is reached. These conflicts often either peter out or are marginalized by political developments, with the militants neither seizing power nor surrendering. Unlike regular warfare, irregular conflicts are unlikely to turn on having the most advanced technology or the imposition of overwhelming force. The military role may be quite limited, with key tasks in the hands of intelligence agencies and the police, and with even leaders and intellectuals who frame and describe the core issues at the heart of the struggle.[4]

Given the fundamental differences between conventional and counterinsurgent warfare, Arreguin-Toft concludes that each requires its own force structure and doctrine:

Strategic interaction theory shows why the two missions demand two different kinds of armed forces: one to defend U.S. interests in conventional wars, and one to defend them in small wars against terrorists. It also highlights the importance of politics and diplomacy in combating insurgencies and terrorists. Determined insurgents and terrorists are difficult to defeat. But where strong actors have succeeded, they have done so most dramatically by preceding *discriminate* military attacks with political and economic reforms—reforms that effectively isolated guerrillas and terrorists from their base of social support.[5]

Whatever the arguments for the establishment of MOOTW-dedicated forces (and there are serious arguments against), such forces are not likely to find favor in the Pentagon, which, like any other large bureaucracy, has organizational preferences based upon what it likes to do and does well. The Pentagon is exceptionally good at conventional warfare but not particularly good at fighting irregular adversaries to a politically decisive finish. Marine Corps small-war expert Thomas X. Hammes points out that though war against an unconventional enemy "is the only kind of war America has ever lost," the Defense Department "has largely ignored unconventional warfare. As the only Goliath in the world, we should be worried that the world's Davids have found a sling and stone that work. Yet the internal DOD debate has largely ignored this striking difference between the outcomes of conventional and unconventional warfare."[6] Strategic Studies Institute analysts Steven Metz and Raymond Millen observe that while "the strategic salience of insurgency for the United States is higher than it has been since the height of the Cold War, [insurgency] remains challenging for the United States because two of its dominant characteristics—protractedness and ambiguity—mitigate the effectiveness of the American military."[7]

Institutional resistance is especially strong inside the army, notwithstanding recent growth in its special operations force components. Though the Marine Corps is comfortable with counterinsurgency because of its long history of small wars and policing operations (in 1990 it reissued its classic 1940 *Small Wars Manual*), the army, notwithstanding considerable experience in small wars, has never viewed counterinsurgency as anything other than a diversion from its main mission of conventional combat against like enemies.

In a landmark 1986 assessment of the U.S. Army's performance in Vietnam, Andrew Krepinevich, a serving army officer, set out to answer the question,

> How could the army of the most powerful nation on Earth, materially supported on a scale unprecedented in history, equipped with the most sophisticated technology in an age when technology had assumed the role of a god of war, fail to emerge victorious against a numerically inferior force of lightly armed irregulars?[8]

Krepinevich contended that the army, in the person of Gen. William C. Westmoreland, insisted on applying its own concept of war in an Indochinese strategic, operational, and tactical environment for which the concept was not suited; the army neither understood nor wanted to understand the nature of the war it was entering. The concept, rooted in the army's victories of World War II, had two characteristics: "a focus on . . . conventional war and reliance on high volumes of firepower to minimize casualties." Unfortunately,

> the Army's experience in war did not prepare it well for counterinsurgency, where the emphasis is on light infantry formations, not heavy divisions;

on firepower restraint, not its widespread application; on the resolution of political and social problems within the nations targeted by insurgents, not closing with and destroying the insurgent's field forces.[9]

Army leaders looked upon irregulars with disdain and believed that conventional forces that had defeated German armies could readily handle a bunch of rag-tag Asian guerrillas, an attitude reflected in Army Chief of Staff (1962–64) Gen. George Decker's assurance to a skeptical President John F. Kennedy that "any good soldier can handle guerrillas" and in Chairman of the Joint Chiefs of Staff (1964–70) Gen. Earle Wheeler's declaration in 1964 that "the essence of the problem in Vietnam is military."[10]

Westmoreland rejected of a strategy of isolating the insurgents militarily and politically from the population in favor of a "search-and-destroy" strategy of attrition that boiled down to killing as many Communists as possible in the hope of pushing the enemy to the point where he could no longer replace his losses and would therefore quit. In so doing Westmoreland displayed an utter obliviousness to the political nature of the war—that the war was at bottom a contest for political allegiance. Westmoreland's strategy failed not only because it misread the nature of the war but also because it mistakenly assumed that the enemy would lose control of his own losses because U.S. forces would retain the tactical initiative. In fact, the Communists initiated 80–90 percent of all firefights and were thus in a position to control their losses, which, given North Vietnam's population and birth rate, never approached the "irreplaceable" crossover point.[11]

Attrition was not without its critics even inside the army. The Marines opposed Westmoreland's strategy and, to Westmoreland's great dismay, exploited their experience of pacification by pursuing instead in their area of operations in Vietnam (the I Corps Tactical Zone, which encompassed South Vietnam's five northernmost provinces) a population protection strategy that integrated civil and military operations as well as Marine Corps rifle squads into South Vietnamese regional force platoons. These "Combined Action Platoons" lived among the locals and concentrated on pacification activities while other Marine Corps units patrolled and conducted civic action programs. The commander of Marine Corps forces in the Pacific defended population protection by pointing to the improved security it delivered and by pointing out that Westmoreland's body count strategy "can be a dubious index of success since, if their killing is accompanied by devastation of friendly areas, we may end up having done more harm than good."[12]

There were limits to the Marine Corps' strategy as well, however. Even had Westmoreland supported a population protection strategy countrywide, prospects for successful counterinsurgency were always limited in South Vietnam by pervasive governmental corruption at the national and provincial levels and the questionable political legitimacy of a Saigon government that was largely the creation of the United States and run by military officers who were disproportionately Catholic and who had served on the French side during the First Indochina War. Marine Corps forces in I Corps also had to contend with conventional military threats posed by PAVN units, and it is not clear that the Marines ever resolved the dilemma—the same the British faced in America—of dealing simultaneously and effectively with regular and irregular threats.[13] And of course counterinsurgency offered no solution to the conventional PAVN invasion that brought down South Vietnam in 1975.

The Marines were not the only ones to question Westmoreland's attrition strategy. U.S. Army Chief of Staff Gen. Harold K. Johnson also had such doubts that he commissioned a study, "A Program for the Pacification and Long-Term Development of Vietnam"—known as PROVN—in the spring of 1965. The study, which was conducted by ten carefully chosen officers under the leadership of Gen. Creighton Abrams (Westmoreland's successor in South Vietnam), was charged with "developing new courses of action to be taken in South Vietnam by the United States and its allies, which will, in conjunction with current actions, modified as necessary, lead in due time to successful accomplishment of U.S. aims and objectives."[14] The final report of the PROVN study, which was submitted to General Johnson in March 1966, essentially repudiated Westmoreland's search-and-destroy strategy and called instead for a population protection strategy. The report declared that success in Vietnam could be achieved only "through bringing the individual Vietnamese, typically a rural peasant, to support willingly the GVN [Government of Vietnam]. The critical actions are those that occur at the village, district, and provincial levels. This is where the war must be fought; this is where that war and the object which lies beyond it must be won."[15] Those who conducted the PROVN study clearly recognized what Westmoreland did not: that the object of war extends beyond defeat of the enemy's military forces to the securing of the political object for which war is waged.

Predictably, the PROVN study was rejected by Westmoreland, who subsequently mentioned it in neither his memoirs nor his official report on the war, and by Wheeler, who never saw the war in any but narrowly military terms and who was in any event, along with the air force and navy chiefs, much more preoccupied with obtaining a relaxation of White House restrictions on the air war against North Vietnam than in the fighting in the South. As for General Johnson, although he believed that the PROVN study was valid, he could not, in the end, bring himself to overrule the strategy choice of a commander in the field.[16]

Sixteen years after Andrew Krepinevich's *The Army and Vietnam* appeared, another serving Army officer, John Nagl, published *Learning to Eat Soup with a Knife: Counterinsurgency Lessons from Malaya and Vietnam*, which examined how "two armies learned when they were confronted with situations for which they were not prepared by training, organization, and doctrine: the British army in the Malayan Emergency and the American army in the Vietnam War."[17] Nagl concluded that organizational culture was the key to the ability to learn from unanticipated conditions and that the British army's organizational culture produced successful counterinsurgency in Malaya whereas the U.S. Army's failed to do so in Vietnam. More disturbingly, he also concluded that though thirty years had passed since the last U.S. combat forces departed Vietnam, "the U.S. Army has failed to form a consensus on the lessons of Vietnam and has not accepted the idea that revolutionary war requires a qualitatively different response from the conventional warfare it knows so well how to fight."[18] If anything, much of the army's leadership drew the worst possible lessons from the war, at least to the extent that Col. Harry G. Summers Jr.'s highly influential 1982 book, *On Strategy: A Critical Analysis of the Vietnam War*, became, as Nagl asserts, "the U.S. Army's approved version of why it lost the Vietnam War."[19]

Summers, a combat veteran of Korea and Vietnam serving on the staff of the Strategic Studies Institute of the U.S. Army War College, used Carl von Clausewitz's *On War* as the yardstick for judging U.S. political and military performance, and he mercilessly condemned both. He censured the Johnson administration for failing to mobilize the national political will via dramatic exhortation and a formal declaration of war, and he indicted the military for having lost touch with the art of war, including the imperative not to confuse the administrative requirements involved in preparing for war with the operational requirements for waging war. Summers argued that the United States waged a halfhearted war with no intention of winning; it lacked even a concept of victory, notwithstanding repeated official proclamations of the vitality of U.S. interests in Vietnam.

Though Summers reintroduced the army to Clausewitz, he did so by rewriting history to confirm the army's rejection of counterinsurgency. He argued—in complete contradiction to the historical record—that the army failed in Vietnam because it was not sufficiently *conventional* in fighting the war! He claimed that the army in the early 1960s had become mesmerized by counterinsurgency to the point of doctrine becoming dogma and, accordingly, that the army focused on the internal insurgent threat in South Vietnam (which in his view the South Vietnamese should have handled) rather than the external conventional threat from North Vietnam. Summers even denied that the Communists' strategy of protracted irregular warfare was a strategy at all, suggesting that it was a ruse to deflect U.S. attention away from the external conventional threat.

> [Our] basic mistake . . . was that we saw their guerrilla operations as a strategy in and of itself. Because we saw it as a strategy, we attempted to understand it in terms of "people's war" theories of Mao Tse-tung, and devised elaborate theories of counterinsurgency. . . . [I]nstead of orienting on North Vietnam—the source of the war—we turned our attention to the symptom—the guerrilla war in the south. Our new "strategy" of counterinsurgency blinded us to the fact that the guerrilla war was tactical and not strategic. It was a kind of economy of force operation on the part of North Vietnam to buy time and to wear down superior U.S. forces.[20]

Summers conveniently ignored two facts: that the Vietnamese Communists understood their own strategy in terms of the people's war theories of Mao Tse-tung and that it was the Communists' "economy-of-force" operation that was decisive in destroying America's political will to fight on to a military victory. The Johnson administration's post–Tet Offensive decision to abandon the main U.S. war aim—defeating the Communists militarily—in favor of seeking a way to extricate the United States from Vietnam, was made in 1968 and was not contested by the incoming Nixon administration, which not only accepted (for three years) an inherited suspension of the bombing of North Vietnam but also initiated a series of unilateral troop withdrawals without reciprocal concessions on the part of Hanoi. Summers did not acknowledge that in 1968 PAVN forces accounted for only 20 percent of armed Communist strength in the South and that it took Hanoi another seven years to muster the conventional military strength to win the war. Summers also ignored South Vietnam's abject political and military incapacity to deal with the internal insurgent threat. It was that incapacity, after all, that prompted U.S. ground combat intervention in the first place. As Robert Osgood observed,

> In the final analysis, all of the controversies over how the Vietnam War should have been fought are less significant in explaining defeat or the prospect of victory than the likelihood that no military success could have enabled the government of South Vietnam to maintain independence by its own efforts, or perhaps even with the continued presence of American forces.[21]

Finally, Summers failed to recognize that the strength of U.S. interest in the outcome of the conflict was limited, which necessarily imposed limits on the amount of blood and treasure any political administration could expend on behalf of winning the war. (Was Summers unaware of Andrew Mack's seminal 1975 article, "Why Big Nations Lose Small Wars: The Politics of Asymmetric Conflict," or did Summers choose simply to ignore it?)

It is little wonder that the Vietnam War reinforced the army's aversion to counterinsurgency. If Summers's book was the approved version of why the army lost the war, the Weinberger-Powell doctrine was the army's prescription for avoiding another Vietnam. Rather than confront the painful truth that the army failed in Vietnam because it rejected counterinsurgency, was it not better to focus on avoiding the mission altogether? "No more Vietnams" meant no more lost wars but it also meant no more counterinsurgency. The Weinberger tests for using force, including the presence of vital interests, the assurance of public support, a determination to win militarily, and use of force only as a last resort, coupled with Powell's insistence that force, when used, be used overwhelmingly, represent the distillation of the professional military's take on the lessons of the Vietnam War. The doctrine deserves recapitulation and further discussion because it was the Vietnam "syndrome" prescribed as official doctrine, because it essentially rejected limited use of force, and because it reflected the traditional American preference for divorcing the military from the political.

Weinberger enunciated his doctrine two years after Summers's book was published, in a November 1984 speech before the National Press Club. The doctrine consisted of six "tests" (his term) to be passed before the United States committed force—tests that by implication were flunked in Vietnam and in the subsequent case of disastrous U.S. intervention in Lebanon (which Weinberger had vigorously opposed):

1. The United States should not commit forces to *combat* overseas unless the particular engagement or occasion is deemed vital to our national interest or that of our allies.
2. If we decide that it *is* necessary to put *combat* troops in a given situation, we should do so wholeheartedly and with the clear intention of winning.
3. If we *do* decide to commit forces to combat overseas, we should have clearly defined political and military objectives.
4. The relationship between our objectives and the forces we have committed—their size and composition—must be continually reassessed and re-adjusted if necessary.
5. Before the U.S. commits combat forces abroad, there must be reasonable assurance [that] we will have the support of the American people and their elected representatives in Congress.
6. The commitment of U.S. forces to combat should be a last resort.[22]

Weinberger identified "gray area conflicts" as "the most likely challenge to peace," yet warned that they were "precisely the most difficult challenges to which a democracy must respond." He further cautioned that if "we are certain that force is required in any given situation, we run the risk of inadequate national will to apply the resources needed." He reserved his heaviest fire, however, for those "theorists [who] argue that military force can be brought to bear in any crisis," who "are eager to advocate its use even in limited amounts simply because they believed that if there are American forces of *any* size present they will somehow solve the problem." The United States had to abandon the employment of force "as a regular and customary part of our diplomatic efforts" because to not do so "would surely plunge us headlong into the sort of domestic turmoil we experienced during the Vietnam War." Weinberger viewed the "intermixture of diplomacy and the military" as inherently dangerous because it meant "that we should not hesitate to put a battalion or so of American forces in various places in the world where we desired . . . stability, or changes of government, or support of governments or whatever else." Weinberger, in sum, saw force not as an arm of diplomacy, but rather as a substitute for it—something to be used only when diplomacy failed.

Weinberger's doctrine was carried into the George H. W. Bush administration by Gen. Colin Powell, who became chairman of the Joint Chiefs of Staff in 1989 and a key player in the Persian Gulf crisis of 1990–91. Indeed, his allegiance during the crisis to the doctrine and his emphasis on the application of overwhelming force and minimal U.S. casualties led many commentators to start using the term "Weinberger-Powell" doctrine. Powell had, in fact, served as Weinberger's military aide and helped the secretary of defense draft his famous speech. "War should be the politics of last resort," he wrote in his bestselling memoirs. "And when we go to war, we should have a purpose that our people understand and support; we should mobilize the country's resources to fulfill that mission and then go on to win. In Vietnam, we entered a half-hearted war, with much of the nation opposed or indifferent, while a small fraction carried the burden."[23]

These words essentially restated the Weinberger doctrine. Use of force should be highly restricted. It should be avoided in situations where political restrictions threaten to impede its effective use, where a clear and quick military win is not attainable, and where public and congressional opinion is hostile or even indifferent to the purpose for which force is being used. Except in cases of enemy attack, force, in short, should be used only in ideal political and military conditions. Weinberger-Powell was in effect a recipe for military inaction for fear of embracing the inherent risks of military action. It is no coincidence that Powell opposed the use of force to reverse Iraq's aggression against Kuwait, to stop Serbian genocide in Bosnia, and to overthrow the Saddam Hussein regime. His doctrine reflects "a strategic frame of mind that is both apolitical and absolute. The absolutism reflects and all-or-nothing approach that has dominated past strategy, and it disassociates itself with politics because the only satisfactory outcome is a military victory." As such, it "is a paradigm that is inappropriate for the entire spectrum of conflict, especially those missions that have emerged in the post–Cold War era."[24]

Thus the army ignored counterinsurgency until it encountered insurgency again in Iraq. The army studiously avoided any systematic appraisal of counterinsurgent lessons learned in Vietnam because such an appraisal would have suggested a responsibility to prepare for future insurgencies. One insurgency out of sight was all insurgencies out of mind. "Iraq underscores . . . the overwhelming organizational tendency within the U.S. military not to absorb historical lessons when planning and conducting counterinsurgency operations," concluded a 2005 Rand Corporation study delivered to Secretary of Defense Donald Rumsfeld. The study proceeded to recommend,

> In the future, U.S. military forces engaged in counterinsurgency operations must [be] composed of personnel with training and skills similar to special operations forces, i.e., the language and culture of the country, and in the critically important political, economic, intelligence, organizational, and psychological dimensions of counterinsurgency warfare. Serious attention should also be given to creating in the Army a dedicated cadre of counterinsurgency specialists and a program to produce such experts.[25]

As if to confirm the army's willful refusal to learn lessons of past counterinsurgency campaigns, Krepinevich returned to the fray in 2005 with a condemnation of U.S. counterinsurgent operations in Iraq. Asserting that the failed search-and-destroy strategy continues to exert a strong pull on the U.S. military because it is about killing the enemy rather than performing potentially more effective but less heroic tasks, Krepinevich argued that, as in Vietnam, U.S. operations against insurgents in Iraq

> put too great an emphasis on destroying insurgent forces and minimizing U.S. casualties and too little on providing enduring security to the Iraqi people; too much effort into sweeping maneuvers and no enduring presence and too little into effective coordination of security and reconstruction efforts; and too high a priority on quickly fielding large numbers of Iraq security forces and too low a priority on ensuring their effectiveness.[26]

A senior British officer serving in Iraq was even more critical of the U.S. Army's bull-in-the-china-shop counterinsurgency operations in Iraq and published his scathing observations in, surprisingly, *Military Review*, the journal of the U.S.

Army Command and General Staff College. "Granted, modern technology enables lethal force to be applied more precisely, thus helping to minimize collateral damage and reduce the potential for inadvertent alienation of the civilian population," conceded Brigadier Nigel Aylwin-Foster.

> Nonetheless, the characteristic U.S. military intent has remained one of uncompromising destruction of the enemy's forces, rather than a more finely tuned harnessing of military effect to serve political intent—a distinction in the institutional understanding of military purpose that becomes highly significant when an army attuned to conventional warfare suddenly needs to adapt to the more subtle political framework of a COIN [counterinsurgency] campaign.
>
> In short, the U.S. Army has developed over time a singular focus on conventional warfare, of a particular swift and violent style, which left it ill-suited to the kind of operation it encountered as soon as conventional warfighting ceased to be the primary focus of OIF.[27]

The argument here is not that the Defense Department is hopelessly unadaptable to the deconventionalized global strategic environment—only that its force-structural bias toward conventional combat is long standing and well entrenched and that overcoming it will entail fundamental change in how U.S. military forces are organized, equipped, manned, and trained. For examples, personnel policies that constantly rotate individuals from one assignment to another and promotion policies prejudiced against development of specialized knowledge and language skills are antithetical to the requirements of successful counterinsurgency.

Bureaucratic opposition may be sufficiently powerful to block requisite change absent forceful outside intervention by the White House or Congress, and even outside intervention is no guarantee of change. In the early 1960s the army essentially blew off President John F. Kennedy's demand that it take counterinsurgency seriously.[28] Two decades later, however, Congress successfully jammed jointness down the screaming throats of the "Joint" Chiefs of Staff and the secretary of defense.[29] What was once anathema to the Pentagon became mantra. Indeed, jointness can claim much credit for America's conventional military effectiveness.

Perhaps it is time for Congress to intervene again in the form of legislation that would impose upon the interagency process the measure of jointness that Goldwater-Nichols imposed upon the armed services.

The strong, especially democracies, lose to the weak when the latter brings to the test of war a stronger will and superior strategy reinforced by external assistance. In the case of the United States in Vietnam, a weaker will and inferior strategy was reinforced by an apolitical conception of war itself and a specific professional-military aversion to counterinsurgency. In the case of Iraq, the jury remains out on the issues of will and strategy, but the unexpected political and military difficulties the United States has encountered there seem to have arisen in part because of a persistent view of war as a substitute for policy and an abiding antipathy to preparing for war with irregular adversaries.

6

Conclusion

Examination of Goliath defeats reveals the limits of material preponderance and the importance of political will, strategy, and, in the case of an insurgent enemy, isolation from external assistance. Conventional military strength is indispensable in big wars, but it has limited utility in small wars, which involve combat against irregular adversaries. Conversely, the weaker side risks swift defeat if it attempts to fight the stronger side on conventional military terms; to survive and prevail, the weak are driven to strategies of indirection and protraction.

Andrew Mack, Ivan Arreguin-Toft, and Gil Merom have made critical contributions to the literature on weak-actor victories over the strong, though they have either downplayed the significance of external assistance or ignored it altogether. An extensive assessment of their work, combined with my own previously published research on the Vietnam and Iraq wars and subsequent research on other asymmetric wars, leads me to the following conclusions:

1. The stronger side usually wins; the best strategy, therefore, is to be strong.

Clausewitz was right. It is always good to be strong and never good to be weak. The United States has an unusual record of military success in large part because it has been—or has been *on*—the stronger side in virtually all of its major wars. Even in the case of the American War of Independence, it is arguable that Great Britain lost its status as the stronger side, at least in the North American theater of operations, once the French intervened in full financial, military, and naval force. The British were certainly the weaker side at Yorktown, by which time ally-less Britain was at war with Spain and the Netherlands as well as the French and the Americans. The only major war Americans lost was the Confederacy's futile attempt to achieve decisive conventional military victory over a materially preponderant Union.

Overwhelming force is inherently desirable, though it is easier to state as an objective than it is to achieve on the battlefield. The United States and its coalition partners enjoyed overwhelming force in the Gulf War of 1991; no amount of will, strategic legerdemain, or foreign help could have sustained an Iraqi defense of Kuwait against the coalition juggernaut assembled by President George H. W. Bush. Twelve years later, however, a much smaller, "transformed" U.S. force, supported by a politically less impressive coalition than that of 1991, swept aside minimal Iraqi conventional military resistance but failed to secure the country against the effects of the Iraqi state's abrupt disintegration, especially catastrophic looting and an eruption of insurgent violence. Numbers count. The cold war Soviet threat in Central Europe, which was the primary focus of NATO force planning and justification of its nuclear first-use policy, was the sheer enormity of Soviet forces deployed opposite NATO Center and readily reinforceable from the Soviet Union's western military districts.

2. Weaker-side victories are exceptional and almost always rest on some combination of stronger political will, superior strategy, and foreign help.

Single-factor explanations of asymmetric war outcomes are rarely satisfactory. There are simply too many variables at play in war—the most complex of all human enterprises. The American rebels and the Vietnamese Communists prevailed because both had a stronger will *and* a better strategy *and* massive foreign help. Will, absent capacity to act effectively, counts for little; Osama bin Laden cannot will his way to victory using a strategy hitched to political objectives that provoke resistance beyond al Qaeda's ability to overcome.

With respect to successful insurgencies, their common reliance on irregular warfare, at least until they move from being the weaker side to becoming the stronger, reflects recognition of their own conventional military weakness. Irregular warfare is a strategy of necessity, and against a strong and determined enemy it implies—indeed, mandates—superior political will because without a greater readiness to sacrifice time and blood an insurgency has little reason to hope for victory against its materially stronger foe. Only against exceptionally feckless and inept governments can insurgents expect relatively easy wins, but in such cases it is the regime that is the weaker side. If state power is left lying in the street, the first politically and organizationally prepared claimant is likely to pick it up, as did the Bolsheviks in Leningrad in 1917, the Black Shirts in Rome in 1922, and the Fidelistas in Havana in 1959.

3. External assistance is a common enabler of victorious insurgent wars, though certainly no guarantee of success.

The literature seeking to explain weak-actor success against the strong pays insufficient attention to the factor of foreign help. Mack ignores it altogether, whereas Arreguin-Toft preposterously dismisses it as a significant factor in the Vietnam War's outcome on the grounds that the war was politically over by 1965—before massive U.S. intervention and Chinese and Soviet counterintervention. The U.S. cause in South Vietnam might have been politically doomed from the start, but the political contest could not be settled—and was not going to be settled—without a military fight, and that was a fight in which North Vietnam could not even participate, much less prevail, without foreign help and a lot of it. The Vietnam War was, after all, an *armed* conflict. To discount or ignore the importance of external assistance may serve arguments for other explanations of how the weak win, but it can and does distort the historical record.

External assistance can blur the very distinction between the strong and weak, especially if analysis is confined to the material balance in the actual theater of military operations. The importance of foreign help is evident in the scarcity of unassisted insurgent victories; the strong-willed Boer and Confederate insurgents were effectively isolated from foreign help, as were, finally, the FLN fighters in Algeria. All were defeated militarily, as were the isolated Chinese insurgents in Malaya and the Hukbalahaps in the Philippines—two prominent examples of suc-cessful counterinsurgent warfare conducted by modern democracies.

Foreign help is no substitute for sound strategy, however. Soviet- and Cuban-backed insurgencies in Africa and Central America fared poorly because they could never gain sufficient political traction among indigenous populations. The material boost afforded to an insurgency by foreign help also can be offset by corresponding external assistance to the enemy government. During the cold war, both Soviet and U.S. client states in the developing world profited from such help. Until the 1980s, the dominant paradigm was U.S. support of non-Communist governments against Soviet-backed insurgencies; in the cold war's last decade, the paradigm shifted to U.S. support of anti-Communist insurgencies against Soviet-backed regimes.

4. Modern democracies have limited political tolerance for protracted overseas wars against irregular enemies.

This is a common judgment, and it is supported by most of the available evidence. European colonial empires disintegrated in the decades following the end of World War II largely because metropolitan governments lacked the political stamina to sustain them; colonial unrest, and in some cases outright rebellion, raised the price of empire beyond the metropole's willingness to pay. The post–World War II American record of involvement in protracted irregular warfare has not been impressive: a lost war in Vietnam, humiliation in Lebanon and Somalia, and a seemingly endless counterinsurgent war in Iraq. In Vietnam, Lebanon, and Somalia, the United States faced enemies in possession of superior will and strategy—enemies who understood that democracy's center of gravity is public opinion and that democratic opinion can be favorably influenced for withdrawal by bloody and stalemated hostilities.

Democratic-regime vulnerability to political exhaustion via prolonged irregular warfare is supported by much recent research, including that of Thomas X. Hammes, Gil Merom, and Robert A. Pape. Pape's analysis of suicide bombing as a rational strategic choice reveals that practitioners of this particular brand of irregular warfare believe that democracies are politically much more vulnerable than dictatorships to these tactics. That said, democracies appear to be much less vulnerable to what some would call self-defeat when confronted with such attacks on their own territory; homeland security is the core vital security interest of any state and accordingly calls forth far grater willingness to sacrifice than in the case of distant wars waged for limited objectives. American resolve to do whatever is necessary to hunt down Osama bin Laden and to destroy al Qaeda and its affiliated terrorist organizations shows no sign of waning five years after the 9/11 attacks. American will to defeat Islamist terrorism directed against the United States and its interests overseas must not be confused with declining public support for the war in Iraq; there was no evidence of Iraqi complicity in the 9/11 attacks and no convincing evidence of a collaborative relationship of any kind between the overthrown Baathist regime and al Qaeda.

As I argued in *Bounding the Global War on Terrorism*, a monograph published in December 2003 by the U.S. Army's Strategic Studies Institute, the conflation of the two quite different threats posed by al Qaeda and Saddam Hussein's Iraq was a strategic error of the first order because it propelled the United States into an unnecessary war against Iraq that has provided the al Qaeda network a major strategic opportunity in the Middle East. Though al Qaeda was effectively repressed in Baathist Iraq, it is operating in post-Baathist Iraq in the form of affiliated and inspired terrorist organizations, whose spectacular attacks, hostage-takings, and beheadings have contributed to declining American public support for the Iraq War. If al-Zarqawi's terrorism and other insurgent violence in Iraq succeed in driving the United States out of Iraq without accomplishing its declared objectives there, the effect will be to validate prewar al Qaeda claims, accompanied by repeated references to Vietnam, Lebanon, and Somalia, that the American democratic superpower has feet of clay. By unintentionally converting Iraq into "the central front of the war on terrorism," the United States has exposed itself to the risk of another defeat at the hands of a weak actor.

A modern democracy's vulnerability to defeat in protracted hostilities against irregular adversaries is evident not only in the U.S. performance in Vietnam, Lebanon, Somalia, and Iraq. Israel, the only genuine democracy in the Middle East, was arguably driven out of southern Lebanon and Gaza because the strategic value of an entrenched Israeli presence in those two places proved unworthy of the actual and anticipated blood and treasure costs of sustaining it. These two evacuations, coupled with Prime Minister Ariel Sharon's stunning abandonment—shortly before his crippling stroke—of the Likud Party and the probability of eventual Israeli acceptance of an independent Palestinian state on the West Bank, testify to another democracy's limited tolerance for protracted war against a determined irregular foe.

5. For the United States, the impact of anticipated and incurred casualties on political will is a function primarily of military action's perceived costs, benefits, and chances of success.

The belief that Americans are casualty intolerant irrespective of stakes and circumstances held sway among U.S. civilian and military elites during the 1980s and 1990s. It also emboldened Saddam Hussein to believe that he could get away with his conquest of Kuwait and Osama bin Laden to think he could escape effective retaliation for the 9/11 attacks. Extensive research before and after 9/11, however, reveals much more conditional public attitudes toward casualties as well as the importance of presidential leadership in shaping public opinion in given instances of threatened or actual use of force. If the *perceived* stakes at hand and chances of success are high, then support for military action is also likely to be high; conversely, if stakes and feasibility are seen as low, public support is likely to be weak or even nonexistent. Pearl Harbor and 9/11 instantly mobilized public opinion for all-out war, even though the road to victory was understood to be long and arduous. In contrast, public tolerance for casualties in Lebanon, Somalia, and the Balkans was low because most Americans did not regard the stakes involved as worth much bloodshed; in each case, presidential explanations for launching and sustaining U.S. military intervention were confusing or unpersuasive.

Public support for the Vietnam and Iraq wars was initially high because presidents Lyndon Johnson and George W. Bush, respectively, persuaded most Americans that vital interests were threatened. In the case of Iraq, the Bush administration also apparently persuaded itself as well as most Americans that military success would be quick, cheap, and decisive. Support for war in both cases declined over time as casualties mounted against a backdrop of seemingly stalemated military operations. Support for the Iraq War declined more rapidly because U.S. occupation of Iraq sparked an unexpected insurgent reaction and exposed the hollowness of prewar Iraqi threats postulated by the Bush administration as justifications for war.

Swift military success tends to overcome doubts about the wisdom and costs of intervention. The U.S. invasion of Grenada in 1983 for purposes not made altogether clear was nonetheless popular because it was over quickly and because it boosted America's military self-respect in the wake of the deadly terrorist attack on the U.S. Marine Corps headquarters in Beirut, Lebanon. The 1998 war against Serbia over Serbian ethnic cleansing in Kosovo commanded tepid public support because it lasted much longer than expected and because President Bill Clinton failed to articulate a convincing case for making war over endangered U.S. interests in the former Yugoslavia. Indeed, presidential pronouncements are critical in mobilizing and sustaining support for military action, especially in the face of mounting casualties. It is not objective interests and chances of success that count, but rather public perceptions of them, and it is the political leadership that "educates" those perceptions. Casualties cannot be divorced from perceptions of costs, benefits, and prospects for success.

6. America's political system and Jominian (scientific-technological) approach to war greatly impede U.S. success in counterinsurgent warfare; accordingly, the United States should avoid direct military involvement in foreign internal wars.

Such wars are primarily political struggles and only secondarily military contests, and the very presence of foreign combat forces can provoke insurgent attacks. Avoidance of such wars means abandonment of regime-change wars that saddle the United States with responsibility for establishing political stability and state-building. Neither the Pentagon nor the U.S. government as a whole is properly organized or sufficiently motivated to meet the challenges of political reconstruction in foreign lands, especially under conditions of persistent insurgent violence. Notwithstanding the exceptional cases of post–World War II Germany and Japan, the United States has demonstrated—in Vietnam, Somalia, Haiti, Bosnia, Kosovo, and Afghanistan—that it lacks the patience and skills required to effect the enduring rehabilitation of failed states. U.S. success in Germany and Japan was the product of unique military, political, and strategic conditions that have not since been repeated and are most unlikely to reappear in the future.

America's strategic culture and way of war are hostile to politically messy wars and to military operations other than war. Counterinsurgency and imperial policing operations demand forbearance, personnel continuity, foreign language skills, cross-cultural understanding, minimal employment of force, and robust interagency involvement and cooperation. None of these are virtues of American statecraft and war-making. Americans view war as a suspension of politics; they want to believe that the politics of war will somehow sort themselves out once military victory is achieved. Thus the Department of Defense was handed complete responsibility for regime change in Iraq; predictably, it immersed itself in planning to accomplish the first (and easiest) half of regime change—toppling the Baathist regime by force—at the expense of thinking about, much less seriously planning for, the far more difficult half of securing the country and establishing the stability requisite for Iraq's successful political reconstruction.

The forty-year record that starts in Vietnam, runs through Lebanon, Somalia, Bosnia, and Kosovo, and is now playing out in Iraq suggests that modern American democracy is not particularly good—indeed, is severely disadvantaged—

at waging small wars. If this is the case, then the logical policy choice is to refuse intervention in such wars. Why should the United States continue to enter wars it is no good at winning? A policy of abstention from small wars of choice would mandate a foreign policy that placed the protection of concrete strategic interests ahead of crusades to promote the overseas expansion of abstract American political values. A foreign policy based on realism would have spared the United States the agonies of Vietnam, Lebanon, and Somalia, where the United States lacked strategic interests justifying intervention; realism also would have prevented the expansion of a necessary war against al Qaeda into an unnecessary war in Iraq.

7. The United States has become a victim of its conventional military success.

America's unchallenged mastery of conventional warfare has afforded it a capacity to deter conventional military attack—no mean feat given the poor record of conventional deterrence during the twentieth century. Yet that same mastery has driven America's conventionally weak enemies into developing and refining compensatory modes of violence ranging from transnational terrorism to acquisition of weapons of mass destruction and their effective means of delivery. This is not the first instance in which effective conventional deterrence has provoked inevitable sub- and supra-conventional responses: Israel's repeated demonstrations—in 1948, 1956, 1967, and 1973—of irresistible conventional military prowess left its Arab enemies no choice but to fall back on the options of terrorism and nuclear weapons. Indeed, it is the specter of terrorism armed with nuclear weapons—of an undeterrable enemy in possession of destructive power heretofore monopolized by states—that the George W. Bush administration has rightly defined as the gravest threat to U.S. security.

Precisely because terrorism and nuclear weapons represent asymmetric responses to conventional military supremacy, that supremacy has limited utility against unconventional threats. Conventional forces, especially those fielded by modern democracies, do not have impressive records in defeating determined insurgent challenges; and a policy of preventive conventional war against enemy states seeking to acquire nuclear weapons is fraught with unacceptable dangers because it presumes exceptionally good intelligence, rests on the false premise that such states are undeterrable, promotes America's strategic isolation, and invites precisely the kind of unintended outcomes the United States has encountered in Iraq.

Notes

Introduction

1. Carl von Clausewitz, *On War*, ed. and trans. Michael Howard and Peter Paret (Princeton, NJ: Princeton University Press, 1976), 194, 204.
2. C. E. Callwell, *Small Wars: Their Principles and Practice*, 3rd ed. (Lincoln: University of Nebraska Press, 1996), 21.
3. *Small Wars Manual* (Washington, DC: U.S. Marine Corps, 1990), 1–2.
4. See "Letter from al-Zawahiri to al-Zarqawi," July 9, 2005, released October 11, 2005, by the Office of the Director of National Intelligence, http://www.dni.gov/release_letter_101105.html.
5. Jeffrey Record and W. Andrew Terrill, *Iraq and Vietnam: Differences, Similarities, and Insights* (Carlisle, PA: Strategic Studies Institute, U.S. Army War College, May 2004).

Chapter 1: Explaining Goliath Defeats: Will, Strategy, and Type of Government

1. Clausewitz, *On War*, 75.
2. Andrew Mack, "Why Big Nations Lose Small Wars: The Politics of Asymmetric Conflict," *World Politics* 27, no. 2 (1975), 175.
3. Ibid., 177 (emphasis in original).
4. Ibid., 179.
5. Ibid., 180.
6. Ibid., 181–182.
7. Piers Mackesy, *The War for America, 1775–1783* (Lincoln: University of Nebraska Press, 1993), 515.

8. The chief argument for intervention in Vietnam was that failure to intervene would undermine the credibility of U.S. defense commitments elsewhere. There is no evidence, however, that any major U.S. ally in Europe or Asia saw Vietnam as a test of U.S. credibility. On the contrary, many regarded U.S. intervention in Southeast Asia as a mistake that undermined U.S. capacity to defend its commitments worldwide.

9. The calculation is the average for years 1965–74 and based on figures appearing in Jeffrey Record, *Revising U.S. Military Strategy: Tailoring Means to Ends* (Washington, DC: Pergamon-Brassey's, 1984), 100.

10. Quoted in Doris Kearns, *Lyndon Johnson and the American Dream* (New York: Harper and Row, 1976), 251–52.

11. Quoted in George McT. Kahin, *Intervention: How America Became Involved in Vietnam* (New York: Alfred A. Knopf, 1986), 249.

12. Quoted in Tom Wells, *The War Within: America's Battle Over Vietnam* (New York: Henry Holt, 1994), 99.

13. Dean Rusk, *As I Saw It*, with Richard Rusk and Daniel S. Papp (New York: W. W. Norton, 1990), 472.

14. William C. Westmoreland, interview with Tom Wells, in Wells, *The War Within*, 99.

15. Spencer C. Tucker, ed., *Encyclopedia of the Vietnam War: A Political, Social, and Military History* (New York: Oxford University Press, 1998), 64.

16. Jeffrey Record, *The Wrong War: Why We Lost in Vietnam* (Annapolis, MD: Naval Institute Press, 1998), 36–37; and John E. Mueller, "The Search for the 'Breaking Point' in Vietnam: The Statistics of a Deadly Quarrel," *International Studies Quarterly* 24, no. 4 (December 1980): 465–96. The number of Vietnamese Communist civilian dead is not known, though their inclusion with military dead would almost certainly yield a total loss proportional to population less than that sustained by the Soviet Union in World War II.

17. Robert A. Doughty, *Pyrrhic Victory: French Strategy and Operations in the Great War* (Cambridge, MA: Belknap Press, 2005), 508–11.

18. Record, *The Wrong War*, 37.

19. Richard K. Betts, "Interests, Burdens, and Persistence: Asymmetries Between Washington and Hanoi," *International Studies Quarterly* 24, no. 4 (December 1980): 523.

20. Mack, "Why Big Nations Lose Small Wars," 184.

21. Ibid., 185.

22. Ibid., 200.

23. Steven Peter Rosen, "War Power and the Willingness to Suffer," in Bruce M. Russett, ed., *Peace, War, and Numbers* (Beverly Hills, CA: Sage Publications, 1972), 167.

24. Ibid., 107–8.

25. Ibid., 183.

26. Colin S. Gray, *Another Bloody Century: Future Warfare* (London: Weidenfeld and Nicholson, 2005), 224.

27. See Richard C. Eichenberg, "Victory Has Many Friends: U.S. Public Opinion and the Use of Military Force, 1981–2005," *International Security* 30, no. 1 (Summer 2005): 140–77.

28. Ivan Arreguin-Toft, *How the Weak Win Wars: A Theory of Asymmetric Conflict* (New York: Cambridge University Press, 2005).

29. Ibid., 22.

30. Ivan Arreguin-Toft, "How the Weak Win Wars: A Theory of Asymmetric Conflict," *International Security* 26, no. 1 (Summer 2001): 95.

31. Ibid., 100, 101.

32. Ibid., 101–2, 103.

33. Ibid., 103.

34. Ibid., 105.

35. Ibid., 105–6.

36. Ibid., 107.

37. Arreguin-Toft, *How the Weak Win*, 72–108.

38. Ibid., 228–32.

39. Ibid., 193–94.

40. Ibid., 45–46.

41. Gil Merom, *How Democracies Lose Small Wars: State, Society, and the Failures of France in Algeria, Israel in Lebanon, and the United States in Vietnam* (New York: Cambridge University Press, 2003), 15.

42. Ibid., 26.

43. Ibid., 24.

44. Ibid.

45. Ibid., 230–31.

46. Eichenberg, "Victory Has Many Friends," 174.

47. Christopher Gelpi, Peter D. Feaver, and Jason Reifler, "Success Matters: Casualty Sensitivity and the War in Iraq," *International Security* 30, no. 3 (Winter 2005–6): 8.

48. Merom, *How Democracies Lose Small Wars*, 246–47.

49. Ibid., 22.

50. Ibid., 27.

51. Ibid., 44–45.

52. Quoted in ibid., 22.

53. See Norman Cigar, "Iraq's Strategic Mindset and the Gulf War: Blueprint for

Defeat," *Journal of Strategic Studies* 15, no. 1 (March 1992): 2–14; and Jeffrey Record, "Defeating Desert Storm (and Why Saddam Didn't)," *Comparative Strategy* 12, no.2 (April–June 1993): 125–40.

54. Osama bin Laden, "Declaration of War Against the Americans Occupying the Land of the Two Holy Places," first published in *Al Quds Al Araby*, a London newspaper in August 1996 and reprinted in Online News Hour with Jim Lehrer, http://www.pbs.org/newshour/terrorism/international/fatwa_1996.html.

55. Statements by Osama bin Laden and his lieutenants released by al Jazeera satellite television, October 10, 2001, reprinted in http://www.ict.org.il/spotlight/det.cfm?id=688.

56. See Dan Reiter and Allan C. Stam, *Democracies at War* (Princeton, NJ: Princeton University Press, 2002).

Chapter 2: The Role of External Assistance

1. Arreguin-Toft, *How the Weak Win*, 162, 163.

2. Niccolo Machiavelli, *The Prince,* trans. W. K. Marriott (New York: Alfred A. Knopf, 1992), 100.

3. Larry H. Addington, *The Patterns of War Since the 18th Century* (Bloomington: Indiana University Press, 1984), 16.

4. For perhaps the best analysis of the supply challenges the British faced during the Revolutionary War, see R. Arthur Bowler, *Logistics and the Failure of the British Army in America, 1775–1783* (Princeton, NJ: Princeton University Press, 1975). Also see Norman Baker, *Government and Contractors: The British Treasury and War Supplies, 1775–1783* (London: University of London, 1971); David Syrett, *Shipping and the American War, 1775–1783* (London: University of London, 1970); and Anthony James Joes, *America and Guerrilla Warfare* (Lexington: University Press of Kentucky, 2000), 14–16.

5. Theodore Ropp, *War in the Modern World* (New York: Collier Books, 1962), 92–93.

6. Quoted in Mackesy, *The War for America*, 512.

7. Addington, *The Patterns of War*, 15.

8. Neil Longley York, *Turning the World Upside Down: The War of Independence and the Problem of Empire* (Westport, CT: Praeger, 2003), 118.

9. Donald M. Snow and Dennis M. Drew, *From Lexington to Desert Storm and Beyond: War and Politics in the American Experience*, 2nd ed. (Armonk, NY: M. E. Sharpe, 2000), 30; Addington, *The Patterns of War*, 15.

10. Ropp, *War in the Modern World*, 89.

11. John D. Waghelstein, "Regulars, Irregulars and Militia: The American Revolution," *Small Wars and Insurgencies* 6, no. 2 (Autumn 1995): 136.

12. Piers Mackesy, "What the British Army Learned," in Ronald Hoffman and Peter J. Albert, eds., *Arms and Independence: The Military Character of the American Revolution* (Charlottesville: University Press of Virginia, 1984), 195.

13. See John Shy, "The American Revolution: The Military Conflict Considered as a Revolutionary War," in Stephen G. Kurtz and James H. Hutson, eds., *Essays on the American Revolution* (Chapel Hill: University of North Carolina Press, 1973), 121–56.

14. Mackesy, *The War for America*, 198.

15. See Bowler, *Logistics and the Failure of the British Army*, 167–211.

16. T. Harry Williams, *The History of American Wars From Colonial Times to World War I* (New York: Alfred A. Knopf, 1981), 63.

17. Snow and Drew, *From Lexington to Desert Storm*, 39.

18. Allan R. Millett and Peter Maslowski, *For the Common Defense: A Military History of the United States of America*, rev. ed. (New York: Free Press, 1994), 70.

19. Addington, *The Patterns of War*, 15.

20. Ibid.

21. Joes, *America and Guerrilla Warfare*, 22–23.

22. See Mackesy, *The War for America*, 181–89, 219–22.

23. Quoted in Stanley Weintraub, *Iron Tears: America's Battle for Freedom, Britain's Quagmire* (New York: Free Press, 2005), 126.

24. Quoted in ibid., 283.

25. Ibid., 45

26. Joes, *America and Guerrilla Warfare*, 47.

27. Clausewitz, *On War*, 479–83.

28. See Robert Hughes, *Goya* (New York: Alfred A. Knopf, 2003), 261–319.

29. For two excellent recent works on the war, both by Charles J. Esdaile, see *The Peninsular War: A New History* (New York: Palgrave MacMillan, 2003), and *Fighting Napoleon: Guerrillas, Bandits and Adventurers in Spain, 1808–14* (New Haven, CT: Yale University Press, 2004).

30. Clausewitz, *On War*, 480.

31. Ibid.

32. Esdaile, *The Peninsular War*, 108.

33. David Gates, *The Spanish Ulcer: A History of the Peninsular War* (New York: W. W. Norton, 1986), 30.

34. John R. Elting, *Swords Around a Throne: Napoleon's Grand Armee* (New York: Free Press, 1988), 509.

35. Anthony James Joes, *Resisting Rebellion: The History and Politics of Counterinsurgency* (Lexington: University Press of Kentucky, 2004), 64.

36. Elting, *Swords Around a Throne*, 512, 515.

37. Figures for French and Anglo-Portuguese troop strengths are calculations based on orders of battle appearing in Gates, *The Spanish Ulcer*, 481–530.

38. Joes, *Resisting Rebellion*, 66.

39. David G. Chandler, *The Campaigns of Napoleon* (New York: Macmillan, 1966), 611.

40. Gates, *The Spanish Ulcer*, 468.

41. Chandler, *The Campaigns of Napoleon*, 611, 659; Alan Schom, *Napoleon Bonaparte* (New York: HarperCollins, 1997), 469.

42. Letter of transmittal from Secretary of State Dean Acheson to President Harry Truman, July 30, 1949, reprinted in *The China White Paper*, August 1949 (Stanford, CA: Stanford University Press, 1967), xiv. Originally issued as *United States Relations with China with Special Reference to the Period 1944–1949*, Department of State Publication 3573, Far Eastern Series 30.

43. Robert B. Asprey, *War in the Shadows: The Guerrilla in History* (New York: William Morrow, 1994), 440–441,

44. For a detailed breakdown of U.S. financial, economic, and military assistance to China during the period 1945–49, see *The China White Paper*, 969–1054.

45. Walter Laqueur, *Guerrilla Warfare: A Historical and Critical Study* (New Brunswick, NJ: Transaction Publishers, 1998), 259.

46. Bard E. O'Neill, *Insurgency and Terrorism: Inside Modern Revolutionary Warfare* (Washington, DC: Brassey's, 1990), 35.

47. Ian F. W. Beckett, *Modern Insurgencies and Counter-Insurgencies: Guerrillas and Their Opponents Since 1750* (London: Routledge, 2001), 77.

48. *The China White Paper*, 311–23.

49. Ibid., 116–18. The treaty gave Russia commercial port rights and facilities in Dairen, naval use of Port Arthur, and co-ownership and operation of the Chinese Eastern and South Manchurian railways for thirty years. See also Tang Tsou, *America's Failure in China: 1941–50* (Chicago: University of Chicago Press, 1963), 270–87.

50. See Chen Jian, *Mao's China and the Cold War* (Chapel Hill: University of North Carolina Press, 2001), 24–29; and Sergei N. Goncharov, John W. Lewis, and Xue Litai, *Uncertain Partners: Stalin, Mao, and the Korean War* (Stanford, CA: Stanford University Press, 1993), 6–14.

51. For a detailed examination of the factors underlying the Truman administration's refusal to contemplate direct U.S. military intervention in China, see Tsou, *America's Failure in China*, 356–75.

52. Michael M. Sheng, *Battling Western Imperialism: Mao, Stalin, and the United States* (Princeton, NJ: Princeton University Press, 1997), 110–11.

53. Ibid., 110; and Gonchorov, Lewis, and Litai, *Uncertain Partners*, 14.

54. Steven I. Levine, *Anvil of Victory: The Communist Revolution in Manchuria, 1945–1948* (New York: Columbia University Press, 1987), 240.

55. Ibid., 240.

56. Quoted in *The China White Paper*, 382.

57. Qiang Zhai, *China and the Vietnam Wars, 1950–1975* (Chapel Hill: University of North Carolina Press, 2000), 47–49.

58. Ibid., 20.

59. See Jian, *Mao's China and the Cold War*, 118–27; and Melvin Gurtov, *The First Vietnam Crisis: Chinese Communist Strategy and United States Involvement, 1953–1954* (New York: Columbia University Press, 1967), 6–19.

60. Martin Windrow, *The Last Valley: Dien Bien Phu and the French Defeat in Vietnam* (London: Cassell, 2005), 152, 154.

61. Arthur J. Dommen, *The Indochinese Experience of the French and the Americans: Nationalism and Communism in Cambodia, Laos, and Vietnam* (Bloomington: Indiana University Press, 2001), 200.

62. Bernard B. Fall, *Hell in a Very Small Place: The Siege of Dien Bien Phu* (New York: Harper and Row, 1967), 451–52.

63. Windrow, *The Last Valley*, 151; and Bernard B. Fall, *Street Without Joy* (Mechanicsburg, PA: Stackpole Books, 1961), 32, 322.

64. Fall, *Hell in a Very Small Place*, 454–55; and Zhai, *China and the Vietnam Wars*, 47–49.

65. Snow and Drew, *From Lexington to Desert Storm*, 32.

66. At the conclusion of the First Indochina War in 1954 Communist cadres in southern Vietnam buried or otherwise hid stocks of weapons and ammunition for future use.

67. See John Prados, *The Blood Road: The Ho Chi Minh Trail and the Vietnam War* (New York: John Wiley and Sons, 1999), 109–10; Michael Lee Lanning and Dan Cragg, *Inside the VC and NVA: The Real Story of North Vietnam's Armed Forces* (New York: Ivy Books, 1992), 310; and "France in Vietnam, 1954, and the U.S. in Vietnam, 1965—A Useful Analogy?" Memorandum from McGeorge Bundy to President Lyndon Johnson, June 30, 1965, Document No. 11, John F. Kennedy School of Government Case Study on Americanizing the Vietnam War (Cambridge, MA, 1983).

68. Mark Clodfelter, *The Limits of Air Power: The American Bombing of North Vietnam* (New York: Free Press, 1989), 25, 134–35.

69. For representative declarations of optimism by administration officials and military leaders in late 1967, see Peter Braestrup, *Big Story: How the American Press and Television Reported and Interpreted the Crisis of Tet 1968 in Vietnam and Washington* (Novato, CA: Presidio Press, 1977), 48–55.

70. See Lewis Sorley, *A Better War: The Unexamined Victories and Final Tragedy of America's Last Years in Vietnam* (New York: Harcourt Brace, 1999); and William Colby, *Lost Victory: A Firsthand Account of America's Sixteen-Year Involvement in Vietnam* (Chicago: Contemporary Books, 1989).

71. Sorley, *A Better War.*

72. Earl H. Tilford Jr., *What the Air Force Did in Vietnam and Why* (Maxwell AFB, AL: Air University Press, June 1991), xvii.

73. See Xiaoming Zhang, "Communist Powers Divided: China, the Soviet Union, and the Vietnam War," in Lloyd C. Gardiner and Ted Gittinger, eds., *International Perspectives on Vietnam* (College Station: Texas A&M Press, 2000), 77–97.

74. Ibid., 82, 83.

75. Zhai, *China and the Vietnam Wars*, 132.

76. Zhang, "Communist Powers Divided," 87

77. Zhai, *China and the Vietnam Wars*, 134–35. Also see Chen Jian, "China's Involvement in the Vietnam War, 1964–1969," *China Quarterly* 42 (1995), 356–87.

78. Based on figures appearing in Zhai, *China and the Vietnam Wars*, 136. Numbers rounded off to nearest ten.

79. Zhang, "Communist Powers Divided," 90.

80. See John W. Garver, "The Chinese Threat in the Vietnam War," *Parameters* 22, no. 1 (Spring 1992): 73–85.

81. Guenter Lewy, *America in Vietnam* (New York: Oxford University Press, 1978), 393.

82. See Ilya V. Gaiduk, *The Soviet Union and the Vietnam War* (Chicago: Ivan R. Dee, 1996), 57–72.

83. Oleg Sarin and Lev Dvoretsky, *Alien Wars: The Soviet Union's Agressions Against the World, 1919–1989* (Novato, CA: Presidio Press, 1996), reprinted in Zhang, "Communist Powers Divided," 92.

84. See Lanning and Cragg, *Inside the VC and NVA*, 140; and Prados, *Blood Road*, 374.

85. Lanning and Cragg, *Inside the VC and NVA*, 138.

86. See Stephen T. Hosmer, Konrad Kellen, and Brian M. Jenkins, *The Fall of South Vietnam: Statements by Vietnamese Military and Civilian Leaders* (Santa Monica, CA: Rand Corporation, December 1978); and Col. William E. Le Gro, *Vietnam From Cease-Fire to Capitulation* (Washington, DC: U.S. Army Center of Military History, 1985).

87. William J. Duiker, "Foreword," in *Victory in Vietnam: The Official History of the People's Army of Vietnam, 1954—1975*, trans. Merle L. Pribbenow (Lawrence: University Press of Kansas, 2002), xvi.

88. Lester W. Grau and Michael A. Gress, ed. and trans., *The Soviet-Afghan War, How a Superpower Fought and Lost: The Russian General Staff* (Lawrence: University Press of Kansas, 2002), 304–5.

89. Robert S. Litwak, "The Soviet Union in Afghanistan," in Ariel E. Levite, Bruce W. Jentleson, and Larry Berman, eds, *Foreign Military Intervention: The Dynamics of Protracted Conflict* (New York: Columbia University Press, 1992), 77.

90. Grau and Gress, *The Soviet-Afghan War*, 310.

91. Ibid., xix.

92. Litwak, "The Soviet Union in Afghanistan," 80.

93. Grau and Gress, *The Soviet-Afghan War*, 24; and Litwak, "The Soviet Union in Afghanistan," 81.

94. Grau and Gress, *The Soviet-Afghan War*, 20–22; and Litwak, "The Soviet Union in Afghanistan," 84.

95. Arreguin-Toft, *How the Weak Win*, 181. See also Hassan M. Kakar, *Afghanistan: The Soviet Invasion and the Afghan Response, 1979–1982* (Berkeley: University of California Press, 1995), 129.

96. Arreguin-Toft, *How the Weak Win*, 193, 194.

97. Grau and Gress, *The Soviet-Afghan War*, 23, 213.

98. Peter W. Rodman, *More Precious Than Peace: The Cold War and the Struggle for the Third World* (New York: Charles Scribner's Sons, 1994), 339.

99. For a concise account of the history of the Stinger decision, see James M. Scott, *Deciding to Intervene: The Reagan Doctrine and American Foreign Policy* (Durham, NC: Duke University Press, 1996), 46–62.

100. Thomas Pakenham, *The Boer War* (New York: Random House, 1980), 607.

101. Merom, *How Democracies Lose Small Wars*, 87; Alf Andrew Heggoy, *Insurgency and Counterinsurgency in Algeria* (Bloomington: Indiana University Press, 1972), 179; and John Ambler, *The French Army in Politics, 1945–1962* (Columbus: Ohio State University Press, 1966), 156.

102. Laqueur, *Guerrilla Warfare*, 295; and Merom, *How Democracies Lose Small Wars*, 100–101.

103. Alistair Horne, *A Savage War of Peace: Algeria 1954–1962* (New York: Viking Press, 1977), 183–207.

104. Ibid., 263–65.

105. Ibid., 266.

106. Merom, *How Democracies Lose Small Wars*, 85–86; and John Talbott, *The War Without a Name: France in Algeria, 1954–1962* (New York: Alfred A. Knopf, 1980), 191–96.

107. Colin S. Gray, *Irregular Enemies and the Essence of Strategy: Can the American Way of War Adapt?* (Carlisle, PA: Strategic Studies Institute, U.S. Army War College, March 2006), 20–21.

108. Robert Thompson, *Defeating Communist Insurgency: The Lessons of Malaya and Vietnam* (New York: Frederick A. Praeger, 1966), 19. For other assessments of the Malayan Emergency, see Richard L. Clutterbuck, *The Long, Long War: The Emergency in Malaya 1948–1960* (London: Cassell, 1966); Brian Drohan, "British Political-Military Strategy in the Malayan Emergency," *Armor* 65, no. 1 (January–February 2006): 34–38; Robert Jackson, *The Malayan Emergency: The Commonwealth's Wars 1948–1966* (London: Routledge, 1991); Robert W. Komer, *The Malayan Emergency in Retrospect: Organization of Successful Counterinsurgency Effort* (Santa Monica, CA: Rand Corporation, 1972); and Donald MacKay, *The Malayan Emergency 1948–1960: The Domino That Stood* (Washington, DC: Brassey's, 1997).

109. John A. Nagl, *Learning to Eat Soup With a Knife: Counterinsurgency Lessons From Malaya and Vietnam* (Chicago: University of Chicago Press, 2002).

110. Ibid., 103; and Richard Stubbs, *Hearts and Minds in Guerrilla Warfare: The Malayan Emergency 1948–1960* (New York: Oxford University Press, 1989), 256.

111. O'Neill, *Insurgency and Terrorism*, 111.

112. Millett and Maslowski, *For the Common Defense*, 163–68.

113. Ibid., 205.

114. Arreguin-Toft, *How the Weak Win Wars*, 24.

115. See Norman Graebner, "Northern Diplomacy and European Neutrality," in David Donald, ed., *Why the North Won the Civil War* (New York: Collier Books, 1960), 55–78; and Howard M. Hensel, *The Sword of the Union: Federal Objectives and Strategies During the American Civil War* (Montgomery, AL: USAF Air Command and Staff College, 1989), 91–105.

116. Anthony James Joes, "After Appomattox: The Guerrilla War That Never Was," *Small Wars and Insurgencies* 8, no. 1 (Spring 1997): 52–70.

Chapter 3: The Iraqi Insurgency: Vietnam Perspectives

1. John E. Mueller, "The Iraq Syndrome," *Foreign Affairs* 84, no. 6 (November–December 2005): 50–51.

2. For insightful analyses of the Iraqi insurgency, see Ian F. Beckett, *Insurgency in Iraq: An Historical Perspective* (Carlisle, PA: Strategic Studies Institute, U.S. Army War College, January 2005); Zaki Chehab, *Inside the Resistance: The Iraqi Insurgency and the Future of the Middle East* (New York: Nation Books, 2005); Anthony H. Cordesman, *Iraqi Security Forces: A Strategy for*

Success (Westport, CT: Praeger Security International, 2006), 237–314; Alastair Finlan, "Trapped in the Dead Ground: US Counter-Insurgency Strategy in Iraq," *Small Wars and Insurgencies* 16, no. 1 (March 2005): 1–21; Ahmed S. Hashim, *Insurgency and Counter-Insurgency in Iraq* (Ithaca, NY: Cornell University Press, 2006); Loretta Napoleoni, *Insurgent Iraq: Al Zarqawi and the New Generation* (New York: Seven Stories Press, 2005); and Steven Metz, "Insurgency and Counterinsurgency in Iraq," *Washington Quarterly* 27, no. 1 (Winter 2003–4): 25–36.

3. For an extensive discussion of Iraqi insurgent motivations and political objectives, see Hashim, *Insurgency and Counter-Insurgency*, 59–124.

4. Ibid., 99, 170–76.

5. "President Outlines Strategy for Victory in Iraq," speech before the U.S. Naval Academy, Annapolis, MD, November 30, 2005, http://www.whitehouse.gov/news/releases/2005/11/print/20051130-2.html.

6. Hashim, *Insurgency and Counter-Insurgency*, 214.

7. Napoleoni, *Insurgent Iraq*, 22, 160.

8. Chehab, *Inside the Resistance*, 264.

9. Napoleoni, *Insurgent Iraq,* 150.

10. Ibid., 178–82.

11. Louise Roug and Richard Boudreaux, "Deadly Rift Grows Among Insurgents," *Los Angeles Times*, January 29, 2006; Philip Sherwell, "Insurgents Fight Back Against Al-Qaeda's Foreign Zealots," *London Sunday Telegraph*, January 15, 2006; and Sabrina Tavernise and Dexter Filkins, "Local Insurgents Tell of Clashes With Al Qaeda's Forces in Iraq," *New York Times*, January 12, 2006.

12. *Small Arms Survey 2004* (Oxford, UK: Oxford University Press, 2004), 3.

13. Napoleoni, *Insurgent Iraq*, 170.

14. *In Their Own Words: Reading the Iraqi Insurgency*, Middle East Report No. 50. (Brussels: International Crisis Group, February 15, 2006), 5; and Michael R. Gordon and Bernard E. Trainor, *Cobra II: The Inside Story of the Invasion and Occupation of Iraq* (New York: Pantheon Books, 2006), 504–5.

15. Anton La Guardia, "Foreign Fighters Only a Tiny Part of the Rebellion," *London Daily Telegraph*, June 30, 2005; Jonathan Finer, "Among Insurgents in Iraq, Few Foreigners Are Found," *Washington Post*, November 17, 2005; Anthony H. Cordesman, "Iraq and Foreign Fighters," Working Draft: Updated as of November 17, 2005 (Washington, DC: Center for Strategic and International Studies), 2.

16. Bryan Bender, "Study Cites Seeds of Terror in Iraq," *Boston Globe*, July 17, 2005; and Mia Bloom, "Grim Saudi Export—Suicide Bombers," *Los Angeles Times*, July 17, 2005.

17. Cordesman, "Iraq and Foreign Fighters," 5.

18. Murad al-Shishani, "The Salafi-Jihadist Movement in Iraq: Recruitment Methods and Arab Volunteers," *Terrorism Monitor*, December 2, 2005, 3.

19. Murad al-Shishani, "Al-Zarqawi's Rise to Power: Analyzing Tactics and Targets," *Terrorism Monitor*, November 17, 2005, 1.

20. Cordesman, "Iraq and Foreign Fighters," 7.

21. For an assessment of the influence of the Munich and Vietnam analogies on U.S. uses of force since 1950, see Jeffrey Record, *Making War, Thinking History: Munich, Vietnam, and Presidential Uses of Force From Korea to Kosovo* (Annapolis, MD: Naval Institute Press, 2002). For a reassessment of the lessons of Munich, see Jeffrey Record, *The Specter of Munich: Reconsidering the Lessons of Appeasing Hitler* (Washington, DC: Potomac Books, 2006).

22. See, for example, Frederick W. Kagan, "Iraq Is Not Vietnam," *Policy Review* 134 (December 2005–January 2006): 3–14; and Stephen Biddle, "Seeing Baghdad, Thinking Saigon," *Foreign Affairs* 85, no. 2 (March–April 2006): 2–14.

23. Tucker, *Encyclopedia of the Vietnam War*, 396, 453; Pribbenow, *Victory in Vietnam*, 211, 431; James J. Wirtz, *The Tet Offensive: Intelligence Failure and War* (Ithaca, NY: Cornell University Press, 1991), 247–51; and Phillip B. Davidson, *Vietnam at War: The History, 1946–1975* (Novato, CA: Presidio Press, 1988), 475.

24. Douglas Pike, *Viet Cong: The Organization and Techniques of the National Liberation Front of South Vietnam* (Cambridge, MA: MIT Press, 1966). In 1986 Pike also published *PAVN: People's Army of Vietnam* (New York: Da Capo Press, 1986).

25. See discussion in Cordesman, *Iraqi Security Forces*, 249–50.

26. Sharon Behn, "50,000 Iraqi Insurgents Dead, Caught," *Washington Times*, July 26, 2005.

27. Shelby Stanton, *Vietnam Order of Battle* (Washington, DC: U.S. News Books, 1981), 333; and David L. Anderson, *The Columbia Guide to the Vietnam War* (New York: Columbia University Press, 2002), 286–88.

28. See Michael Ware, "The New Rules of Engagement," *Time*, December 15, 2005.

29. Record and Terrill, *Iraq and Vietnam*, 11–12.

30. Based on data appearing on the "Iraq Coalition Casualty Count" website, http://icasualties.org/oif.

31. Rick Jervis, "Attacks in Iraq Jumped in 2005," *USA Today*, January 23, 2006.

32. W. Andrew Terrill and Conrad C. Crane, *Precedents, Variables, and Options in Planning a U.S. Military Disengagement From Iraq* (Carlisle, PA: Strategic Studies Institute, U.S. Army War College, October 2005), v–vi.

33. Tyler Marshall and Mark Mazzetti, "Bush Is Now in Step With His Generals," *Los Angeles Times*, December 1, 2005.

34. The literature on U.S. mistakes regarding the decision to invade Iraq and the handling of events in post-Baathist Iraq is voluminous. See, for examples, Gwynne Dyer, *Ignorant Armies: Sliding Into War in Iraq* (Toronto: McClelland and Stewart, 2003); Jeffrey Record, *Dark Victory: America's Second War Against Iraq* (Annapolis, MD: Naval Institute Press, 2004); David L. Phillips, *Losing Iraq: Inside the Postwar Reconstruction Fiasco* (Boulder, CO: Westview Press, 2005); Larry Diamond, *Squandered Victory: The American Occupation and the Bungled Effort to Bring Democracy to Iraq* (New York: Henry Holt, 2005); George Packer, *The Assassins' Gate: America in Iraq* (New York: Farrar, Straus and Giroux, 2005); James Kitfield, "The Moment of Truth," *National Journal*, May 15, 2004, 1484–1490; James Fallows, "Bush's Lost Year in Iraq," *Atlantic Monthly* 294, no. 33 (October 2004): 68–84; Joseph Galloway, et al., "The Iraq War: Miscalculation and Misstep," Three-part series, *Philadelphia Inquirer*, October 17–19, 2004; Michael R. Gordon, "Catastrophic Success," Three-part series, *New York Times*, October 19–21, 2004; and Anthony H. Cordesman, "American Strategic, Tactical, and Other Mistakes in Iraq: A Litany of Errors" (Washington, DC: Center for Strategic and International Studies, April 19, 2006).

35. Francis Fukuyama, "After Neoconservatism," *New York Times Magazine*, February 19, 2006, 64, 65.

36. *National Strategy for Victory in Iraq* (Washington, DC: National Security Council, November 2005), 3.

37. Gordon and Trainor, *Cobra II*, 506.

38. See David C. Hendrickson and Robert W. Tucker, "Revisions in Need of Revising: What Went Wrong in the Iraq War," *Survival* 47, no. 2 (Summer 2005): 7–32.

39. See Andrew Krepinevich Jr., "How to Win in Iraq," *Foreign Affairs* 84, no. 5 (September–October 2005): 87–104.

40. See Lawrence F. Kaplan, "Clear and Fold," *New Republic* 233 (December 19, 2005): 12–15; and Frederick W. Kagan, "Fighting to Win," *Weekly Standard* 11, no. 14 (December 19, 2005): 21–26.

41. See Ang Chen Guan, *Ending the Vietnam War: The Vietnamese Communists' Perspective* (New York: Routledge Curzon, 2005), 150–65; and Van Tien Dung, *Our Great Spring Victory: An Account of the Liberation of South Vietnam*, trans. John Spragens Jr. (New York: Monthly Review Press, 1977), 6–25.

42. The departure of U.S. combat forces left about 550,000 South Vietnamese regulars and 525,000 territorials to face a PAVN estimated at 600,000 troops,

about 220,000 of which were in South Vietnam. Jeffrey J. Clarke, *Advice and Support: The Final Years, The U.S. Army in Vietnam* (Washington, DC: Center of Military History, U.S. Army, 1988), 485.

43. Joseph Buttinger, *Vietnam: The Unforgettable Tragedy* (New York: Horizon Press, 1977), 148.

44. Cao Van Vien, *The Final Collapse* (Washington, DC: Center of Military History, U.S. Army, 1983), 155.

45. See, for example, Evan Thomas, *The Very Best Men—Four Who Dared: The Early Years of the CIA* (New York: Simon & Schuster, 1995), 328.

46. *The Pentagon Papers: The Defense Department History of the United States Decisionmaking on Vietnam*, vol. 4 (Boston: Beacon Press, 1971), 398–99.

47. Douglas Kinnard, *The War Managers: American Generals Reflect on Vietnam* (New York: Da Capo Press, 1977), 97.

48. Hosmer, et al., *The Fall of South Vietnam*, 31.

49. Stuart A. Herrington, *Peace With Honor? An American Reports on Vietnam, 1973–1975* (Novato, CA: Presidio Press, 1983), 40.

50. Clarke, *Advice and Support*, 341–59.

51. Anthony James Joes, *The War for South Vietnam, 1954–1975*, rev. ed. (Westport, CT: Praeger, 2001), 150–51.

52. Lewy, *America in Vietnam*, 218.

53. William J. Duiker, *The Communist Road to Power in Vietnam*, 2nd ed. (Boulder, CO: Westview Press, 1996), 350, 359.

54. Timothy J. Lomperis, *The War Everyone Lost—and Won: America's Intervention in Vietnam's Twin Struggles*, rev. ed. (Washington, DC: Congressional Quarterly Press, 1993), 160.

55. Henry A. Kissinger, "The Vietnam Negotiations," *Foreign Affairs* 47, no. 2 (January 1969): 230.

56. George C. Herring, *America's Longest War: The United States and Vietnam, 1950–1975*, 3rd ed. (New York: McGraw-Hill, 1996), 298.

57. Terrill and Crane, *Precedents, Variables, and Options*, 13.

58. Ibid., 17.

59. Chris Kraul, "Decline in Oil Output Dims Iraq's Recovery," *Los Angeles Times*, January 25, 2006; and James Glanz, "Iraq Utilities Are Falling Short of Prewar Performance," *New York Times*, February 9, 2006.

60. Napoleoni, *Insurgent Iraq*, 189.

61. Biddle, "Seeing Baghdad, Thinking Saigon," 5.

62. Ethnic Vietnamese accounted for over 80 percent of Vietnam's population in the 1960s. The principal minorities were the Chinese, who lived in the cities,

and the aboriginal tribes, who inhabited the remote Central Highlands. Neither minority sought or wielded political power.

63. Arreguin-Toft, *How the Weak Win Wars*, 146.

64. "Winners and Losers in Iraq," Editorial, *New York Times*, December 26, 2005.

65. Terrill and Crane, *Precedents, Variables, and Options*, 44.

66. See James Fallows, "Why Iraq Has No Army," *Atlantic Monthly* 296, no. 5 (December 2005): 60–77.

67. President George W. Bush, speech before the Naval Academy, November 30, 2005.

68. Fallows, "Why Iraq Has No Army."

69. *National Strategy for Victory in Iraq,* 12.

70. Matt Kelley, "U.S. to Cut Iraq Troop Levels," *USA Today*, December 23, 2005.

71. David S. Cloud, "U.S. Is Sending Reserve Troops to Iraq's West," *New York Times,* May 30, 2006.

72. President George W. Bush, speech before the Naval Academy.

73. Stanley Karnow, "Giap Remembers," *New York Times Magazine*, June 23, 1990, 36.

74. See Record, *The Wrong War*, 54–56; Joes, *The War for South Vietnam*, 101–4; Duiker, *Sacred War*, 295–97; and Lomperis, *The War Everyone Lost*, 76–80.

75. See John E. Mueller, *War, Presidents and Public Opinion* (New York: John Wiley and Sons, 1973), 52–58; and Eric V. Larson, *Casualties and Consensus: The Historical Role of Casualties in Domestic Support for U.S. Military Operations* (Santa Monica, CA: Rand Corporation, 1996), 59–66.

76. Larson, *Casualties and Consensus*, 27–29.

77. See Mueller, *War, Presidents, and Public Opinion*; Larson, *Casualties and Consensus*; and Benjamin C. Schwarz, *Casualties, Public Opinion, and U.S. Military Intervention: Implications for U.S. Regional Strategies* (Santa Monica, CA: Rand Corporation, 1994). Also see discussion in Peter D. Feaver and Christopher Gelpi, *Choosing Your Battles: American Civil-Military Relations and the Use of Force* (Princeton, NJ: Princeton University Press, 2003), 95–148; Richard A. Lacquement Jr., "The Casualty Aversion Myth," *Naval War College Review* 57, no. 1 (Winter 2004): 38–57; John A. Gentry, "Military Force in An Age of National Cowardice," *Washington Quarterly* 21, no. 4 (Autumn 1998): 179–91; and Jeffrey Record, "Force Protection Fetishism: Sources, Consequences, and (?) Solutions," *Aerospace Power Journal* 14, no. 2 (Summer 2000): 4–11.

78. See Peter Feaver and Christopher Gelpi, "Casualty Aversion: How Many Deaths Are Acceptable?" *Washington Post*, November 7, 1999.

79. Larson, *Casualties and Consensus*, 15.

80. Richard K. Betts, "What Will It Take to Deter the United States?" *Parameters* 25, no. 4 (Winter 1995–96): 76.

81. Jeffrey Kimball, *Nixon's Vietnam War* (Lawrence: University Press of Kansas, 1998), 72–74.

82. Linda Bilmes and Joseph E. Stiglitz, *The Economic Costs of the Iraq War: An Appraisal Three Years After the Beginning of the Conflict*, Research Working Papers Series (Cambridge, MA: John F. Kennedy School of Government, Harvard University, January 2006), http://ksgnotes1.harvard.edu/Research/wpaper.nsf/rwp/RWP06-002.

83. Mueller, "The Iraq Syndrome," 44–54.

84. Polling data appearing on the Gallup Organization website, http://institution.gall up.com (accessed on November 20, 2005).

85. Dana Milbank and Claudia Deane, "Poll Finds Dimmer View of Iraq War," *Washington Post*, June 8, 2005.

86. Dick Polman, "Public's Support of the War Faltering," *Philadelphia Inquirer*, August 14, 2005.

87. See Richard Morin and Claudia Deane, "Poll Finds Bush Job Rating at New Low," *Washington Post*, April 11, 2006; and Adam Nagourney and Megan Thee, "Poll Gives Bush Worst Marks Yet on Major Issues," *New York Times*, May 10, 2006.

88. Mueller, "The Iraq Syndrome," 49–50.

Chapter 4: The American Way: War Without Politics

1. Max Boot, "The New American Way of War," *Foreign Affairs* 82, no. 4 (July–August 2003): 42, 44.

2. Max Boot, "No Shortcuts," *Los Angeles Times*, March 22, 2006.

3. Colin S. Gray, "The American Way of War: Critique and Implications," in Anthony D. McIvor, ed., *Rethinking the Principles of War* (Annapolis, MD: Naval Institute Press, 2005), 27–33. Also see Gray, *Irregular Enemies and the Essence of Strategy*.

4. Thomas G. Mahnken, "The American Way of War in the Twenty-First Century," in Efram Inbar, ed., *Democracies and Small Wars* (Portland, OR: Frank Cass, 2003), 74, 75, 77, 78.

5. Clausewitz, *On War*, 605, 607.

6. Reprinted in Jay M. Shafritz, *Words on War: Military Quotations From Ancient Times to the Present* (New York: Prentice Hall, 1990), 425

7. This does not mean that each and every restriction imposed on force is necessary and consistent with the political object being pursued. Civilian decision

makers, especially those prone to err on the side of caution or captivated by notions of finite gradations of coercion, can and do get it wrong.

8. Samuel R. Berger and Brent Scowcroft, "The Right Tools to Build Nations," *Washington Post*, July 27, 2005.

9. Lawrence Freedman, *The Transformation of Strategic Affairs,* Adelphi Paper 379 (London: International Institute for Strategic Studies, March 2006), 49, 51.

10. Francis Fukuyama, *America at the Crossroads: Democracy, Power, and the Neoconservative Legacy* (New Haven, CT: Yale University Press, 2006), 36.

11. Gordon and Trainor, *Cobra II*, 82, 504.

12. See Robert M. Cassidy, "Back to the Street Without Joy: Counterinsurgency Lessons From Vietnam and Other Small Wars," *Parameters* 34, no. 2 (Summer 2004): 73–83; John Waghelstein, "Counterinsurgency Doctrine and Low-Intensity Conflict in the Post-Vietnam Era," in Lawrence E. Grinter and Peter M. Dunn, eds., *The American War in Vietnam: Lessons, Legacies, and Implications for Future Conflicts* (New York: Greenwood Press, 1987), 127–37.

13. Robert M. Cassidy, *Counterinsurgency and the Global War on Terror: Military Culture and Irregular War* (Westport, CT: Praeger Security International, 2006), 21.

14. Antulio J. Echevarria, *Toward an American Way of War* (Carlisle, PA: Strategic Studies Institute, U.S. Army War College, March 2004), 10, 16.

15. David J. Lonsdale, *The Nature of War in the Information Age* (New York: Frank Cass, 2004), 9, 211.

16. Frederick W. Kagan, "War and Aftermath," *Policy Review* 120 (August–September 2003): 27.

17. Ibid., 3–27.

18. Hendrickson and Tucker, "Revisions in Need of Revising," 27.

19. Berger and Scowcroft, "The Right Tools."

20. Colin S. Gray, "How Has War Changed Since the End of the Cold War?" *Parameters* 35, no. 1 (Spring 2005): 21.

21. Ralph Peters, "The Counterrevolution in Military Affairs," *Weekly Standard* 11, no. 20 (February 6, 2006): 18.

22. See Michele A. Flournoy, "Did the Pentagon Get the Quadrennial Defense Review Right?" *Washington Quarterly* 29, no. 2 (Spring 2006): 67–84.

23. *Quadrennial Defense Review* (Washington, DC: Department of Defense, February 6, 2006), 36.

24. Ibid., 44.

25. Frederick W. Kagan, "A Strategy for Heroes," *Weekly Standard*, February 20, 2006, 32. For further commentary on the QDR, see Andrew F. Krepinevich, "Old Remedies for New Evils," *Wall Street Journal*, February 14, 2006; Michael

O'Hanlon, "Quadrennial Defense Review Resonance," *Washington Times*, February 17, 2006; David Von Drehle, "Rumsfeld's Transformation," *Washington Post*, February 12, 2006; and Larry Korb, "Numbers Show Army Too Taxed," *Atlanta Journal-Constitution*, February 13, 2006.

26. Freedman, *The Transformation of Strategic Affairs*, 15.

Chapter 5: The American Way: Search and Destroy

1. Carnes Lord, "American Strategic Culture in Small Wars," *Small Wars and Insurgencies* 3, no. 3 (Winter 1992): 205, 207.

2. Ibid., 208.

3. Beckett, *Insurgency in Iraq*, 26.

4. Freedman, *The Transformation of Strategic Affairs*, 92–93.

5. Arreguin-Toft, *How the Weak Win Wars*, 226.

6. Thomas X. Hammes, *The Sling and the Stone: On War in the 21st Century* (St. Paul, MN: Zenith Press, 2004), 3, 5.

7. Steven Metz and Raymond Millen, *Insurgency and Counterinsurgency in the 21st Century* (Carlisle, PA: Strategic Studies Institute, U.S. Army War College, November 2004), vi.

8. Andrew F. Krepinevich Jr., *The Army and Vietnam* (Baltimore, MD: Johns Hopkins University Press, 1986), 4.

9. Ibid., 5.

10. Ibid., 37.

11. See Record, *The Wrong War*, 80–82.

12. Quoted in Nagl, *Learning to Eat Soup With a Knife*, 157. For an early and well-informed if hardly dispassionate account of the Marine Corps' CAP program in Vietnam, see William R. Corson, *The Betrayal* (New York: W. W. Norton, 1968).

13. See Michael A. Hennessy, *Strategy in Vietnam: The Marines and Revolutionary Warfare in I Corps, 1965–1972* (Westport, CT: Praeger, 1997).

14. Quoted in Nagl, *Learning to Eat Soup With a Knife*, 159.

15. Quoted in ibid.

16. For the best account of General Johnson and the PROVN study, see Lewis Sorley, *Honorable Warrior: General Harold K. Johnson and the Ethics of Command* (Lawrence: University of Kansas Press, 1998), 227–41. See also *The Pentagon Papers*, vol. 2, 501–2, 576–80; and Eric Bergerud, *The Dynamics of Defeat: The War in Hau Nghia Province* (Boulder, CO: Westview Press, 1991), 110–14.

17. Nagl, *Learning to Eat Soup With a Knife*, xxi.

18. Ibid., 205.

19. Ibid., 207.

20. Harry G. Summers Jr., *On Strategy: A Critical Analysis of the Vietnam War* (Novato, CA: Presidio Press, 1982), 86, 88.

21. Quoted in Robert W. Komer, *Bureaucracy at War: U.S. Performance in the Vietnam Conflict* (Boulder, CO: Westview Press, 1986), 12.

22. Excerpts from the Weinberger speech appearing here and in following paragraphs are drawn from "The Uses of Military Power," speech before the National Press Club, Washington, DC, November 28, 1984, reprinted in Caspar W. Weinberger, *Fighting for Peace: Seven Critical Years in the Pentagon* (New York: Warner Books, 1990), 433–45 (emphasis in original).

23. Colin Powell, *My American Journey*, with Joseph E. Persico (New York: Random House, 1995), 148.

24. Matthew J. Morgan, "An Evolving View of Warfare: War and Peace and the American Military Profession," *Small Wars and Insurgencies* 16, no. 2 (June 2005): 154.

25. *Iraq: Translating Lessons Into Future DoD Policies* (Santa Monica, CA: Rand Corporation, February 2005), 7.

26. Krepinevich, "How to Win in Iraq," 92.

27. Brigadier Nigel Aylwin-Foster, "Changing the Army for Counterinsurgency Operations," *Military Review* 2 (November–December 2005): 9. Also see Jason Vest, "Willful Ignorance: How the Pentagon Sent the Army to Iraq Without a Counterinsurgency Doctrine," *Bulletin of Atomic Scientists* 61, no. 4 (July–August 2005): 41–48.

28. See Krepinevich, *The Army and Vietnam*, 27–55.

29. The most comprehensive assessment of the legislative history of the 1986 Defense Reorganization Act and the Pentagon's opposition to it is James R. Locher III, *Victory on the Potomac: The Goldwater-Nichols Act Unifies the Pentagon* (College Station: Texas A&M University Press, 2002).

Glossary

ALN	*Armee de Liberation Nationale* (Algeria)
ARVN	Army of the Republic of Vietnam
CCP	Chinese Communist Party
DRA	Democratic Republic of Afghanistan
FLN	*Front de Liberation Nationale* (Algeria)
IED	improvised explosive device
ISI	Inter-Services Intelligence (Pakistan)
KMT	Kuomintang (Nationalist Government of China)
MCP	Malayan Communist Party
MOOTW	military operations other than war
MRLA	Malayan Races Liberation Army
NATO	North Atlantic Treaty Organization
OAS	*Organisation Armee Secrete* (Algeria and France)
OIF	Operation Iraqi Freedom
PAVN	People's Army of Vietnam
PLA	People's Liberation Army
PROVN	A Program for the Pacification and Long-Term Development of Vietnam
QDR	*Quadrennial Defense Review*
RVN	Republic of Vietnam
RVNAF	Republic of Vietnam Armed Forces

SAM   surface-to-air missile
VC   Vietcong
WMD   weapon of mass destruction

Bibliography

Addington, Larry H. *The Patterns of War Since the 18th Century*. Bloomington: Indiana University Press, 1984.

al-Shishani, Murad. "Al-Zarqawi's Rise to Power: Analyzing Tactics and Targets." *Terrorism Monitor*, November 17, 2005, 1–3.

———. "The Salafi-Jihadist Movement in Iraq: Recruitment Methods and Arab Volunteers." *Terrorism Monitor*, December 2, 2005, 2–4.

Ambler, John. *The French Army in Politics, 1945–1962*. Columbus: Ohio State University Press, 1966.

Anderson, David L. *The Columbia Guide to the Vietnam War*. New York: Columbia University Press, 2002.

Arreguin-Toft, Ivan. "How the Weak Win Wars: A Theory of Asymmetric Conflict." *International Security* 26, no. 1 (Summer 2001): 93–128.

———. *How the Weak Win Wars: A Theory of Asymmetric Conflict*. New York: Cambridge University Press, 2005.

Asprey, Robert B. *War in the Shadows: The Guerrilla in History*. New York: William Morrow, 1994.

Aylwin-Foster, Nigel. "Changing the Army for Counterinsurgency Operations." *Military Review* 2 (November–December 2005): 2–13.

Baker, Norman. *Government and Contractors: The British Treasury and War Supplies, 1775–1783*. London: University of London, 1971.

Beckett, Ian F. *Insurgency in Iraq: An Historical Perspective*. Carlisle, PA: Strategic Studies Institute, U.S. Army War College, January 2005.

————. *Modern Insurgencies and Counter-Insurgencies: Guerrillas and Their Opponents Since 1750.* London: Routledge, 2001.

Behn, Sharon. "50,000 Iraqi Insurgents Dead, Caught." *Washington Times*, July 26, 2005.

Bender, Bryan. "Study Cites Seeds of Terror in Iraq." *Boston Globe*, July 17, 2005.

Berger, Samuel R., and Brent Scowcroft. "The Right Tools to Build Nations." *Washington Post*, July 27, 2005.

Bergerud, Eric. *The Dynamics of Defeat: The War in Hau Nghia Province.* Boulder, CO: Westview Press, 1991.

Betts, Richard K. "Interests, Burdens, and Persistence: Asymmetries Between Washington and Hanoi." *International Studies Quarterly* 24, no. 4 (December 1980): 520–24,

————. "What Will It Take to Deter the United States?" *Parameters* 25, no. 4 (Winter 1995–96): 70–79.

Biddle, Stephen. "Seeing Baghdad, Thinking Saigon." *Foreign Affairs* 85, no. 2 (March–April 2006): 2–14.

Bilmes, Linda, and Joseph E. Stiglitz. *The Economic Costs of the Iraq War: An Appraisal Three Years After the Beginning of the Conflict.* Research Working Papers Series. Cambridge, MA: John F. Kennedy School of Government, Harvard University, January 2006. http://ksgnotes1.harvard.edu/Research/wpaper.nsf/rwp/RWP06-002.

bin Laden, Osama. "Declaration of War Against the Americans Occupying the Land of the Two Holy Places." Reprinted in Online News Hour with Jim Lehrer. http://www.pbs.org/newshour/terrorism/internationalfatwa_1996.html.

Bloom, Mia. "Grim Saudi Export—Suicide Bombers." *Los Angeles Times*, July 17, 2005.

Boot, Max. "The New American Way of War." *Foreign Affairs* 82, no. 4 (July–August 2003): 41–58.

————. "No Shortcuts." *Los Angeles Times*, March 22, 2006.

Bowler, R. Arthur. *Logistics and the Failure of the British Army in America, 1775–1783.* Princeton, NJ: Princeton University Press, 1975.

Braestrup, Peter. *Big Story: How the American Press and Television Reported and Interpreted the Crisis of Tet 1968 in Vietnam and Washington.* Novato, CA: Presidio Press, 1977.

Buttinger, Joseph. *Vietnam: The Unforgettable Tragedy.* New York: Horizon Press, 1977.

Callwell, C. E. *Small Wars: Their Principles and Practice.* 3rd ed. Lincoln: University of Nebraska Press, 1996.

Cassidy, Robert M. "Back to Street Without Joy: Counterinsurgency Lessons From Vietnam and Other Small Wars." *Parameters* 34, no. 2 (Summer 2004): 73–83.

―――. *Counterinsurgency and the Global War on Terror: Military Culture and Irregular War*. Westport, CT: Praeger Security International, 2006.

Chandler, David G. *The Campaigns of Napoleon*. New York: Macmillan, 1966.

Chehab, Zaki. *Inside the Resistance: The Iraqi Insurgency and the Future of the Middle East*. New York: Nation Books, 2005.

The China White Paper, August 1949. Stanford, CA: Stanford University Press, 1967.

Cigar, Norman. "Iraq's Strategic Mindset and the Gulf War: Blueprint for Defeat." *Journal of Strategic Studies* 15, no. 1 (March 1992): 2–14.

Clarke, Jeffrey J. *Advice and Support: The Final Years, The U.S. Army in Vietnam*. Washington, DC: Center of Military History, U.S. Army, 1988.

Clausewitz, Carl von. *On War*. Edited and translated by Michael Howard and Peter Paret. Princeton, NJ: Princeton University Press, 1976.

Clodfelter, Mark. *The Limits of Air Power: The American Bombing of North Vietnam*. New York: Free Press, 1989.

Cloud, David S. "U.S. Is Sending Reserve Troops to Iraq's West." *New York Times*, May 30, 2006.

Clutterbuck, Richard L. *The Long, Long War: The Emergency in Malaya 1948–1960*. London: Cassell, 1966.

Colby, William. *Lost Victory: A Firsthand Account of America's Sixteen-Year Involvement in Vietnam*. Chicago: Contemporary Books, 1989.

Cordesman, Anthony H. "American Strategic, Tactical, and Other Mistakes in Iraq: A Litany of Errors." Washington, DC: Center for Strategic and International Studies, April 19, 2006.

―――. "Iraq and Foreign Fighters." Working Draft: Updated as of November 17, 2005. Washington, DC: Center for Strategic and International Studies.

―――. *Iraqi Security Forces: A Strategy for Success*. Westport, CT: Praeger Security International, 2006.

Corson, William R. *The Betrayal*. New York: W. W. Norton, 1968.

Davidson, Phillip B. *Vietnam at War: The History, 1946–1975*. Novato, CA: Presidio Press, 1988.

Diamond, Larry. *Squandered Victory: The American Occupation and the Bungled Effort to Bring Democracy to Iraq*. New York: Henry Holt, 2005.

Dommen, Arthur J. *The Indochinese Experience of the French and the Americans: Nationalism and Communism in Cambodia, Laos, and Vietnam*. Bloomington: Indiana University Press, 2001.

Doughty, Robert A. *Pyrrhic Victory: French Strategy and Operations in the Great War*. Cambridge, MA: Belknap Press, 2005.

Drohan, Brian. "British Political-Military Strategy in the Malayan Emergency." *Armor* 65, no. 1 (January–February 2006): 34–38.

Duiker, William J. *The Communist Road to Power in Vietnam*. 2nd ed. Boulder, CO: Westview Press, 1996.

———. "Foreword." *Victory in Vietnam: The Official History of the People's Army of Vietnam, 1954–1975*. Translated by Merle L. Pribbenow. Lawrence: University Press of Kansas, 2002.

———. *Sacred War: Nationalism and Revolution in a Divided Vietnam*. New York: McGraw-Hill, 1993.

Dung, Van Tien. *Our Great Spring Victory: An Account of the Liberation of South Vietnam*. Translated by John Spragens Jr. New York: Monthly Review Press, 1977.

Dyer, Gwynne. *Ignorant Armies: Sliding Into War in Iraq*. Toronto: McClelland and Stewart, 2003.

Echevarria, Antulio J. *Toward an American Way of War*. Carlisle, PA: Strategic Studies Institute, U.S. Army War College, March 2004.

Eichenberg, Richard C. "Victory Has Many Friends: U.S. Public Opinion and the Use of Military Force, 1981–2005." *International Security* 30, no. 1 (Summer 2005): 140–77.

Elting, John R. *Swords Around a Throne: Napoleon's Grand Armee*. New York: Free Press, 1988.

Esdaile, Charles J. *Fighting Napoleon: Guerrillas, Bandits and Adventurers in Spain, 1808–14*. New Haven, CT: Yale University Press, 2004.

———. *The Peninsular War: A New History*. New York: Palgrave MacMillan, 2003.

Fall, Bernard B. *Hell in a Very Small Place: The Siege of Dien Bien Phu*. New York: Harper and Row, 1967.

———. *Street Without Joy*. Mechanicsburg, PA: Stackpole Books, 1961.

Fallows, James. "Bush's Lost Year in Iraq." *Atlantic Monthly* 294, no. 33 (October 2004): 68–84.

———. "Why Iraq Has No Army." *Atlantic Monthly* 296, no. 5 (December 2005): 60–77.

Feaver, Peter D., and Christopher Gelpi. "Casualty Aversion: How Many Deaths Are Acceptable?" *Washington Post*, November 7, 1999.

———. *Choosing Your Battles: American Civil-Military Relations and the Use of Force*. Princeton, NJ: Princeton University Press, 2003.

Finer, Jonathan. "Among Insurgents in Iraq, Few Foreigners Are Found." *Washington Post*, November 17, 2005.

Finlan, Alastair. "Trapped in Dead Ground: U.S. Counter-Insurgency Strategy in Iraq." *Small Wars and Insurgencies* 16, no. 1 (March 2005): 1–21.

Flournoy, Michele A. "Did the Pentagon Get the Quadrennial Defense Review Right?" *Washington Quarterly* 29, no. 2 (Spring 2006): 67–84.

"France in Vietnam, 1954, and the U.S. in Vietnam, 1965—A Useful Analogy?" Memorandum from McGeorge Bundy to President Lyndon Johnson, June 30, 1965. Document No. 11, John F. Kennedy School of Government Case Study on Americanizing the Vietnam War. Cambridge, MA, 1983.

Freedman, Lawrence. *The Transformation of Strategic Affairs*. Adelphi Paper 379. London: International Institute for Strategic Studies, March 2006.

Fukuyama, Francis. "After Neoconservatism." *New York Times Magazine*, February 19, 2006, 62–67.

———. *America at the Crossroads: Democracy, Power, and the Neoconservative Legacy*. New Haven, CT: Yale University Press, 2006.

Gaiduk, Ilya V. *The Soviet Union and the Vietnam War*. Chicago: Ivan R. Dee, 1966.

Galloway, Joseph, et al. "The Iraq War: Miscalculation and Misstep." Three-part series. *Philadelphia Inquirer*, October 17–19, 2004.

Garver, John W. "The Chinese Threat in the Vietnam War." *Parameters* 22, no. 1 (Spring 1992): 73–85.

Gates, David. *The Spanish Ulcer: A History of the Peninsular War*. New York: W. W. Norton, 1986.

Gelpi, Christopher, Peter D. Feaver, and Jason Reifler. "Success Matters: Casualty Sensitivity and the War in Iraq." *International Security* 30, no. 3 (Winter 2005–6): 7–46.

Gentry, John A. "Military Force in an Age of National Cowardice." *Washington Quarterly* 21, no. 4 (Autumn 1998): 179–91.

Glanz, James. "Iraq Utilities Are Falling Short of Prewar Performance." *New York Times*, February 9, 2006.

Goncharov, Sergei, John W. Lewis, and Xue Litai. *Uncertain Partners: Stalin, Mao, and the Korean War*. Stanford, CA: Stanford University Press, 1993.

Gordon, Michael R. "Catastrophic Success." Three-part series. *New York Times,* October 19–21, 2004.

———, and Bernard E. Trainor. *Cobra II: The Inside Story of the Invasion and Occupation of Iraq*. New York: Pantheon Books, 2006.

Graebner, Norman. "Northern Diplomacy and European Neutrality." *Why the North Won the Civil War*. Edited by David Donald. New York: Collier Books, 1960.

Grau, Lester W., and Michael A. Gress, ed. and trans. *The Soviet-Afghan War, How a Superpower Fought and Lost: The Russian General Staff*. Lawrence: University Press of Kansas, 2002.

Gray, Colin S. "The American Way of War: Critique and Implications." *Rethinking the Principles of War*. Edited by Anthony D. McIvor. Annapolis, MD: Naval Institute Press, 2005.

———. *Another Bloody Century: Future Warfare*. London: Weidenfeld and Nicholson, 2005.

———. "How Has War Changed Since the End of the Cold War?" *Parameters* 35, no. 1 (Spring 2005): 14–26.

———. *Irregular Enemies and the Essence of Strategy: Can the American Way of War Adapt?* Carlisle, PA: Strategic Studies Institute, U.S. Army War College, March 2006.

Guan, Ang Chen. *Ending the Vietnam War: The Vietnamese Communists' Perspective*. New York: Routledge Curzon, 2005.

Gurtov, Melvin. *The First Vietnam Crisis: Chinese Communist Strategy and United States Involvement, 1953–1954*. New York: Columbia University Press, 1967.

Hammes, Thomas X. *The Sling and the Stone: On War in the 21st Century*. St. Paul, MN: Zenith Press, 2004.

Hashim, Ahmed S. *Insurgency and Counter-Insurgency in Iraq*. Ithaca, NY: Cornell University Press, 2006.

Heggoy, Alf Andrew. *Insurgency and Counterinsurgency in Algeria*. Bloomington: Indiana University Press, 1972.

Hendrickson, David C., and Robert W. Tucker. "Revisions in Need of Revising: What Went Wrong in the Iraq War." *Survival* 47, no. 2 (Summer 2005): 7–32.

Hennessy, Michael A. *Strategy in Vietnam: The Marines and Revolutionary Warfare in I Corps, 1965–1972*. Westport, CT: Praeger, 1997.

Hensel, Howard M. *The Sword of the Union: Federal Objectives and Strategies During the American Civil War*. Montgomery, AL: USAF Air Command and Staff College, 1989.

Herring, George C. *America's Longest War: The United States and Vietnam, 1950–1975*. 3rd ed. New York: McGraw-Hill, 1996.

Herrington, Stuart A. *Peace With Honor? An American Reports on Vietnam, 1973–1975*. Novato, CA: Presidio Press, 1983.

Horne, Alistair. *A Savage War of Peace: Algeria 1954–1962*. New York: Viking Press, 1977.

Hosmer, Stephen T., Konrad Kellen, and Brian M. Jenkins. *The Fall of South*

Vietnam: Statements by Vietnamese Military and Civilian Leaders. Santa Monica, CA: Rand Corporation, December 1978.

Hughes, Robert. *Goya.* New York: Alfred A. Knopf, 2003.

In Their Own Words: Reading the Iraqi Insurgency. Middle East Report No. 50. Brussels: International Crisis Group, February 15, 2006.

Iraq: Translating Lessons Into Future DoD Policies. Santa Monica, CA: Rand Corporation, February 2005.

Jackson, Robert. *The Malayan Emergency: The Commonwealth's Wars 1948–1966.* London: Routledge, 1991.

Jervis, Rick. "Attacks in Iraq Jumped in 2005." *USA Today*, January 23, 2006.

Jian, Chen. "China's Involvement in the Vietnam War, 1964–1969." *China Quarterly* 42 (1995): 356–87.

———. *Mao's China and the Cold War.* Chapel Hill: University of North Carolina Press, 2001.

Joes, Anthony James. "After Appomattox: The Guerrilla War That Never Was." *Small Wars and Insurgencies* 8, no. 1 (Spring 1997): 52–70.

———. *America and Guerrilla Warfare.* Lexington: University Press of Kentucky, 2000.

———. *Resisting Rebellion: The History and Politics of Counterinsurgency.* Lexington: University Press of Kentucky, 2004.

———. *The War for South Vietnam, 1954–1975.* Rev. ed. Westport, CT: Praeger, 2001.

Kagan, Frederick W. "Fighting to Win." *Weekly Standard* 11, no. 14 (December 19, 2005): 21–26.

———. "Iraq Is Not Vietnam." *Policy Review* 134 (December 2005–January 2006): 3–14.

———. "A Strategy for Heroes." *Weekly Standard*, February 20, 2006.

———. "War and Aftermath." *Policy Review* 120 (August–September 2003): 3–27.

Kahin, George McT. *Intervention: How America Became Involved in Vietnam.* New York: Alfred A. Knopf, 1986.

Kakar, Hassan M. *Afghanistan: The Soviet Invasion and the Afghan Response, 1979–1982.* Berkeley: University of California Press, 1995.

Kaplan, Lawrence F. "Clear and Fold." *New Republic* 233 (December 19, 2005): 12–15.

Karnow, Stanley. "Giap Remembers." *New York Times Magazine*, June 23, 1990.

Kearns, Doris. *Lyndon Johnson and the American Dream.* New York: Harper and Row, 1976.

Kelley, Matt. "U.S. to Cut Iraq Troop Levels." *USA Today*, December 23, 2005.

Kimball, Jeffrey. *Nixon's Vietnam War*. Lawrence: University Press of Kansas, 1998.

Kinnard, Douglas. *The War Managers: American Generals Reflect on Vietnam*. New York: Da Capo Press, 1977.

Kissinger, Henry A. "The Vietnam Negotiations." *Foreign Affairs* 47, no. 2 (January 1969): 211–34.

Kitfield, James. "The Moment of Truth." *National Journal*, May 15, 2004, 1484–1490.

Komer, Robert W. *Bureaucracy at War: U.S. Performance in the Vietnam Conflict*. Boulder, CO: Westview Press, 1986.

———. *The Malayan Emergency in Retrospect: Organization of Successful Counterinsurgency Effort*. Santa Monica, CA: Rand Corporation, 1972.

Korb, Larry. "Numbers Show Army Too Taxed." *Atlanta Journal-Constitution*, February 13, 2006.

Kraul, Chris. "Decline in Oil Output Dims Iraq's Recovery." *Los Angeles Times*, January 25, 2006.

Krepinevich, Andrew F., Jr. *The Army and Vietnam*. Baltimore, MD: Johns Hopkins University Press, 1986.

———. "How to Win in Iraq." *Foreign Affairs* 84, no. 5 (September–October 2005): 87–104.

———. "Old Remedies for New Evils." *Wall Street Journal*, February 14, 2006.

La Guardia, Anton. "Foreign Fighters Only a Tiny Part of the Rebellion." *London Daily Telegraph*, June 30, 2005.

Lacquement, Richard A., Jr. "The Casualty Aversion Myth." *Naval War College Review* 57, no. 1 (Winter 2004): 38–57.

Lanning, Michael Lee, and Dan Cragg. *Inside the VC and NVA: The Real Story of North Vietnam's Armed Forces*. New York: Ivy Books, 1992.

Laqueur, Walter. *Guerrilla Warfare: A Historical and Critical Study*. New Brunswick, NJ: Transaction Publishers, 1998.

Larson, Eric V. *Casualties and Consensus: The Historical Role of Casualties in Domestic Support for U.S. Military Operations*. Santa Monica, CA: Rand Corporation, 1996.

Le Gro, William E. *Vietnam From Cease-Fire to Capitulation*. Washington, DC: U.S. Army Center of Military History, 1985.

"Letter from al-Zawahiri to al-Zarqawi." July 9, 2005. Released October 11, 2005, by the Office of the Director of National Intelligence. http://www.dni.gov/release_letter_101105.html.

Levine, Steven I. *Anvil of Victory: The Communist Revolution in Manchuria, 1945–1948.* New York: Columbia University Press, 1987.

Lewy, Guenter. *America in Vietnam.* New York: Oxford University Press, 1978.

Litwak, Robert S. "The Soviet Union in Afghanistan." *Foreign Military Intervention: The Dynamics of Protracted Conflict.* Edited by Ariel E. Levite, Bruce W. Jentleson, and Larry Berman. New York: Columbia University Press, 1992.

Locher, James R., III. *Victory on the Potomac: The Goldwater-Nichols Act Unifies the Pentagon.* College Station: Texas A&M Press, 2002.

Lomperis, Timothy J. *The War Everyone Lost—and Won: America's Intervention in Vietnam's Twin Struggles.* Rev. ed. Washington, DC: Congressional Quarterly Press, 1993.

Lonsdale, David J. *The Nature of War in the Information Age.* New York: Frank Cass, 2004.

Lord, Carnes. "American Strategic Culture in Small Wars." *Small Wars and Insurgencies* 3, no. 3 (Winter 1993): 205–16.

Machiavelli, Niccolo. *The Prince.* Translated by W. K. Marriott. New York: Alfred A. Knopf, 1992.

Mack, Andrew. "Why Big Nations Lose Small Wars: The Politics of Asymmetric Conflict." *World Politics* 27, no. 2 (1975): 175–200.

MacKay, Donald. *The Malayan Emergency 1948–1960: The Domino That Stood.* Washington, DC: Brassey's, 1997.

Mackesy, Piers. *The War for America, 1775–1783.* Lincoln: University of Nebraska Press, 1993.

———. "What the British Army Learned." *Arms and Independence: The Military Character of the American Revolution.* Edited by Ronald Hoffman and Peter J. Albert. Charlottesville: University of Virginia Press, 1984.

Mahnken, Thomas G. "The American Way of War in the Twenty-First Century." *Democracies and Small Wars.* Edited by Efram Inbar. Portland, OR: Frank Cass, 2003.

Marshall, Tyler, and Mark Mazzetti. "Bush Is Now in Step With His Generals." *Los Angeles Times,* December 1, 2005.

Merom, Gil. *How Democracies Lose Small Wars: State, Society, and the Failures of France in Algeria, Israel in Lebanon, and the United States in Vietnam.* New York: Cambridge University Press, 2003.

Metz, Steven. "Insurgency and Counterinsurgency in Iraq." *Washington Quarterly* 27, no. 1 (Winter 2003–4): 25–36.

———, and Raymond Millen. *Insurgency and Counterinsurgency in the 21st*

Century. Carlisle, PA: Strategic Studies Institute, U.S. Army War College, November 2004.

Milbank, Dana, and Claudia Deane. "Poll Finds Dimmer View of Iraq War." *Washington Post*, June 8, 2005.

Millett, Allan R., and Peter Maslowski. *For the Common Defense: A Military History of the United States of America*. Rev. ed. New York: Free Press, 1994.

Morgan, Matthew J. "An Evolving View of Warfare: War and Peace and the American Military Profession." *Small Wars and Insurgencies* 16, no. 2 (June 2005): 147–69.

Morin, Richard, and Claudia Deane. "Poll Finds Bush Job Rating at New Low." *Washington Post*, April 11, 2006.

Mueller, John E. "The Iraq Syndrome." *Foreign Affairs* 84, no. 6 (November–December 2005): 44–54.

———. "The Search for the 'Breaking Point' in Vietnam: The Statistics of a Deadly Quarrel." *International Studies Quarterly* 24, no. 4 (December 1980): 465–496.

———. *War, Presidents and Public Opinion*. New York: John Wiley and Sons, 1973.

Nagl, John A. *Learning to Eat Soup With a Knife: Counterinsurgency Lessons From Malaya and Vietnam*. Chicago: University of Chicago Press, 2002.

Nagourney, Adam, and Megan Thee. "Poll Gives Bush Worst Marks Yet on Major Issues." *New York Times*, May 10, 2006.

Napoleoni, Loretta. *Insurgent Iraq: Al Zarqawi and the New Generation*. New York: Seven Stories Press, 2005.

National Strategy for Victory in Iraq. Washington, DC: National Security Council, November, 2005.

O'Hanlon, Michael. "Quadrennial Defense Review Resonance." *Washington Times*, February 17, 2006.

O'Neill, Bard E. *Insurgency and Terrorism: Inside Modern Revolutionary Warfare*. Washington, DC: Brassey's, 1990.

Packer, George. *The Assassins' Gate: America in Iraq*. New York: Farrar, Straus and Giroux, 2005.

Pakenham, Thomas. *The Boer War*. New York: Random House, 1980.

The Pentagon Papers: The Defense Department History of the United States Decisionmaking on Vietnam. 5 vols. Boston: Beacon Press, 1971.

The Pentagon Papers: The Defense Department History of the United States Decisionmaking on Vietnam. The Senator Gravel Edition. Vol. 4. Boston: Beacon Press, 1995.

Peters, Ralph. "The Counterrevolution in Military Affairs." *Weekly Standard* 11, no. 20 (February 6, 2006): 18–24

Phillips, David L. *Losing Iraq: Inside the Postwar Reconstruction Fiasco*. Boulder, CO: Westview Press, 2005.

Pike, Douglas. *PAVN: People's Army of Vietnam*. New York: Da Capo Press, 1986.

———. *Viet Cong: The Organization and Techniques of the National Liberation Front of South Vietnam*. Cambridge, MA: MIT Press, 1966.

Polman, Dick. "Public's Support of the War Faltering." *Philadelphia Inquirer*, August 14, 2005.

Powell, Colin. *My American Journey*. With Joseph E. Persico. New York: Random House, 1995.

Prados, John. *Blood Road: The Ho Chi Minh Trail and the Vietnam War*. New York: John Wiley and Sons, 1999.

"President Outlines Strategy for Victory in Iraq." Speech before the U.S. Naval Academy, Annapolis, MD, November 30, 2006. http://www.whitehouse.gov/news/releases/2005/11/print/20051130-2.html.

Quadrennial Defense Review. Washington, DC: Department of Defense, February 6, 2006.

Record, Jeffrey. *Dark Victory: America's Second War Against Iraq*. Annapolis, MD: Naval Institute Press, 2004.

———. "Defeating Desert Storm (and Why Saddam Didn't)." *Comparative Strategy* 12, no. 2 (April–June 1993): 125–40.

———. "Force Protection Fetishism: Sources, Consequences, and (?) Solutions." *Aerospace Power Journal* 14, no. 2 (Summer 2000): 4–11.

———. *Making War, Thinking History: Munich, Vietnam, and Presidential Uses of Force From Korea to Kosovo*. Annapolis, MD: Naval Institute Press, 2002.

———. *Revising U.S. Military Strategy: Tailoring Means to Ends*. Washington, DC: Pergamon-Brassey's, 1984.

———. *The Specter of Munich: Reconsidering the Lessons of Appeasing Hitler*. Washington, DC: Potomac Books, 2006.

———. *The Wrong War: Why We Lost in Vietnam*. Annapolis, MD: Naval Institute Press, 1998.

———, and W. Andrew Terrill. *Iraq and Vietnam: Differences, Similarities, and Insights*. Carlisle, PA: Strategic Studies Institute, U.S. Army War College, May 2004.

Reiter, Dan, and Allan C. Stam. *Democracies at War*. Princeton, NJ: Princeton University Press, 2002.

Rodman, Peter W. *More Precious Than Peace: The Cold War and the Struggle for the Third World.* New York: Charles Scribner's Sons, 1994.

Ropp, Theodore. *War in the Modern World.* New York: Collier Books, 1962.

Rosen, Steven Peter. "War Power and the Willingness to Suffer." *Peace, War, and Numbers.* Edited by Bruce M. Russett. Beverly Hills, CA: Sage Publications, 1972.

Roug, Louise, and Richard Boudreaux. "Deadly Rift Grows Among Insurgents." *Los Angeles Times,* January 29, 2006.

Rusk, Dean. *As I Saw It.* With Richard Rusk and Daniel S. Papp. New York: W. W. Norton, 1990.

Schom, Alan. *Napoleon Bonaparte.* New York: HarperCollins, 1997.

Schwarz, Benjamin C. *Casualties, Public Opinion, and U.S. Military Intervention: Implications for U.S. Regional Strategies.* Santa Monica, CA: Rand Corporation, 1994.

Scott, James M. *Deciding to Intervene: The Reagan Doctrine and American Foreign Policy.* Durham, NC: Duke University Press, 1996.

Shafritz, Jay M. *Words on War: Quotations From Ancient Times to the Present.* New York: Prentice Hall, 1990.

Sheng, Michael M. *Battling Western Imperialism: Mao, Stalin, and the United States.* Princeton, NJ: Princeton University Press, 1997.

Sherwell, Philip. "Insurgents Fight Back Against Al-Qaeda's Foreign Zealots." *London Sunday Telegraph,* January 15, 2006.

Shy, John. "The American Revolution: The Military Conflict Considered as a Revolutionary War." *Essays on the American Revolution.* Edited by Stephen G. Kurtz and James H. Hutson. Chapel Hill: University of North Carolina Press, 1973.

Small Arms Survey 2004. Oxford, UK: Oxford University Press, 2004.

Small Wars Manual. Washington, DC: U.S. Marine Corps, 1990.

Snow, Donald M., and Dennis M. Drew. *From Lexington to Desert Storm and Beyond: War and Politics in the American Experience.* 2nd ed. Armonk, NY: M. E. Sharpe, 2000.

Sorley, Lewis. *A Better War: The Unexamined Victories and Final Tragedy of America's Last Years in Vietnam.* New York: Harcourt Brace, 1999.

———. *Honorable Warrior: General Harold K. Johnson and the Ethics of Command.* Lawrence: University of Kansas Press, 1998.

Stanton, Shelby. *Vietnam Order of Battle.* Washington, DC: U.S. News Books, 1981.

Stubbs, Richard. *Hearts and Minds in Guerrilla Warfare: The Malayan Emergency 1948–1960.* New York: Oxford University Press, 1989.

Summers, Harry G., Jr. *On Strategy: A Critical Analysis of the Vietnam War.* Novato, CA: Presidio, 1982.

Syrett, David. *Shipping and the American War, 1775–1783.* London: University of London, 1970.

Talbott, John. *The War Without a Name: France in Algeria, 1954–1962.* New York: Alfred A. Knopf, 1980.

Tavernise, Sabrina, and Dexter Filkins. "Local Insurgents Tell of Clashes With Al Qaeda's Forces in Iraq." *New York Times*, January 12, 2006.

Terrill, W. Andrew, and Conrad C. Crane. *Precedents, Variables, and Options in Planning U.S. Military Disengagement From Iraq.* Carlisle, PA: Strategic Studies Institute, U.S. Army War College, October 2005.

Thomas, Evan. *The Very Best Men—Four Who Dared: The Early Years of the CIA.* New York: Simon & Schuster, 1995.

Thompson, Robert. *Defeating Communist Insurgency: The Lessons of Malaya and Vietnam.* New York: Frederick A. Praeger, 1966.

Tilford, Earl H., Jr. *What the Air Force Did in Vietnam and Why.* Maxwell AFB, AL: Air University Press, June 1991.

Tsou, Tang. *America's Failure in China: 1941–50.* Chicago: University of Chicago Press, 1963.

Tucker, Spencer C., ed. *Encyclopedia of the Vietnam War: A Political, Social, and Military History.* New York: Oxford University Press, 1998.

Van Slyke, Lyman. *The China White Paper, August 1949.* Stanford, CA: Stanford University Press, 1967.

Vest, Jason. "Willful Ignorance: How the Pentagon Sent the Army to Iraq Without a Counterinsurgency Doctrine." *Bulletin of Atomic Scientists* 61, no. 4 (July–August 2005): 41–48.

Vien, Cao Van. *The Final Collapse.* Washington, DC: Center of Military History, U.S. Army, 1983.

Von Drehle, David. "Rumsfeld's Transformation." *Washington Post*, February 12, 2006.

Waghelstein, John D. "Counterinsurgency Doctrine and Low-Intensity Conflict in the Post-Vietnam Era." *The American War in Vietnam: Lessons, Legacies, and Implications for Future Conflicts.* Edited by Lawrence E. Grinter and Peter M. Dunn. New York: Greenwood Press, 1987.

———. "Regulars, Irregulars and Militia: The American Revolution." *Small Wars and Insurgencies* 6, no. 2 (Autumn 1995): 133–58.

Ware, Michael. "The New Rules of Engagement." *Time*, December 15, 2005.

Weinberger, Caspar W. *Fighting for Peace: Seven Critical Years in the Pentagon.* New York: Warner Books, 1990.

Weintraub, Stanley. *Iron Tears: America's Battle for Freedom, Britain's Quagmire*. New York: Free Press, 2005.

Wells, Tom. *The War Within: America's Battle Over Vietnam*. New York: Henry Holt, 1994.

Williams, T. Harry. *The History of American Wars From Colonial Times to World War I*. New York: Alfred A. Knopf, 1981.

Windrow, Martin. *The Last Valley: Dien Bien Phu and the French Defeat in Vietnam*. London: Cassell, 2005.

"Winners and Losers in Iraq." Editorial. *New York Times*, December 26, 2005.

Wirtz, James J. *The Tet Offensive: Intelligence Failure and War*. Ithaca, NY: Cornell University Press, 1991.

York, Neil Longley. *Turning the World Upside Down: The War of Independence and the Problem of Empire*. Westport, CT: Praeger, 2003.

Zhai, Qiang. *China and the Vietnam Wars, 1950–1975*. Chapel Hill: University of North Carolina Press, 2000.

Zhang, Xiaoming. "Communist Powers Divided: China, the Soviet Union, and the Vietnam War." *International Perspectives on Vietnam*. Edited by Lloyd C. Gardiner and Ted Gittinger. College Station: Texas A&M Press, 2000.

Index

About the Author

Well-known defense policy critic Jeffrey Record teaches strategy at the U.S. Air Force's Air War College in Montgomery, Alabama. He received his doctorate at the Johns Hopkins School of Advanced International Studies and is the author of eight books and a dozen monographs, including *Dark Victory: America's Second War Against Iraq*; *Making War, Thinking History: Munich, Vietnam, and Presidential Uses of Force From Korea to Kosovo*; *Hollow Victory: A Contrary View of the Gulf War*; *The Wrong War: Why We Lost in Vietnam*; *Bounding the Global War on Terrorism*; and *The Specter of Munich: Reconsidering the Lessons of Appeasing Hitler*. Dr. Record served as a pacification adviser in the Mekong Delta during the Vietnam War, and he has since served as a Rockefeller Younger Scholar on the Brookings Institution's Defense Analysis Staff and as a senior fellow at the Institute for Foreign Policy Analysis, the Hudson Institute, and the BDM International Corporation. He also has extensive Capitol Hill experience, having served as legislative assistant for national security affairs to Senators Sam Nunn and Lloyd Bentsen and later as a professional staff member of the Senate Armed Services Committee. He lives in Atlanta, Georgia, with his wife, Leigh.